How
COMPETITIVE EXCELLENCE
can help you and your team...

"As a coach who has spent 13 years on the high school level, four years on the junior college level, and 17 years on the Division I level, I think this book would be of great value to coaches in determining guidelines by which to help develop a philosophy of successful team building. The past experiences of successful coaches has been beneficial to me and I'm certain this book will prove helpful to all of us."

Lute Olson, Head Basketball Coach
University of Arizona

"I believe the efforts made by Steve to guide new coaches is truly needed. There are so many confusing situations that arise in our field that hopefully coaches will find some solutions as well as some inspiration in this book."

Marilyn McReavy, Head Volleyball Coach
University of Florida

"A great book for coaches in examining a variety of ways to deal with today's student-athlete. Learning about motivation to mental tough-ness from the top coaches in the country makes COMPETITIVE EXCELLENCE a one-of-a-kind team building book."

Tom Apke, Head Basketball Coach
Appalachian State University

COMPETITIVE EXCELLENCE

The Psychology and Strategy of Successful Team Building

Stephen J. Brennan, M.Ed., M.P.E.

Peak Performance Publishing
Omaha, Nebraska

Other books by Stephen J. Brennan:

THE MENTAL EDGE: BASKETBALL'S PEAK PERFORMANCE WORKBOOK

BASKETBALL RESOURCE GUIDE   (co-author with Jerry V. Krause)

ISBN 0-9619230-1-6

Peak Performance Publishing
A Division of Peak Performance Consultants, Inc.
14728 Shirley Street
Omaha, Nebraska 68144   U.S.A.

Dedication

To all team builders

in the athletic, academic, and corporate domains.

Contents

Foreword

There is something special about the "sport experience." It goes beyond the playing of the game, the physical exertion and the final outcome of the contest. Although some see it only as a game, many see it as an experience bordering on the spiritual.

The spiritual part of athletics is the psychological part, long ignored but rapidly being recognized as critical on its own. In the past several decades, we have seen a rise in the interest in sport psychology, a field still in its infancy, but rapidly growing.

One of the most profound parts of the sport experience is teamwork, that awareness of where you fit into the total picture. The shared experience of working together as a single unit committed to a common end is a great teacher.

Ironically, there has been little done in the area of teamwork in athletics. Every coach would readily agree that it is of utmost importance and yet few have a specific, outlined plan of how to attain it or what to do about it. That team feeling, everywhere from a group of athletes on a team involving individual sports such as tennis to a team needing to think as one such as basketball, provides a support system that is hard to compare.

Steve Brennan's work provides a major step in compiling, analyzing and condensing teamwork into understandable and practical terms. The format of taking 29 successful coaches and asking them to relate their approach to motivation, team cohesion, discipline, mental preparation, mental toughness and communication provides a format that all coaches can understand and to which they can relate.

As the reader will notice, despite the different sports, diversity of ideas and the different definitions by the various coaches of the different terms, there is a commonality that stands out very clearly. Successful coaches have a clear plan beyond the techniques of the game and that plan involves mental preparation, athlete interaction, and specific exercises where athletes work together to get to know each other and share an emotional experience. That emotional experience, teamwork, more often than not produces success and is NOT a result of success.

This book can be used as a guide to help coaches begin to think, not only about team building, but more specifically about developing the six elements Brennan discusses in building a team. The variety of coaching approaches outlined can provide each coach with a drill, a technique, a style or an idea to begin to develop a team in his/her own personal way.

This avant garde book is a big step in what will be a major coaching change of the 1990's, a movement in developing the psychological part of the game as well as the technical part. Many coaches will look back and see this book as having made a major impact on their coaching career.

Tom Tutko, Ph. D.

Preface

As a coach, I was highly interested in the psychological aspects of athletic competition. I always surrounded myself with extremely competent assistant coaches who were specialists in the X's and O's and in scouting opponents. I considered my strengths to be organization and mental preparation of the players. Combining the talents of the coaching staff made for successful programs.

In 1988, using my interest in sport psychology and my expertise as a performance consultant as a catalyst, I began compiling mental preparation techniques from the most successful coaches in the nation. My intent was to produce a sport psychology coaching text that would be beneficial to both aspiring and veteran coaches.

Midway through the research, it occurred to me that the subject matter that each coach was discussing were components of the team-building process: motivation, team cohesion, discipline, mental preparation, mental toughness and communication. *COMPETITIVE EXCELLENCE* is the result of this study.

It was also my intent for this book to spotlight coaches in many sports, coaches of male and female teams, and coaches with high and low profiles. The key element for inclusion in the book was the proven ability of the coach to build a winning program from the bottom up. As you read through each chapter, the team-building skills of each coach are very evident.

The book is organized with each coach occupying a separate chapter. Each chapter begins with a cover page, which includes the coaching position, career record and educational background of the coach. The cover page also summarizes personal and team highlights.

An Introduction precedes the main text in each chapter. The purpose of the Introduction is to give the reader some biographical and career-development data on the coach, establishing a smooth transition into the discussion of the coach's philosophy on motivation, team cohesion, discipline, mental preparation, mental toughness and communication.

Finally, the book is intended to provide insight into team-building strategies for not only athletic coaches, but academic and corporate personnel as well. Educational administrators may find some team-building techniques useful, while corporate executives, managers, supervisors, personnel directors and human resource specialists may gain some ideas applicable to their environments.

COMPETITIVE EXCELLENCE should not be considered the definitive study of team-building strategies because it was never intended to be. However, the book can be considered a pragmatic guide for individuals and organizations seeking to build and maintain a winning team within their specific work groups.

Steve Brennan

ACKNOWLEDGMENTS

I want to give my heartfelt thanks to all those who helped make this book possible: Steve Beideck, a journalist and former student, for his editorial expertise and skillful manuscript editing; the sports information and public relations departments of the schools and teams; the always helpful and pleasant support staff personnel in the athletic offices; and my family, Lorna, Anne, Bradley and Stephanie, for their constant support and encouragement to complete this project.

Finally, I want to give special thanks to my friends, the coaches, who contributed so much of their valuable time, wisdom and energy, and who believe that teamwork is the key to success.

JANE ALBRIGHT
Northern Illinois University

Position
Head Women's Basketball Coach

Career Record
97-74   (6 seasons)

Education
B.S. 1977 Appalachian State University
M.S. 1983 University of Tennessee

Team and Personal Highlights

* 1989-90 North Star Conference Coach of the Year Award; Women's Basketball Coaches Association (WBCA) Region IV Coach of the Year Award; North Star Conference Regular Season and Tournament Championships; First-ever NCAA Tournament appearance; Final national ranking: Associated Press-17th, USA Today-16th.

* 1988-89 23-7 Record; Top 25 ranking in the country; New Orleans Holiday Tournament Championship; North Star Conference Regular Season Championship.

* 1979-80 South Carolina Region II High School Coach of the Year Award.

*   3 All-American players.

*   14 All-Conference players.

Jane Albright

Introduction...

The secret is out in DeKalb, Illinois. After winning 49 of 61 games in the past two years and participating in the first NCAA tournament in the school's history in 1990, the Nothern Illinois Huskies women's basketball program under the direction of Jane Albright has skyrocketed into national prominence.

Albright has been associated with winning throughout her coaching career. As an assistant coach at the University of Tennessee (1981-83), she learned about developing winning attitudes and habits from her mentor, Pat Summitt. Jane has combined Summitt's ideas with her own to construct a strong philosophical base for successful team building.

Jane's mental approach to coaching is strengthened by her Masters degree in sport psychology. She is a Master Teacher-Coach, having built the Northern Illinois women's basketball program into a national contender in just six years. The highly personable coach of the Huskies is a strong proponent of the mental approach to success. Here are Coach Albright's thoughts...

...on Motivation

Motivation is a prime ingredient for success in every organization, and it is a non-stop, daily attitude needed in order to be successful in every endeavor in life.

"Motivation," Albright says, "is the ability to make yourself do things day in and day out which are necessary to help you achieve a significant goal - even when you don't feel like it."

The key element is having the perseverance to attain team and personal goals.

"Motivation gives direction to accomplish your goals," she adds.

There are different techniques you can use to motivate your players. Some techniques are more effective than others, she says. Jane's most effective motivational technique revolves around the concept of communication with her players.

"I have found that the most effective motivation tool is sitting down with the student-athletes, both individually and as a team, and discussing goals," she says. "It's also imperative that everyone is involved. I don't want to leave anyone out because that could hurt our team unity."

Jane talks to the players about forming goals, about individual goals, and the importance of regular communication among the group.

"We talk about their expectations, my expectations, and accountability to the program," she states.

Coach Albright makes it a point to meet regularly with the team as a group and with the players individually to discuss their progress, to make any revisions or possible changes, and to share her thoughts and goals with them.

"I praise them as much as I can, whenever I can," she says.

Albright believes the least effective motivational tool involves self-motivation.

"I've found that expecting each of my players to get motivated entirely on their own is impossible!" she says.

Albright believes that intrinsic motivation from the players, without any type of feedback from her, cannot be sustained for any length of time.

"I need to give them constant feedback on my thoughts and feelings," she concludes.

Expecting players to be motivated entirely on their own, all the time, is not an expectation you'll find in Coach Albright's philosophy. In summary, two-way comunication is the key to Jane's motivational techniques.

* * * * * * * * * *

...on Team Cohesion

Team chemistry is a vital ingredient for ultimate team success. Albright defines team cohesion this way: "It's the ability of a group of completely different individuals to put a common goal above themselves and to strive daily to accomplish it."

She adds that individual wants or pet peeves aren't important to a close-knit team "because the group wants to succeed and they know they all need each other." Team chemistry, she says, can't happen unless there is an air of unselfishness among team members.

Coach Albright utilizes several techniques to enhance team unity.

"First, you must talk to them a lot, daily, about the importance of team goals," she says.

"Next, I believe you need to require each player to support each teammate by specific actions."

So what are some of these "specific actions?"

"We do a number of things at Northern Illinois to indicate respect and support for our players," she says. "For example, we ask each player to point to the passer that enabled her to score. This shows the passer that you appreciated the pass.

"We have our team huddle before a foul shot to set strategy. Also, we like the players along the lane to slap hands with our free throw shooter after her shot. These are just a few things we do during games and practices."

Jane mentions another innovation that has helped team unity.

"We have individuals draw the name of an opponent for a specific game and allow them to do a pre-game motivational project that is fun. This is a great way to stress the importance of a game, have the team working together, and having fun in the process," she states.

But the key element to team chemistry at Northern Illinois, Coach Albright points out , is requiring players to be supportive in their actions and their words, especially when they don't feel like it.

"We want those support actions instinctive in our players and I make sure we keep doing it all the time," she says.

In summary, cohesion is built in Coach Albright's teams by stressing the importance of "team" and "common goals" and by requiring specific actions during practices and games. She states that team cohesion cannot be taken for granted. It is an on-going process in which all team and coaching staff members benefit.

* * * * * * * * * *

...on Discipline

Discipline is a trait of the championship team and individual. Coach Albright's philosophy on team discipline is exact and unwavering.

"We have kids sign contracts that include team rules and we insist that they abide by them," she says.

Ideally, Jane would like the senior players to make the rules, "but we haven't used that system yet."

She adds that they praise the kids who do the little things correctly within the program.

"This shows us who the self-disciplined players are," she says.

Preaching values and accountability is extremely important to Coach Albright.

"We talk to kids often on the value systems for both individuals and the team. We explain accountability and responsibility. A team that lacks accountability to itself and its members will not be successful. I really believe that,"she concludes.

In recapping Coach Albright's philosophy on team discipline, she stresses signed contracts that include team rules and the consequences of breaking those rules. Value systems are an important part of the program, accountability and responsibility are ingrained in every team member, and she praises the players who do the little things necessary for success.

When it comes to utilizing disciplinary methods with her team, Coach Albright has found that some methods are more effective than others.

"Peer pressure is one of the most effective methods of discipline, even though I'm not directly involved," she states. "The two most effective forms of discipline I've used are extra running and taking away a starting position or cutting down on playing time."

The least effective methods of discipline, in Albright's estimation, involves activities away from the court.

"First of all, yelling at a player has no long-lasting effect and she probably tunes me out anyway," she says. "So I make it a rule with myself to really watch reactions when I yell to see if it has more effect on some players than others. But mostly I've found yelling in itself is non-productive."

Coach Albright has also found that extra study hall time and specific work hours for players have little or no effect.

"Today's athletes react more quickly to disciplinary methods that take them out of the spotlight," she says. "For example, cutting down on playing time or taking a starting spot away usually grabs a player's attention.

"And", she adds, "no one likes extra running."

In summarizing Coach Albright's methods of discipline with her Huskie teams, the most effective methods include a reduction of playing time, eliminating a starting position, extra running, and team peer pressure. Least effective methods of discipline are excessive yelling at the athlete, extra study hall duty, and additional working hours away from the team.

* * * * * * * * * *

...on Mental Preparation

All successful coaches say that mental preparation is essential to team and individual success, and Coach Albright concurs. Mental preparation, she states, means having the kids ready to play, whether it's during practice or games.

"It's basically a matter of concentration," she says. "The player must have her mind in the present tense, in the here and now. She cannot be preoccupied with outside distractions. In order to be mentally prepared, she needs to know exactly what must be done in every situation during practice and games. She also must work on her concentrations skills at all times."

With the length of the intercollegiate season and the time commitment demanded of the players and coaching staff, it is extremely important that sound mental preparation techniques are utilized throughout the season.

To handle the grind of pre-season practices and home and away non-conference and conference games, Albright's approach is consistent with her overall philosophy.

"We are constantly communicating with the kids, talking, encouraging," she states. "We set individual and team goals for each part of our season, from pre-season practices to post-season tournaments."

To keep the players sharp, and as an aid to the coaching staff, practices and games are charted extensively and the significance of those statistics are discussed with each player, she says.

"Finally we talk about seeing the big picture and how our goals are centered on winning our conference or holiday tournament and getting into post-season play."

In summary, Coach Albright mixes communication, statistics, and visualization to mentally prepare the players for the season.

Late-game strategy is also a part of mentally preparing a team, and Albright is a master teacher-coach in this department.

"We have our own way of preparing for late-game strategy that can ultimately help us win," she says, "and we win those games because we practice winning those games."

Coach Albright's method incorporates repetition and game-like situations. The team runs isolated plays against all types of pressure to see which ones are most effective against what defenses, she says.

"Mainly we try to put the players in a position to succeed," she continues. "We want to put them in a situation that builds confidence and not fear. That's really the key."

Albright makes each late-game situation as real as possible. They use the clock all the time and try to use a referee or one of the coaches as a referee to keep things realistic, she says.

"We talk to the kids on how to win and explain to them why the things we are doing will help them win," she says.

In summarizing Coach Albright's mental preparation techniques, she utilizes communication skills, concentration skills, goal setting and charting, visualization and specific game-like situations that conditions her players for success.

* * * * * * * * * *

...on Mental Toughness

Mental toughness is a trait found in all high achievers, and the mentally-tough student-athlete is usually successful in the classroom and on the court.

Albright defines mental toughness as the ability to overcome all obstacles in order to accomplish a goal.

"The mentally tough person," she says, "can overcome physical pain or any situation because that person is focused on what she really wants."

Coach Albright believes there are specific characteristics or traits that help distinguish a mentally tough individual.

"The mentally tough person never quits," she emphasizes.

Intensity is also a trait of the mentally tough person, she says. She also likes to see a very confident player ("almost cocky") and concludes her definition of a mentally tough person by evaluating the work ethic.

She believes that a mentally tough person is a hard worker, in the classroom and on the court, adding, "hard workers are the ones who usually end up with something to show for their efforts."

In summarizing mental toughness, Coach Albright believes that a mentally tough individual is focused and can overcome all obstacles, including physical pain, in order to accomplish a goal. Mental toughness traits include a never-say-die attitude, a burning intensity and desire to be successful, an air of confidence that borders on cockiness, and a work ethic second to none.

* * * * * * * * *

...on Communication

Communication with your athletes and staff and effectively dealing with adversity are important psychological factors needed for the success of a team.

Coach Albright has no specific procedures for inspiring her team if they are losing at halftime or behind in the closing minutes of a game.

"It really depends on the situation," she says.

At halftime, if the team is ahead and they're cocky about it, Jane will cut them down to size.

"But if they're trying very hard and just can't seem to make things happen, I'll praise and encourage them," she says.

Jane's late-game communication usually stresses technical information to the players.

"I'll try to give them a clear direction, using specific X's and O's," she says. "We'll make whatever changes are necessary in order to rectify the situation and get things going in our favor."

When it comes to dealing with tough losses or poor performance by the team, Jane tries to read the situation objectively before deciding on her plan of action.

"If it was a tough loss, I'll try to empathize with them," she says, stressing that the tone must be positive and upbeat. "I'll tell them to look ahead and make this tough loss a learning experience. Then we evaluate what we did right, what we did wrong, and what we need to work on."

Poor game performance of the team is addressed in a variety of ways, depending upon Coach Albright's state of mind, the players reactions, assistant coaches recommendations, and any other factors she believes can be useful.

"Sometimes I don't say a word. I just look at them," she says, "and other times I'll express my disappointment in their performances."

Losing her temper is also a technique she has found effective.

"Since I rarely scream or lose my temper, when I do lose it, the kids take notice very quickly," she notes.

At other times, she just gives the team the cold shoulder for a while before addressing the team. She also will conduct individual conferences with specific players to get problem areas resolved.

In summarizing communication and dealing with adversity, Albright believes late-game and halftime strategy talks should be more technical in nature than inspirational, using encouragement and praise where needed and making appropriate changes in X's and O's.

In dealing with a tough loss, empathy and praise are the most important forms of behavior that the coach should exhibit. She believes you need to stress the positive aspects of the game and learn from the experience.

Coach Albright handles poor team performance in a number of ways, ranging from silence to anger to "the cold shoulder." She rarely loses her temper, but when she does, it's calculated to get a specific response from the players. She also incorporates talks with individuals if she thinks this will be helpful.

* * * * * * * * * *

TOM APKE

Appalachian State University

Position
Head Men's Basketball Coach

Career Record
251-198   (16 seasons)

Education
B.A. 1965 Creighton University
M.Ed. 1967 University of Cincinnati

Team and Personal Highlights

* Current member of NCAA Committee for Basketball Issues.
* Teams have participated in three NCAA and one NIT post-
      season tournaments.
* Southern Conference Coach of the Year Award in 1988.
* Missouri Valley Conference Coach of the Year Award in 1978.
* National Association of Basketball Coaches (NABC) District 5
      Coach of the Year Award in 1978.
* Omaha Sportsman of the Year Award in 1979.
* Omaha Man of the Year Award in 1974.
* Director of NCAA College World Series from 1974-80.
* Member of USA BASKETBALL Games Committee for
      Olympiads 1980 and 1984.
* Member of USA BASKETBALL Council from 1984-88.
* Member of NCAA Basketball Rules Committee from 1980-84.
* Coach of the North Team at National Sports Festival in 1979.
* Member of NABC Committee on Officiating from 1987-89.

Tom Apke

Introduction...

Tom Apke has produced winners everywhere he has coached on the major college level. These coaching stops include Creighton University in Omaha, the University of Colorado in Boulder, and his current position as head basketball coach at Appalachian State University in Boone, North Carolina.

While serving as Athletic Director at Creighton, Apke's team compiled a record of 130-64 from 1974-81, winning two Missouri Valley Conference Championships and participating in three NCAA post-season tournaments and one NIT tournament.

During his five year stop in Boulder, Tom's 1983-84 team finished fourth in the tough Big Eight Conference. At Appalachian State, Tom has established himself once again as a builder of winning teams, guiding the 1988-89 Mountaineer team to a 20-8 record, only the fifth time an ASU team has won 20 games. The 1989-90 team finished 19-11.

A native of Cincinnati and the second of seven children, Apke has always built his winning organization on the "family" theme. Highly respected among his coaching peers, Tom personifies the "nice guy" image in college athletics. He is married to the former Eileen Blazek and they have two children, Mike, 16, and Karin, 12.

His positive outlook on life was in evidence as he enthusiastically talked about the psychology and strategy of successful team building.

Here are Coach Apke's thoughts...

...on Motivation

Motivation in Coach Apke's system is a prime ingredient for success, and it is an on-going process.

"Motivation is the ability to get players to perform at or near their maximum ability," he says. "Basically, it's the ability to get them ready to play."

Over the years, Apke has found motivational techniques and strategies that are both effective and not effective. He is most vocal when discussing ineffective motivational techniques.

"The tyrant approach is totally ineffective when it comes to motivating today's athlete," he stresses. "The old way of trying to get players to do something 'because I say so' is not effective in this day and age."

Effective motivational strategies center around communication and justifications, he says.

"I believe that a coach should most often give reasons why he is trying to get the players to do a certain thing."

This method is not only good for the players, but it's also very beneficial to the coach.

"This method also keeps me fresh," he says, "because I am forced to evaluate the rationale behind why we are doing something or else our players won't accept what I am telling them."

In summary, Tom defines motivation as the ability to get the players ready to perform at or near their maximum ability. He says that the most effective motivational technique is to communicate and explain the rationale behind ideas presented to the players.

The most ineffective method for motivating today's players, he states, is the tyrant approach, forcing the players to action "because I say so."

* * * * * * * * * *

...on Team Cohesion

Even though Apke's teams are always considered cohesive by opposing coaches, he stills admits to being amused by the disparity of the team chemistry "phenomenon."

"This area is always somewhat of a mystery to most coaches," he begins. "I have seen teams made up of mostly bandits which had team chemistry, and I've seen others made up of really good kids who didn't have it."

Do the players have to like each other?

"I don't think that the players absolutely have to get along with one another off the court, but I do believe that it generally helps if they do," he concludes.

Tom's definition of team chemistry revolves around the idea of each athlete showing respect to one another.

"I think that the more you can do to make them get along as people, the better chance they have of getting along as players," he says.

Apke's "family" approach to team cohesion has always been a major part of his philosophy, and has proved to be a very effective recruiting tool in the process.

"Parents are most interested in how their son is going to be treated while a student-athlete at our university, and I point out to them that we are all a part of a basketball family," Apke says. "Because I feel so strongly about that aspect of the team, parents and the athlete himself are willing to take a closer look at our program."

The "family" approach has paid dividends for Coach Apke.

"I can say that we've recruited several players over the years because of our 'family' approach to team cohesion," he states proudly.

The "family" approach to team chemistry has three major components to it, Coach Apke says.

"The first thing is that I try to make our players have some fun," he says. "We work hard and our practices are not a 'junior high picnic,' but I believe that they are playing the game in college because they love basketball, and if a coach can keep the entire atmosphere enjoyable to them, they are more likely to be a 'together' group."

Some of those "fun" activities usually involve unique drills that spotlight the player's abilities or a general "looseness" during practice.

"What's nice about it is that the players know when it is fun time and when it is work time," Apke says.

Another extremely critical ingredient for team cohesion is honest communication between the coach and the athlete.

"I think that honest communication about what each person's role on the team is can be important," he states. "The 12th man might not like his role, but if he understands it, he is more likely to accept it and contribute to the team in his own way."

Tom credits the work of a sport pychologist with the third element of building team cohesion.

"One of the things I learned from the sport psychologist who worked with my team at a previous school is the importance of goal setting," he says. "I think getting a team to state what it is they want to accomplish 'as a group' helps to keep team cohesion and chemistry positive."

In summarizing Coach Apke's thoughts on team cohesion, he believes that making the effort to get players to get along as individuals will have a positive effect on how they get along as players.

Apke's formula for building a "family" atmosphere includes establishing a fun environment at practice, communicating with players in a totally honest fashion, and utilizing team goal setting strategies, he states.

* * * * * * * * * *

...on Discipline

Team discipline is a trait of the successful team and individual, but the days of absolute dictatorship by the head coach is no longer an effective tool.

"Don't get me wrong," he begins. "I believe you need rules, but I also believe that each individual case needs to be reviewed separately."

Coach Apke reinforces the belief that team rules need to be established by both the players and coaches, but that the head coach also has the discretion and powers to act within his capacity as head coach concerning specific situations.

"First, I believe that the absolute dictator type of discipline is no longer as effective when dealing with players today," he says. "Therefore, I have few rules, and the rules I do have are voted on by the players or are very general by me."

Least effective disciplinary methods are a result of "absolute" rules, he says.

"I don't like the absolute rule like anyone caught drinking during the season is suspended for one game. I believe we are educators, and as such, we need to look at each situation on an individual basis."

Absolute rules can also be an easy way out for coaches.

"Sometimes having absolute rules makes it easier for us as coaches," he says. "But different player's circumstances may dictate different actions by us as coaches."

Coach Apke believes that the best method in dealing with discipline are establishing general rules and then handling each disciplinary case on an individual basis.

"An example of one of my general rules is regarding hair length," he states. "I tell them to be neat and well-groomed, and that I will be the judge of that. This way, I have some leeway in dealing with each player as an individual."

Another example of dealing with the student-athlete on an individual basis concerns the method of getting released from study hall responsibilities.

"Someone who may have a "C" average but is vastly underachieving may have to continue to go to study hall," he says. "But another with a "C" average may no longer be required to go to study hall. I think each case has to be examined under its own merits."

In summary, Coach Apke believes that discipline needs to be enforced, but that absolute rules should not be the basis for the disciplinary action.

Rules should be established by both team and coaches, he says, but the head coach should also establish general team rules that he can deal with on an individual basis.

Finally, a dictator-type of discipline is not an effective way in dealing with today's players, he believes. The most effective method is setting general rules and reviewing each case on its own merit.

* * * * * * * * * *

...on Mental Preparation

Mental preparation is essential for team and individual success, and Coach Apke begins this aspect of team preparation on the first day of practice.

"Mental preparation involves many things," he begins. "I ask our players to play hard and play smart. Therefore, the mental aspect of playing with your head is always stressed to the players."

This mental approach is part of a daily regimen.

"I try to emphasize the specifics of what is meant by smart play every day in practice," he says.

Coach Apke also believes that mental preparation impacts physical performance.

"I tell them that if they will begin to concentrate ahead of time on what things they will have to do to win tonight, they will be sharper, quicker and physically better," he states.

Coach Apke also believes that teams that play "flat" physically are teams that had poor mental preparation.

Mentally preparing for the physical grind of a non-conference and conference season takes on the same approach in his teaching methodology during pre-season practice.

"To me, variety is the spice of life in pre-season practice," he begins. "We try to have lots of ways to teach the same things. We also talk about mental toughness and concentration when we think they are beginning to drag."

The same mental training approach is utilized during both non-conference and conference games.

"For me, most preparation has taken place in practice," he says.

Specific items must be covered during practices, however.

"We show them exactly what we want, we show them what the other team is likely to try to do, we teach them the powers of concentration, and then we try to give them the confidence that they can be successful," he concludes.

Coaches must also be aware of one other element of preparation.

"After all this preparation, you now have to let them play and be careful not to over-coach," he says.

Late-game strategy and mental preparation go hand-in-hand.

"We try to practice all of our late-game strategy frequently during practice," he says. "One technique is to put three minutes on the scoreboard and give Team A a lead against Team B. Now Team A must learn to apply your techniques for protecting the lead, while Team B must learn how to play catch-up."

Special strategy plays are also practiced frequently, and for good reason.

"I don't think you can draw up something during a timeout late in a game and expect your team to go out and do it," he says. Therefore, we go over everything that we think could happen during a game at practice."

In summarizing Coach Apke's thoughts on mental preparation, he stresses that each individual play hard and play smart. He explains on a daily basis the specifics of what he means by "smart" play.

He also emphasizes that correct mental preparation can have a powerful effect on physical performance, saying that the mentally-ready team is usually sharper, quicker and physically better. He also points out that a team that plays "flat" had poor mental preparation.

Variety in drills is the key to keeping mentally fresh during the grind of pre-season practice, he says. Mental preparation during practice sessions also helps a team prepare for all non-conference and conference games.

Finally, late-game strategy is practiced frequently. Special plays must also be a part of every practice session, he says, because he doesn't think you can draw up something new late in a game and expect successful execution from the players.

* * * * * * * * * *

...on Mental Toughness

Coach Apke associates mental toughness with the ability to concentrate and put distractions aside in order to perform efficiently. He also believes that mental toughness is a trait that most student-athletes do not possess, but can be taught.

"Mental toughness is the ability to concentrate while under pressure and the ability to block out distractions," he says. He continues by adding, "I don't think it happens naturally to a lot of players, but I think you can teach some of the things that will help their mental toughness."

He illustrates the need for mental toughness with his players on a daily basis.

"When the players complain that the gym is too hot or cold or that the track team up on the balcony is distracting them, I talk to them about mental toughness and concentration," he states.

Reference is always made to one of the Mountaineer's big rivals when Apke feels mental toughness is lacking.

"I tell them that when we are at East Tennessee State that their fans will be yelling and booing and trying to distract us, but we're not going to let it bother us," he says.

Coach Apke utilizes a drill in practice to help build concentration and mental toughness in his players.

"It's nothing major, but we do drills where we have Group A versus Group B in a free throw shooting contest. Each team is allowed to yell and try to distract their opponent while they are shooting. We stress that if they concentrate, they won't be affected by the yelling," he concludes.

He reiterates his belief that the student-athlete can be taught concentration techniques that will help them build their mental toughness.

In summarizing mental toughness, Coach Apke defines the term by listing the traits of a mentally tough player. He says that the mentally tough player has the ability to focus all of his powers of concentration on the job at hand while under pressure and to have the ability to block out all distractions. Tom also believes that mental toughness skills can be taught to all student-athletes.

* * * * * * * * * *

...on Communication

Coach Apke has always had the remarkable ability to effectively communicate his thoughts to a wide range of audiences, be it players, administrators, or alumni groups. That ability to articulate his thoughts to his audiences has been a key to success in his organization.

"I try to honestly tell the players that all I want them to do is play hard and smart...and smart implies playing together...and that winning will take care of itself," he points out. "Then if someone who is just better than us beats us and we have played hard and smart, I tell them it was a good effort. However, if we win, but didn't play hard or smart, then I'll go after them pretty hard."

Playing with the heart in addition to the head is also something that Tom tries to instill in his players.

"I always try to remind them that playing well is not always possible, but that playing with your head and you heart is always possible," he says. By consistently adhering to this philosophy, Coach Apke believes that his players feel they are being treated consistently in what is expected of them.

Halftime comments are dictated by the effort and smartness exhibited by the players during the first half.

"If the team simply has made some technical mistakes, I might calmly show them which adjustments need to be made," he says.

But if the first half problems are a result of lack of effort or concentration, he will take a less calm approach.

"If we are losing bacause of lack of effort or lack of what we are supposed to be doing, then I will get on them about playing hard and smart, with their heads and their hearts," he says.

Coach Apke is also quick to admit his mistakes if his strategy didn't work.

"If some piece of strategy by me backfired, I will explain to them why I decided on the strategy. I will also tell them that a loss was my fault if I did make a decision that cost us a game," he says.

In the end however, communication is only effective if it is honest and sincere when conveyed.

"I believe that if the players are treated with honesty and respect from the coach, that they in turn will do their best to earn that respect," he states.

In summary, communication is most important when dealing daily with players and staff and in times of adversity. Coach Apke's philosophy of playing hard and smart is the backbone of his message to his players. The only time he will admonish his players during halftime is when a lack of effort and concentration is present, he says.

Another message that Tom stresses to the players is that while playing well is not always possible, that playing with the head and the heart is always possible.

When strategy has backfired, he is quick to admit fault to the players and explain why he decided upon that strategy. If a coaching decision was instrumental in the team losing, Coach Apke will take the blame and again explain why it was his fault.

Finally, the key to communicating effectively, Tom says, is to be honest with the players and staff in all discussions and to show respect to everyone in the organization. He believes that if the head coach treats every person with respect and honesty, they in turn will do their best to earn that respect.

* * * * * * * * * *

CEAL BARRY
University of Colorado

Position
Head Women's Basketball Coach

Career Record
199-131 (11 seasons)

Education
B.S. 1977 University of Kentucky

Team and Personal Highlights

* 1988-89   27-4 Overall Record; Big Eight Conference Champion;
First Big Eight team to go undefeated in conference
play; Big Eight Post-Season Tournament Champion;
NCAA Tournament; Top Ten final ranking in country.

* 1988   Head Coach, United States Select Team at the Jones
Cup in Taiwan.

* 1987   Head Coach, United States Olympic Festival East
Team.

Ceal Barry

Introduction...

Ceal Barry has been building winning programs since her first coaching stop at the University of Cincinnati in 1979. After compiling a record of 83-42 during her four years in Ohio, she moved her winning philosophy to Boulder to revive the sagging Lady Buffs program. In her seven seasons on the Colorado campus, she has produced three 20-plus win seasons and guided her teams to Big Eight Championships and NCAA tournaments.

A native of Louisville, Kentucky, Ceal played guard for the Wildcat basketball team and lettered in field hockey for three years. The vivacious coach loves talking about building successful teams, so let's begin exploring Coach Barry's winning thoughts...

...on Motivation

Motivation plays a big part in the success of Ceal Barry's teams, and is a prime ingredient for success within all organizations. Motivating today's female student-athlete takes a special talent. Barry says that it is no easy task.

"Motivating people means getting people to do what they naturally don't have a desire to do," she says.

From a basketball approach, some of those things may include running, playing defense, and maintaining the proper weight. But there is a key element to this talent.

"You have to be able to get each individual to not only do what they probably don't like doing, but you also have to get them to do those things with enthusiasm," she states. "And you must be able to get them to do those things consistently, every day, all the time."

So how do you get someone to do things that they may not naturally want to do? Barry thinks there are effective ways to handle the motivation of her players.

"My teams have always had a feeling of trust among the players," she says. "That trust has built itself into a mutual respect between the coaches and players."

Coach Barry says that you build trust through effective communications with the players.

"I talk to the kids individually on a daily basis, making sure that I cover topics that are important to each person," she says. "And that includes personal and academic problems, not just basketball problems."

There are specific things you don't do when trying to motivate the female student-athlete.

"I've found that yelling at the kids is very counter-productive."

It's also very important that you never humiliate the person in front of her peers.

"Degrading their effort in front of the team," Barry points out, "is the worst thing you can do."

Another ineffective motivational technique concerns accusations surrounding attitude.

"Telling them that they don't care about the team or their teammates or the program simply carries no weight around here," she says.

In summary, Barry believes that motivation is a matter of getting people to do things that they naturally have no desire to do, and being able to get them to do it with enthusiasm and consistency.

Least effective motivational techniques for Coach Barry include excessive yelling, public degradation, and accusations of a lack of caring about the program.

Effective motivational techniques include ocmmunicating with the group, developing trust among team members and the coaching staff, and building a mutual respect for all members of the program, including players, coaches, and support personnel.

* * * * * * * * * *

...on Team Cohesion

Team chemistry played a vital role in the success of Coach Barry's 1988-89 team, and she enjoys telling about it.

"My philosophy on team cohesion is pretty basic," she begins. "I believe that no player should have a feeling that her role or position or contributions on the team is any more or any less important than anyone else on the team."

Respect and self-esteem play a big role in team cohesion at Colorado.

"Team cohesion is built on self-esteem," she says. "That self-esteem builds respect for each other as contributing members of the team."

Barry uses a number of effective techniques that helps build team unity.

"We do a number of things at Colorado that has helped build team unity over the years," she states. "One method I've used concerns earning a letter. My team rule states that everyone letters, regardless of minutes played."

Theoretically, promising someone a reward without meeting certain performance standards can lead to inconsistency or lack of effort.

"But we've found this to have no negative effect at all," she says.

Barry also utilizes different methods of fostering team unity while on road trips during the season.

"Everyone rooms together with each team member at least once on the road," she says. "I let the computer randomly select the roommates."

Each person is also delegated responsibilities on every road trip and those responsibilities are rotated among the players.

"Regardless of status, each player must assist our manager in carrying the extra uniform bag and the VCR equipment."

Coach Barry follows a general rule of showing no favoritism to team members, in practice or on the road.

"In fact, we make it a point to recognize second-team members after a big win so they know that their contributions during practice preparations were vital to our success," she says.

In summarizing Barry's thoughts on team cohesion, she believes team chemistry is a result of a healthy self-esteem on the part of each person which translates into a mutual respect for each team member. It's also important that each player feels her contributions are seen as important to the team.

Effective methods of building team cohesion include a variety of techniques. In Coach Barry's system, all players earn a varsity letter regardless of total minutes played. All team members room together at least once during all road trips during the season.

Barry also delegates responsibilities to team members on road trips and rotates those duties throughout the season. No favoritism is shown toward any player, regardless of status, during practice or on the road, and finally, second-team members are recognized after big wins to emphasize the importance of their contributions during game preparations.

* * * * * * * * * *

...on Discipline

Coach Barry believes that discipline is a way of living, and without it, a person will not be successful in any aspect of his or her life.

"Discipline is really reaching a standard that has been set," she says, "and you reach it through playing by the rules."

The rules that Barry mentions include the rules of society, the rules defining the game of basketball, or the rules set by the coaching staff. The disciplined student- athlete functions well in society, she says, because they know what the rules are and how to react to them.

Coach Barry has found that there are some disciplinary methods that won't work in the Colorado program.

"One method that just doesn't work pertains to my setting team rules but not giving any reasoning or justification as to the importance of those rules," she says. "It took me the first few years of coaching to figure that out."

But Barry points out that team rules without a solid foundation of reasoning behind them carries no weight with today's student-athletes.

"Hey, they (the players) want to know why you're doing something," she says. "And you better be able to tell them the answer!"

Another least effective technique centers around not enforcing rules fairly.

"This has to be one of the most difficult jobs as a coach," Barry says. "You try to judge every disciplinary situation on its own merits and see where it falls along the team rules continuum and then act accordingly."

The problem arises when the team or the individual doesn't believe you're being consistent or fair, she says, "and you really have to be able to explain your position."

A third method that is not very effective in disciplining the student-athlete involves negative punishment. Negative punishment usually centers around extra conditioning or extra study hall hours.

"What I've discovered," Barry emphasizes, "is that negative punishment usually makes them more angry." She says this anger can linger and make things even worse.

So what is an effective method of disciplining a student-athlete? Coach Barry's method involves sitting the player down.

"I believe that benching the player has the most positive effect," she states. "By positive, I mean that any time you take away something that the player enjoys the most will surely make her change her ways."

Barry's philosophy has always centered around the team concept. It's important that all players conform to team rules, she says, because if they don't, "you have a problem brewing that will ultimately destroy the team."

In summary, Barry's definition of discipline includes meeting the standards that have been set for you, whether they are society's rules, the rules surrounding the game of basketball, or the rules established by the coaching staff.

Establishing team rules without explanation or justification as to their importance to the team is a very ineffective method for team discipline. Also ineffective is the enforcement of team rules in what is perceived by team members to be inconsistent and unfair. Finally, Coach Barry says that using negative punishment in the form of extra conditioning or extra time commitments is deeply resented and can lead to long-term anger on the part of the student-athlete.

The most effective disciplinary method utilized in the University of Colorado program is benching the player and taking away playing time. Coach Barry feels that this method brings about conformity to team rules in the best possible way because it deprives the player of what she enjoys the most, displaying her skills in front of a crowd.

* * * * * * * * * *

...on Mental Preparation

Mental preparation is an essential ingredient for success for both teams and individuals. Without some kind of mental preparation, a good team can never become great.

Coach Barry defines mental preparation as an ability to focus in on what is important.

"Mental preparation is focusing in mentally on the task at hand," she says. That includes the ability to concentrate and keep attention on what is happening around you.

"You cannot allow any kind of distractions to affect you because distractions hamper performance," she states.

Mental preparation is addressed in different ways during the course of the season.

"During pre-season practices, we talk a lot about our schedule, our goals for the coming season, and our past accomplishments," Barry states.

It is during these references to the schedule that any kind of fear factor is addressed.

"If we're playing a big-time program with national stature, I want to make sure that the players understand that our opponents are human and can be beaten if we play our best and think of the opponent as just another team on our schedule," she says.

During pre-season practices, Coach Barry speaks often to the players about improving individually in all aspects of the game. It is through individual improvement, she says, that a team becomes competitive and ultimately highly successful.

"Accomplishing our pre-season goals has been a major factor in this program getting to where it is today," she states.

Pre-season practices are also a time for the players and staff to reflect positively on previous accomplishments.

"When things get slow and monotonous for the players and staff during pre-season, we like to have the players reflect on a big win or tournament victory from the previous season," Barry explains.

The psychological reasoning for this type of behavior is to build a sense of pride in the players.

"We really stress the pride aspect to the kids," she says, "and it seems to have a very positive influence on them."

In summarizing pre-season mental preparation methods, Coach Barry feels it is important to discuss any fear factor that arises from the schedule and allay those feelings immediately. She also stresses the importance of goal setting, emphasizing that individual improvement results in team improvement. Finally, Barry constantly reminds the players of past accomplishments, shaping and reinforcing a feeling of pride in being a member of the team.

Mental preparation for non-conference games is extremely important to Coach Barry.

"We look at non-conference games as total preparation for our conference season, " she says. "We usually try to find similarities between non-conference teams and our conference teams so that the players get a mental picture of what the conference season is going to be like."

Barry also mentions to the players that the success enjoyed during non-conference games has a bearing on NCAA bids at the end of the season.

"The kids usually get excited about having bragging rights over a team or conference," she says. "A big win over a national contender will weigh in our favor when NCAA bids come out."

The coaches also like to see improvement in execution if the team is playing the same opponent a second consecutive year.

In summarizing mental preparation techniques utilized during non- conference games, Barry and her staff first try to find similarities between non-conference and conference opponents, in either personnel or style of play. This helps reinforce Barry's philosophy of using non-conference games as total preparation for the brutal Big Eight season.

Bragging rights and NCAA tournament bids also receive emphasis during the non-conference portion of the schedule. Defeating a national power and competing successfully during all non-conference games will have a strong bearing on the likelihood of a post-season NCAA tournament invitation, Barry believes.

Finally, if the team is playing an opponent for a second time, the coaching staff wants to see improvement in all phases of the game the second time around.

There are no secrets to what the University of Colorado team wants to accomplish once the Big Eight season begins.

"We want to dominate," Coach Barry states. "We want to be number one in our area."

Mental preparation is critical in late-game strategy development, and Coach Barry has her own way of handling those situations.

"You may think I'm nuts," she states. "But I use a lot of humor in my late-game strategy talks."

Keeping things light at the end of crucial games has worked well for Barry.

"It really fires the team up late in a game," she says.

Another late-game strategy technique includes a momentary mental flash-back for the players.

"I constantly remind the players of what they were willing to sacrifice to prepare for this game, like the early morning runs at 6:30," she states. This type of feedback with the players during important times of the game has been very effective for Barry.

Finally, the most important technique used during late-game strategy talks concerns the attitudes of the players and the type of self-talk they're using.

"When it comes to gut-check time, I want those kids thinking only one thing..'We will win!' "she preaches, "and there are no 'ifs, ands, or buts' about it!"

In summarizing mental preparation techniques utilized during the conference season and during late-game strategy talks with the team, it can be said that Coach Barry is a Master Teacher-Coach. During the conference season, Barry wants her players to be dominatnt in the league, and the practices are indicative of that goal.

Preparing for the Big Eight season means working harder than you ever realized could be possible, she says. Mentally preparing the student-athlete for that kind of season is imperative, and Barry has the ability to prepare her teams so that they can endure the physical and emotional battles associated with Big Eight play.

Humor finds its way into many of Coach Barry's late-game strategy talks with her players. Keeping the situation light seems to be very effective for her. She also reminds the players often of the hard work they've endured to become successful and how that hard work will help them win that particular game.

Finally, positive self-talk is always present during late-game strategy talks. Emphasizing that the team "will win" has conditioned the players into believing that they will be successful in the closing minutes of crucial games.

* * * * * * * * * *

...on Mental Toughness

Many opposing coaches believe the success of the University of Colorado women's basketball team is a result of the mental toughness evident in the players. Coach Barry is appreciative of those kinds of comments from her fellow coaches and enjoys talking about the mental toughness needed to be successful in today's society.

"You've got to be mentally tough in order to survive today," she says.

Mental toughness needs to be exhibited not only on the court, but in the classroom and socially.

"Mental toughness means that a person has the ability to concentrate on the task at hand, regardless of any peripheral distractions of any degree," she says.

Those distractions can be found not only in basketball, but in the university environment and in the social climate of the school.

"I'm extremely proud of my players, watching them grow from being a timid girl as a freshman to being a polished, confident woman as a senior, ready to make her mark in society. And they couldn't have done it without some degree of mental toughness."

What are the characteristics of a mentally tough person? Barry has a list she is happy to share with anyone who will listen.

"I believe you need to be serious-minded toward your goals," she states. "I also think that a mentally tough individual has a very mature outlook about life in general."

Barry adds a competitive nature and a determination to succeed as factors surrounding mental toughness.

"You almost have to have a stubborn streak in you, you're that determined," she concludes.

A positive mental attitude and the ability to commit yourself to a cause are the final two characteristics of a mentally tough individual by Barry's standards.

"Without a positive mental attitude toward life, you'll never be successful in any endeavor," she says. "And without the ability to demonstrate a sense of commitment to others or to personal goals, success will be hard to find for any individual.

In summary, Coach Barry believes that mental toughness is the ability to concentrate on the task at hand regardless of the degree of outside distractions.

The characteristics of a mentally tough individual include being serious-minded, mature in outlook and competitive in nature. Additional traits include a determination that borders on stubbornness, possessing a positive mental attitude toward life and the ability to commit oneself to others and personal goals.

* * * * * * * * * *

...on Comunication

All successful organizations, whether the setting is corporate, educational or athletic, has at the foundation a strong communication channel from the top echelon to the lower levels. This communication is vital during times of crisis and when giving performance evaluations. Coach Barry is very aware of the psychological implications of effective communications with her players and staff.

"At crucial times late in games or at halftime, I try to keep the comments positive in nature," she says.

Inspiration does not have to be vocal in nature to be effective with the players.

"Very rarely do I yell during strategy talks," she says, "because it would be counterproductive for us."

Barry usually discusses the reasons why the team is behind and then makes the necessary technical changes to combat the team's negative slide.

Post-game comments after a tough loss or poor performance are usually handled in the same fashion.

"After either a tough loss or a poor performance, I get angry initially. But by the time I get to the kids, I've gotten the anger under control and I try to react to the game in a constructive, not destructive manner," she says.

Coach Barry believes that losing control and saying things in anger is like trying to build a new bridge after the first one has collapsed.

"It's too short a time between games to lose control and then have to get the team back up emotionally before the next game," she says.

But Barry does not scorn anger as a communication technique all the time.

"I get really angry at least two times a year around game situations," she says.

It's almost cathartic in nature.

"I need to blow off steam just like the players," she says.

In summary, Coach Barry's communication techniques have served her well over the years. During halftime or late in games, she keeps a cool head and calmly discusses technical changes that will help the team change negative momentum.

She rarely yells, but will use anger at specific times during the season to get the attention of the players. At no time will she lose control and say things that can be destructive to team members simply because it's too difficult and time-consuming to repair the damage that has been done.

* * * * * * * * * *

JIM BOLLA
University of Nevada - Las Vegas

Position
Head Women's Basketball Coach

Career Record
197-53   (8 seasons)

Education
B.S. 1975 University of Pittsburgh

Team and Personal Highlights

* 1989-90 Big West Conference Coach of the Year Award; Big West Conference Regular Season and Tournament Champions (7th straight); NCAA Tournament appearance (5th in 7 years); 28-3 overall record; Top Ten Final Ranking.
* 1989 Became winningest coach in Lady Rebel history. Winning percentage (.788) is in top 10 among active collegiate women's basketball coaches.
* 1988-89 27-7 overall record; PCAA Tournament Champion; NCAA Tournament appearance; Top Ten ranking.
* 1982 Married then-UNLV head women's basketball coach, Sheila Strike, and became co-head coach.
* 1980 Official photographer for Eastern Eight Basketball Conference in only year out of coaching.
* 1974 Led University of Pittsburgh basketball team to Final Eight of NCAA Tournament.
* 1971 High school state championship at Cannavin High School in Pittsburgh, Pennsylvania; All-State basketball honors; All-America basketball honors. Participated in prestigious Dapper Dan Classic.

Jim Bolla

Introduction...

Amidst the glitz and the glamour of the Las Vegas strip, another show-stopping performance took place in the Thomas & Mack Center during the 1989-90 Rebels basketball season. The Lady Rebels basketball team, under the direction of Jim Bolla, won their seventh straight Big West Conference Championship, won 28 of 31 games, played in the NCAA Tournament and finished in the Top Ten in the country for the second straight year.

It hasn't taken Bolla long to make his mark in the coaching ranks. In 1989, after only seven seasons at UNLV, Jim became the winningest coach in Lady Rebel history. Following the 1989-90 season, his .788 winning percentage places him in the top ten of active collegiate women's basketball coaches.

He and his wife, Sheila Strike-Bolla, were believed to be the first and only married co-head coaches in the country from 1982-1989. But Sheila was named the Director of Special Projects for the Department of Intercollegiate Athletics at UNLV prior to the 1988-89 season, and Jim became the "sole" head coach.

A native of Pittsburgh, Jim began his coaching career in 1977 at the University of Pittsburgh following a highly successful playing career for the Panthers. A strong believer in the mental aspect of team building, Jim has utilized performance consultants to help the Lady Rebels attain their highest goals. Let's begin to explore Coach Bolla's theories on successful team building by looking at his thoughts...

...on Motivation

Goals and desire play a major role in the motivation of Jim Bolla's teams.

"The kids must have a strong burning desire to be successful," he says. "That inspiration must be directed toward our team goals."

The combination of desire and setting challenging goals has been the trademark of Bolla's successful teams at UNLV.

Through trial and error, Bolla has found some motivational techniques to be better than others.

"Negative feedback of any kind, from myself or my coaches, not only has no motivational effect on our players, but is actually destructive in nature," he points out.

Any kind of criticism that is based on sarcasm or humiliation has no motivational value as far as Coach Bolla is concerned.

"Because of the kind of person we recruit, using any negative feedback or criticism just isn't useful or productive for us," he concludes.

Bolla has found that his most effective motivational technique involves positive communications with the players.

"I've found that positive feedback is the best motivational technique my staff and I can use," he says. "It's just a matter of constantly telling the players they're doing a good job."

In summary, Jim believes that motivation is a combination of desire and inspiration to accomplish team goals. He also stresses that negative feedback and criticism of the student-athlete are the least effective motivational techniques that someone can use.

Finally, the most effective motivational technique is simply a steady dose of positive feedback from the coaches to the players.

* * * * * * * * * *

...on Team Cohesion

Team cohesion is a "family" affair at UNLV. Coach Bolla believes that anything can be accomplished if the team members trust and respect each other.

"Our philosophy concerning team cohesion equates to a family atmosphere," he says. "We are not naive in this matter because we know that every family goes through tough times."

Jim says the key element is trust.

"We have been successful because each player knows that she can count on everyone else to help her out if she needs it."

Coach Bolla builds on the idea of "family" when it comes to effective team cohesion techniques.

"During a recruiting visit by a prospective student-athlete, we place that person with the team for most of the visit, " he says. "We then get feedback from most of the team members after the recruit has left on how they felt about that person and if they believe the person would fit into our program."

Bolla strongly believes that this method of team personnel selection has had a very positive effect on team cohesion.

"We value their judgment on our new people," he says. "It has worked out well for us over the years."

In summarizing Coach Bolla's thoughts on team cohesion, he believes that you need to create a family atmosphere among team members and coaching staff. Also, in order to build team cohesion, you need to reinforce the value of each person's feedback and make them a part of the decision-making process. Combining the family atmosphere with decision-making powers for team members has proven to be a winning combination for the Lady Rebel basketball program.

* * * * * * * * * *

...on Discipline

Discipline has been a strong element in the success of Coach Bolla's teams over the years, and he is quick to explain why.

"Discipline for our team really revolves around two specific rules," he says. "First, you must always do what you say you're going to do and second, you must enforce it on everybody, with no player receiving special treatment."

The effectiveness of the disciplinary process is greatly influenced by the persons doing the disciplining, Bolla says.

"The least effective method involves the coaching staff meting out the discipline," he says.

He continues by saying that no one benefits when the coaches have to determine when a rule has been broken, decide what the punishment will be, and then "having to enforce it."

The most effective method of discipline is when the team makes the rules and enforces them.

"Group pressure is really the best method of taking care of discipline problems," Coach Bolla says.

He goes on to say that when the team makes and enforces the rules, the players respond better than if only one person decided.

"It also takes the coach away from the situation of being the bad guy," he says.

In summary, discipline is a necessaary element of all highly successful organizations. Bolla believes that you must be consistent in all disciplinary matters and that all team rules must be enforced in the same way, with no special treatment for anyone.

Least effective discipline methods involve the coaches making the decisions on violation of team rules. This method is ineffective because Bolla believes the process takes too long, disrupts team cohesion, and damages coach-athlete relations.

The most effective discipline method involves the team making all rules along with the consequences of breaking the rules, and then being responsible for enforcing those rules.

Finally, Coach Bolla believes that when the entire team is involved in the disciplinary process, pressure and resentment toward the coaching staff is removed and the effect on the players is heightened because it is the team doing the disciplining and not one person.

* * * * * * * * * *

.....on Mental Preparation

Mental preparation is essential for team and individual success and Jim believes that the key word in the phrase "mental preparation" is "preparation."

"To me, mental preparation means preparing for your opponent so that there will be no surprises," he says.

That kind of preparation must be intense and it must be comprehensive, he says.

"We will review game film and scouting reports. We also will work on specific game situations, special end-of-game situations, and all little things that might help us, including jump ball plays and free throw situations."

The players need to feel confident going into a game that they have been well-prepared for anything our opponent may throw at us, he concludes.

To mentally prepare the team for the grind of a long season, Coach Bolla believes that practice length has a lot to do with how successful the team will be.

"What I am going to tell you now is heretical in some coaching circles," he says. "During the six weeks of pre-season practices, we very rarely go beyond two hours."

He mentions that he knows of some programs that practice for three hours or more.

"We don't practice long because I not only don't like it, but the players absolutely hate it."

Bolla also points out that once the season begins, practice time diminishes even more.

"Once we start playing games, our practices are usually one and a half hours or less in length," he says.

The Lady Rebels prepare for late-game strategy every day in practice, reinforcing the belief that practice preparation enhances overall mental preparation.

In summarizing Coach Bolla's philosophy on mental preparation, he emphasizes that mental preparation is a product of the overall preparation of the team. This preparation includes reviewing game films and scouting reports. It also includes practicing all end-of-game situations and specific game situations that may arise during a game. Finally, Jim and his staff make sure that all the little things for success are reviewed in practice, specifically jump ball plays and free throw situations.

Mentally preparing the team for the long season has always been handled in the some way. It is Coach Bolla's belief that keeping practice sessions short in time length is the most effective way of combating mental fatigue as the season progresses. Meticulous practice preparation and utilizing shorter practice sessions have been the key to mental preparedness for UNLV teams.

* * * * * * * *

.....on Mental Toughness

Coach Bolla believes that mental toughness is a character trait that can be developed in all persons and is evident in all highly successful individuals.

"A mentally tough person is an individual who has the ability to do what has to be done at whatever the personal cost to that individual," he says.

It is Bolla's strong belief that the mentally tough person is a team-oriented individual.

"A mentally tough individual has the ability to keep her composure in an atmosphere of excitment," Coach Bolla says.

He also states that a mentally tough person has the innate sense to "Give others the opportunity to be successful."

Additional mental toughness traits include consistency and dependability, he says.

In summary, Jim believes that the mentally tough individual has the ability to accomplish what needs to be accomplished, regardless of the personal toll on the individual.

Character traits include composure amidst the element of game excitement, the ability to give others the opportunity to be successful, consistency in performance and dependability in attitude.

* * * * * * * * * *

.....on Communication

Coach Bolla and his staff pride themselves in the ability to effectively communicate with the players in times of adversity during games. Bolla believes that this ability has been instrumental in the overall sucess of the UNLV women's basketball program.

If the Lady Rebels are behind at halftime or late in the game, Jim's procedure for inspiring the team is to take a relaxed, reassuring approach.

"If we are behind at halftime, I take an analytical approach to the situation," he says. "Basically, we analyze what we can do better as a team and then we reinforce what has been working for us."

In a late-game losing situation, the approach is more tactical in nature.

"I emphasize that we need to reduce the deficit slowly, say 5 points in a 5 minute span, if we have that much time to spare. The key is to attack a deficit slowly and methodically, and hopefully things will work out."

After a tough loss or a poor performance by the team, Bolla's comments are brief, with the intention to discuss the game the following day at practice.

"If we've played poorly and lost or we lost a game in the closing seconds, I make it a point to not talk about it right after the game. This time is for the players. They need their space that night. I will analyze the game with my staff, further analyze it myself that night, and then come back the next day and discuss every aspect of the game with the players."

In summary, Coach Bolla does not take a high-intensity approach to inspiring his players in times of adversity during games. Half-time talks include analyses of what isn't working and what is working. A late-game deficit will be attacked in a slow, methodical way if the time permits.

Post-game comments to the team following a poor performance or a last-second loss will be very brief in nature and will contain no specific comments on the game. Jim will analyze the game overnight and will discuss all aspects of the game with the team the next day at practice.

* * * * * * * * * *

BOBBY BOWDEN

Florida State University

Position
Head Football Coach

Career Record
195-72-3 (24 seasons)

Education
B.S. 1953 Samford University

Team and Personal Highlights

* Ranks second in total coaching victories among active NCAA Division I coaches.

* His 195 victories as a head coach places him among the top 15 winningest coaches in NCAA football history.

* Pre-season Number 1 ranking in 1988.

* Winningest bowl coach in terms of percentage and number four on the list of all-time bowl wins.

* Eleven bowl appearances in 14 years at Florida State.

* Ten Top 20 rankings in Final Associated Press polls at Florida State.

* Devout member of the Fellowship of Christian Athletes.

* Little All-American football player at Samford University.

* Three sons coaching college football. Terry is head coach and Jeff is an assistant coach at Samford University. Tommy is an assistant coach at the University of Kentucky.

Bobby Bowden

Introduction...

Bobby Bowden is living proof that nice guys do finish first. A devoted Christian and family man, he has been developing national championship contenders since his arrival in Tallahassee in 1976. But his roots for building winners began long before he accepted the challenge at Florida State University.

The native of Birmingham, Alabama, started his coaching career in 1959 at Howard College (now Samford University), a small Southern school in which he earned Little All-America honors as a player before his graduation in 1953. With his first team at Samford finishing 9-1, Bowden completed a four-year stint with a 31-6 record.

In 1970, Bowden arrived in West Virginia to take the reins of the Mountaineers stumbling football program. During six years in Morgantown, his teams compiled a 42-26 overall record, including Peach Bowl appearances in 1972 and 1975.

Accepting the challenge in 1976 of reviving a Florida State program that had been 4-29 over the previous three seasons, Bobby finished 5-6 in his first year, winning the last three games in dramatic fashion. Those three wins began a string of 13 consecutive winning seasons and have put the Seminole program in the national spotlight.

Bobby Bowden's success as a coach can be attributed to his great love of people and his firm belief that successful teams are built through discipline and mental toughness. The World War II history buff and golf fanatic has always stressed the importance of the mental approach to the game. Let's begin our exploration into the team building strategies of Coach Bobby Bowden with his thoughts...

...on Motivation

Considered by many of his coaching peers as a motivational genius, Coach Bowden believes that motivation begins in the heart.

"Motivation is a state of heart and mind," he says. "You really can't be totally motivated unless both your heart and your mind are in it."

When the player is in the correct state of mind and heart, "he will have the courage and confidence and enthusiasm to give 100% effort all the time," Bowden says. Coach Bowden is a master mental technician when it comes to getting 100% effort from his players.

He has a simple theory when it comes to effective motivational techniques.

"I can tell you what doesn't work, and that's punishment for any kind of failure," he states.

Bowden believes that negative behavior from the coaches when a player makes a mistake only compounds the problem.

"Chewing the kid out won't make it better, for him or me," he says.

The most effective motivational technique that Bobby uses is reward for doing your best.

"We like to keep things positive all the time, so a reward might take the shape of less conditioning for the team or a helmet decal for great individual effort," he says.

The most important aspect, he points out, is that the players know they are loved and respected by the coaches.

In summary, Coach Bowden defines motivation as a state of heart and mind, a combination that gives the players courage, confidence and enthusiasm to give 100% effort at all times.

Least effective motivational techniques include any kind of punishment associated with failure, while the most effective motivational tool includes reward for individual effort.

* * * * * * * * * *

...on Team Cohesion

Team chemistry is a vital ingredient for ultimate team success, and no one knows that better than Coach Bowden. His philosophy concerning team cohesion is built around one word.

"Love is how I define team cohesion and team chemistry," he says. "The sacrifice, commitment, and pain involved with football in insurmountable, and without the players loving each other, you won't find cohesion and winning chemistry."

Building team cohesion, Bowden says, means involving everyone in all team activities.

"I try to build team chemistry by taking the boys to dinner together, to church together, even to banquets together. Wherever there is an easy, free setting where everyone can enjoy themselves is where we'll go."

Coach Bowden's strong Christian faith is also utilized in building team chemistry.

"I encourage the players to be a part of F.C.A. (Fellowship of Christian Athletes) so that they can realize the love of Christ in their lives," he says.

Bobby believes that Christian love has a tremendously positive effect on team building.

"It's mighty powerful in uniting a common bond of love between men," he professes.

In summarizing team cohesion, Coach Bowden defines team chemistry as a love among all the players. This love and respect for each other is the only way there can be winning cohesion on a team, he states.

Effective team building methods include taking the team to places as a group, such as dinners, church and banquets. He also encourages participation in FCA activities to help develop the common bond of love among team members.

* * * * * * * * * *

...on Discipline

Discipline is a trademark of all successful teams and individuals. Discipline is also a way of life at Florida State and many outsiders consider it to be the glue to the success of the Seminole program.

"I am a firm believer in discipline, on and off the field," Coach Bowden emphasizes. "We stress it here and we make a big thing out of it!" But Bowden also makes sure that it is done properly.

There are different ways to discipline a person, and Coach Bowden has his own way of doing things.

"Discipline is great, but you have to make sure that you don't push it too far, that you don't over-do it," he says.

Too much or too little makes any kind of discipline less effective, he believes.

"Hold a bird in your hand too loosely and it will escape," he states. "Hold it too tightly and it will die."

Effective discipline methods again revolve around the concept of love, Bowden says.

"You must convince your squad that discipline is love," he says. Bowden continues with a story to illustrate his point.

"Your dad spanked you as a child when you disobeyed and told you that it hurt him more than it hurt you. He did that because he loved you and wanted to make you a better person."

Coach Bowden puts the finishing touches on that story by stating his philosophy on discipline in no uncertain terms.

"If you don't love the children on your team, then don't discipline them. If you do love them, then you will discipline them, because proper discipline is love."

In summary, Coach Bowden is a firm believer of discipline, both on and off the field. He makes it a big issue with the players, and will not hesitate to exercise his use of disciplinary penalties when they are needed.

He considers too much or too little discipline as ineffective, stressing that a consistent approach must always be utilized. Discipline will be most effective, he believes, when the team is convinced that discipline is another form of love.

Finally, he strongly emphasizes that if you don't love your players, then don't discipline them. Every person on the team must realize that proper discipline is a message of love and that accepting discipline is a way of becoming a better person.

* * * * * * * * * *

...on Mental Preparation

All successful coaches say that mental preparation is essential to team and individual success. Bowden believes that mental preparation is not only a responsibility of the student-athlete, it is a responsibility of the coach as well.

"Mental preparation is transferring the coach's mental attitude and knowledge into the heads of his players," Bobby says.

In Coach Bowden's thoughts, mental preparation also means increasing the powers of concentration.

"Mental preparation means focusing on the priorities of the game and shutting out all distractions," he says.

Coach Bowden thinks that there are no secrets to mentally preparing a team for the long grind of a football season.

"The kids already have a mindset even before they report for fall camp," he says. "We tell them they better show up in excellent physical shape, they better be goal-oriented, and they should expect pre-season practice to be rough."

Every game is important to the Seminoles because they are a major independent school within the CFA.

"Every game is big to us because a loss is a loss, whether it's to Nebraska or Furman," he points out.

So mental preparation means getting ready for all games, not just a few.

"I want the kids to keep a level attitude and not have mountains and valleys mentally," he says. "We must be ready for 11 straight games once the season has started."

Mental preparation for late-game strategy is practiced thoroughly during the week of game preparations.

"We work on our two-minute offense every day," Bowden states. "So if we are behind late in the game, we can still win."

He adds that late-game strategy practice includes both the offense and defense.

"It's important that the kids understand that all late-game situations involve both the offense and the defense. It's a team game no matter how you look at it," he says.

In summarizing mental preparation, Coach Bowden stresses that mental preparation is the responsibility of the player and the coach. It is the coach's duty to get the student-athlete thinking like a coach and keeping a focus on the priorities of the game.

Mental preparation for the season begins long before the players report to fall practice. Coach Bowden communicates his expectations for the pre-season long before the student-athletes arrive on campus. These expectations include reporting in top physical condition, having team and individual goals in mind, and having an understanding that fall practices will be very rough.

Mental preparation for non-conference and conference opponents is identical because Florida State is a college independent. This means that all 11 of their games are important, so mental preparation is ongoing right from the beginning of fall practice.

Finally, to ensure late-game success, the Seminoles practice their two-minute offense each day, incorporating the defense in the preparations as well. The "team" concept is always evident in Coach Bowden's philosophy, so mental preparation will involve all the members of the team.

* * * * * * * * * *

...on Mental Toughness

Mental toughness is a trait found in all highly-skilled athletes, and the team with the most mentally tough players is usually the team that wins. Coach Bowden is very aware of the need for mentally tough players on his teams.

"Mental toughness is also something you can't coach, but you hope that each of your players has it," he says. "I think that mental toughness means allowing the mental to overcome the physical pain associated with football."

Mental toughness is also an attitude, he says.

"It's an attitude that 'no opposing player can physically whip me' and 'no coach is tough enough to run me off'. That's mental toughness."

Coach Bowden believes that there are several traits evident in a mentally tough player.

"He definitely has to be able to play with pain," he states. "That's a critical point."

Reacting to criticism is also a mental toughness trait.

"The player must be able to accept criticism in a positive way," he says. "That is a difficult thing to do for some players."

The final characteristic of mental toughness is persistence.

"The mentally tough player absolutely will not quit at anything he attempts," Coach Bowden says. "Nothing can get in his way to stop him once he's set his mind to accomplish it."

In summary, Coach Bowden believes that mental toughness means having the mental strength to overcome any physical pain associated with football. It is also an attitude of never allowing anyone or anything to influence or intimidate you away from your goals.

Mental toughness traits include playing with pain, accepting criticism in a positive way, and never quitting at anything you do.

* * * * * * * * * *

...on Communication

A major responsibility of a head coach is the ability to effectively communicate with players, fellow coaches, administrators, the media, alumni and the community. Coach Bowden loves talking with people.

"I guess I've always been a talker," he says.

His ability to communicate with his team and coaching staff during critical times of a game puts him in the upper echelon of coaches.

"I very rarely yell or chew the kids out at halftime if the effort was good, but the execution was bad," he says. "But if the effort was bad, I may have a few things to say."

But as most successful coaches do, any inspiration comes from technical responses to adversity.

"There just isn't any time to be jumping up and down and getting emotional late in a close game," he points out. "I have to be able to have the right play called when the game is on the line. The kids expect that and I do, too." So keeping a calm, poised response to adversity is Bowden's way of inspiring his teams late in a close game.

Post-game comments after a tough loss or a poor performance are usually met in a positive way.

"I'm not afraid to tell the kids I'm disappointed," Coach Bowden says. "But no single player or official's call or botched play caused us to lose. It's always a combination of factors and I may touch on only a few of them."

The usual routine is to tell the players that they did the best they could, regroup, learn from our mistakes, and get ready for the next game.

"Now if I see something in the films that I didn't see in the game, well, we'll just have to talk to the team or player about it to get things straightened out." he says.

Always talking, always making sure that everyone understands what needs to be done is the master-teacher approach to communication that has made Coach Bowden one of the best in the country.

In summarizing Coach Bowden's approach to communication, it is apparent that he believes effective communication is an important psychological factor within the program.

Halftime talks will center around technical adjustments for the offense and defense. Only a short time period remains for general comments, and Bowden stresses the importance of effort and concentration during those moments before the team returns to the field.

Reacting to adversity late in a game makes communication vital for success. Coach Bowden takes a calm, poised approach because any kind of emotional scene would be counterproductive to the team. The players expect a professional response from the coaching staff and he makes sure that they get one.

Post-game comments after a tough loss or a poor performance are met in an upbeat tone. Bowden places the blame on no one, and makes it a point to mention the positive aspects of the game. Any additional comments are made to the team after the coaching staff has reviewed the game film.

Coach Bowden ultimately communicates the thought that every game should be a learning experience for the players, whether it is a win or a loss for the Seminoles.

* * * * * * * * * *

JOANNE BRACKER
Midland Lutheran College

Position
Head Women's Basketball Coach
Assistant Professor of Physical Education

Career Record
421-104   (20 seasons)

Education
B.S.   1966 Dana College
M.S.   1970 University of Northern Colorado

Team and Personal Highlights

* Winningest active women's coach in the National Association of Intercollegiate Athletics (NAIA).
* Ranks fourth in the nation for winning percentage among active coaches (.801).
* Team earned national Top Ten ranking six times, finishing number three in 1982-83 season.
* Teams have won eight of the last ten Nebraska Intercollegiate Athletic Conference Championships.
* Teams have captured five consecutive NAIA District 11 titles.
* Assistant Coach for the North Team at the 1989 U.S. Olympic Festival.
* The *Lincoln Journal* 1985 State College Coach of the Year, the first woman to earn that honor.
* Past President of the NAIA Women's Basketball Coaches Association.
* Member of the NAIA All-American Selection Committee.
* Member of the Board of Directors of the Women's Basketball Coaches Association.
* Member of USA BASKETBALL Olympic Games Committee.
* Member of *Coaching Women's Basketball* Editorial Board.

Joanne Bracker

Introduction...

Joanne Bracker has established herself as a coaching legend in Nebraska while guiding Midland Lady Warrior basketball teams for the past 20 seasons.

A soft-spoken individual with a boundless energy level, Coach Bracker has been building winning teams at Midland since her arrival at the Fremont, Nebraska, school in 1970. Her teams have qualified for the national playoffs three times and have dominated the Nebraska Intercollegiate Athletic Conference like no other team.

A sound fundamentalist of the game of basketball, Bracker is a featured speaker at coaching clinics nationwide. Highly respected among her coaching peers, she has been a force behind the rise in popularity of women's basketball while holding national leadership positions within women's coaches associations.

A proven winner and a proponent of the mental aspect of successful team building, Joanne was eager and excited to share her thoughts on this subject. Here are Coach Bracker's thoughts...

...on Motivation

Coach Bracker believes that motivation is the desire to perform well.

"Motivation is the purpose or reason why one is stimulated to perform," she says.

Motivation is also the responsibility of both the player and the coaching staff, she says.

"Since this is a team concept, then everyone needs to be involved," she adds.

Over the course of her illustrious coaching career, Bracker has discovered what elements are effective and what elements are not effective in motivating her players.

"I've found that posting statistical data in itself is not an effective motivational tool for us," Coach Bracker says. "There needs to be some significance in the type of statistics you share with the team, so we take a different approach, which I'll explain later."

Coach Bracker has found that material rewards are not effective in motivating her players.

"Certificates or stars or plaques or ribbons or any of that type of extrinsic reward just hasn't done it for us," she states.

Verbal abuse will not find its way into Coach Bracker's methods of motivating athletes.

"First of all, it's just not in my personality to be a yeller or screamer," she says. "So yelling and screaming would be very emotionally disruptive not only for the players, but for me as well."

Another ineffective motivational technique involves a hyperactive approach to the game.

"I have never used a rah-rah type of speech to motivate the players," she says. "It just isn't a part of my personality and I'd probably only confuse the players if I ever tried it now!"

There are several motivational techniques that Bracker has found to be excellent when dealing with her players over the years, and those techniques include utilizing individuals in addition to visual resources and coaching techniques.

"First of all, I have found that the most effective motivational technique revolves around goal setting," she states. " I need to challenge my players by establishing short-term goals on an individual basis. I also must make sure that those goals are attainable for that player."

She includes specific team goals which are realistic as an extension of the personal goal setting program.

Bracker also believes that being organized and having consistency within the program provides confidence and motivation to the players.

"When the players see that we have a definite plan of attack for each game and that we have won consistently over the years, it has a positive effect," she says.

She now discusses how statistics are utilized within her program as a motivational tool.

"We have what is called a personal accomplishment chart for each player," she states. "We put all the usual types of statistics on the chart, but the program is individualized for each player. From each chart, both the player and I can identify progress or lack of progress throughout the course of the season. This is how I've discovered how statistics can be used as a motivating factor."

Coach Bracker utilizes former players as role models for her current team members, always identifying their successes and accomplishments.

"I want to show the players what hard work and dedication to the team goals can accomplish for an individual," she says. "There's nothing better than showing them living examples of that success."

Media publicity and visual resources are also motivation factors.

"Getting fan support during a game is highly motivating for our players," Bracker says. "We also like to use season highlight videotapes or the Kodak All-America highlight tapes to add a motivational punch during the season."

Scheduling, attractive uniforms and assigning challenges to the players for each game are also motivational techniques that have been effective for Coach Bracker over the years.

"A competitive schedule has been very effective for us in motivating our players and our recruits," she says. "But the schedule must be challenging, not intimidating, for the players. So it's really my responsibility to make sure that our schedule is attractive and competitive."

Attractive, proper-fitting attire is also very motivating for Midland players.

"We take excellent care of our uniforms to make sure they stay attractive and useful for a long period of time."

She adds, "And when we buy new uniforms or warmups, we make sure the players treat the uniforms with respect and sensibility."

Assigning individual challenges and responsibilities for various games has also been a successful motivational technique.

"We'll challenge an individual player or players to improve their performance or shut down an opponent during a game. The players have all responded very positively to personal challenges along these lines."

Occasionally adding new drills, offenses, defenses or special plays during the course of the season can also help motivate the players, Bracker says.

"You need to keep a new idea or drill available when the players begin to lack motivation from the repetition of practice," she says. "Anything new seems to perk them up."

Finally, utilizing a personal touch with each player and keeping pre-game discussions of opponent's perceptions low-key are Bracker's final two motivational techniques.

"I have individual conversations with players each day, not necessarily about team topics," she says.

It's also important to have team discussions and player responses on a wide variety of topics, she says," because we want our players to be complete student-athletes, able to carry on a discussion of a non-athletic nature within the mainstream of the college."

Bracker has also found that keeping a low-key approach to pre-game preparations has been beneficial to the players.

"Before an important game, we'll discuss what I consider to be our opponent's perceptions of us as a team," she states. "If we're an underdog, then we'll stress that we need a great effort from everyone. If we're considered the favorite, then I make sure we keep our minds focused on the game at all times because if we don't, we won't be successful."

In summary, Coach Bracker defines motivation as the desire to perform well. Least effective motivational techniques include posting statistical data and utilizing material rewards such as certificates, stars, plaques or ribbons.

Any type of verbal abuse in the form of yelling or screaming at the athletes is ineffective, as is any display of over-emotional behavior during pre-game talks with the team.

Bracker offers a lengthy list of effective motivational methods. Establishing both short-term, challenging individual goals and specific team goals is a highly effective technique.

Being organized and consistent helps to provide confidence to the players. Personal accomplishment charts identifying player progress is an effective motivational tool, as is using former players as role models.

Motivational videotapes and media publicity can also be highly effective, as can a challenging schedule of games. Individual challenges and responsibilities during games is also an effective method of motivation.

New drills or adjustments to the offense and defense can be effective if used at the right time, and attractive, proper-fitting uniforms and warm-ups also motivate the athletes.

In addition, individual conversations with the players and team discussions on various topics help build pride and motivation. Finally, keeping a low-key approach to the opponent's perceptions of her team is also an effective motivational technique.

* * * * * * * * * *

...on Team Cohesion

Team cohesion is a success ingredient in any organization, and Coach Bracker is proud to point out that one major reason for the success of the Midland women's basketball program is that team chemistry has always been considered excellent among team members.

"We've always recruited conscientious, dependable people, and we're fortunate that they've always put the team ahead of themselves," she says.

Coach Bracker believes that team cohesion is built on mutual respect.

"Team cohesion is the ability of each team member to accept each individual player as a valuable contributor to the whole," she states.

Bracker utilizes several methods to build team cohesion.

"I think you need to establish individual performance roles for each player," she says, adding, "and each role must contribute to the final outcome." If each player reacts to her role in a positive way, then team chemistry is strengthened.

Group activities and open communication lines are instrumental in building team cohesion.

"We have numerous group activities where everyone is involved," Bracker states. "It's important that whenever you have team functions, all members take part."

Keeping communication lines open between the staff and players is crucial if you want to sustain a positive team environment.

"Our players know they can come in and talk to us about anything," she emphasizes. "And we wouldn't have it any other way."

Another effective team building method is switching the roles of the players.

"During practices, we'll have the centers play guard and the guards play the post and the forwards doing both," Coach Bracker says. "It's amazing how team chemistry is improved when each player gets an idea of what it's like to play another position. The players are much more empathetic with their teammates when things go bad because they've been in that same situation."

It's also very important that each team member has something positive to say about her teammates.

"We'll sit down with the team and ask each player to comment positively about a teammate, her strong points and what she likes about her," Bracker says.

Any time you can discuss the positive qualities of each individual in a group setting, only good things can happen, she points out.

Finally team cohesion is built by using team leaders effectively.

"Peer influence is still one of the best ways to build a program, and if you have the type of leader that is admired by other teammates, then you must utilize that player's influence in building team chemistry," she concludes.

In summarizing Coach Bracker's thoughts on team cohesion, she believes that team chemistry is the ability of each member to accept each individual player as a valuable contributor to the team.

Methods of building team cohesion include establishing individual performance roles which contribute to a successful outcome. Numerous group activities and open communication among players is also effective.

Switching roles also builds team unity, as does identifying and discussing the positive qualities of each individual team member. Finally, using team leaders effectively can also build team cohesion.

* * * * * * * * * *

...on Discipline

"To be successful as a team or as an individual, players must be self-disciplined," Coach Bracker states. "We would not be as successful as we have been without our players having some element of self-discipline."

Both the players and coaching staff are involved in establishing team rules.

"Rules and regulations are established with the players for their benefit to assure optimum performance," she says.

Over the years, Bracker has discovered both effective and ineffective methods of disciplining players.

"The most ineffective method is reprimanding a player in the presence of the team," she says. "Any kind of public reprimand is damaging to the player's self-respect and should be avoided."

Coach Bracker lists several methods she has found to be effective when handling player discipline problems.

"Foresight is really the best method," she says. "You can eliminate potential problems by just keeping your eyes and ears open."

She mentions consistent treatment as another effective method of discipline.

"The players respect you when you deal consistently with problems," she states. "Specific penalties for specific rule infractions must be upheld. If players see special treatment, aside from unusual circumstances, they begin to feel you aren't being consistent. And that can really hurt team morale."

Taking immediate action is another effective method when dealing with discipline.

"I've found that you must deal immediately with the problem or it will become worse," Bracker says. "You can't ignore it and hope it goes away on its own, because it won't."

Coach Bracker's final method of handling discipline matters surrounds playing privileges.

"Athletics is a privilege, not a right," she says.

Eliminating playing time during games is highly effective because it takes the player from the spotlight. Even though Coach Bracker will only utilize this option as a last resort, "I'll use it when I must," she says.

In summary, Coach Bracker believes that discipline begins with player self-discipline. Establishing rules and regulations is a joint effort of the team and coaching staff. She believes that the joint effort assures optimum performance by team members and makes them a part of the decision-making process which is good for team morale.

The least effective method of discipline is public reprimand of the player. Bracker believes that irreparable harm can result because of this method and advises that this type of disciplinary action be avoided.

Foresight and consistency are two effective methods of discipline, she says. Keeping eyes and ears open all the time can eliminate potential problems before they develop.

Specific rule infractions should carry specific penalties, and the coach must consistently uphold those penalties. A lack of consistency, she says, can cause additional morale problems.

Dealing immediately with all discipline matters is a third method of effectively handling a problem. Coach Bracker says ignoring the problem or hoping it will disappear only sets the stage for future problems.

The final method that Coach Bracker utilizes when handling discipline problems involves taking away playing time for the athlete. She strongly believes that athletics is a privilege and not a right. Taking away playing privileges, however, is a decision she will make only after exhausting all other options.

* * * * * * * * * *

...on Mental Preparation

Coach Bracker compares mental preparation to motivation in theory.

"I think that both ideas mean having a desire to perform well," she says.

Bracker also stresses the word "preparation" when mentally preparing the team for the grind of a long season.

"During pre-season practice, we mentally prepare the players by establishing short-term goals," she says. "We also begin developing and recording each player's individual progress on their personal charts," she adds.

Another vital area of interest during pre-season is the emphasis on team unity and how important that aspect is to the overall success of our program, she says.

Preparation for non-conference games is enhanced by a competitive schedule, Bracker says.

"Scheduling competitive opponents during non-conference games really helps us because it challenges us to be at our best."

Utilizing all team members during non-conference games is also very important for building team unity, she believes.

"It's important that all the players participate at some time during non-conference games. It not only prepares them for our difficult conference schedule, but keeps team morale high," she concludes.

Mental preparation is solidified during non-conference games through the use of a variety of game strategies.

"We use the non-conference portion of our schedule to implement a variety of game strategies that we know we'll be using during our conference games," she says. "It's also the best time to play a lot of players at different positions and in different combinations to find where the strengths of our team can be found."

Coach Bracker points out that it is important that the team and coaching staff do not over-prepare for teams during the non-conference schedule.

"We will be prepared for each non-conference game, but we won't over-emphasize the preparations. We want to set a preparation pace that leads us up to the conference portion of our schedule," she says.

Preparation for games in the Nebraska Intercollegiate Athletic Conference is likened to preparing for war, Bracker jokes. But her approach is not a laughing matter.

"We are totally and thoroughly prepared for each game we play in our conference," she emphasizes. "Each game plan is concrete, and we make sure that the players are totally confident in what we want them to do and they are in control of each situation they find themselves in during the game."

Conference games also find Bracker and her staff developing a motivational approach for each game.

"We are constantly searching for a specific motivational thought or reason to play well in each contest, kind of a new theme for each game," she says. "This approach has helped us a lot over the years."

Late-game strategy is practiced from the first day of pre-season drills. Bracker is a master technician in the art of late-game preparation and implementation.

"We do a lot of gambling, both offensively and defensively, if we're behind late in a game," she says. "Our approach is to change our traditional patterns to unexpected ones."

The unexpected strategy includes assigning individual responsibilities to players, implementing specific offensive and defensive changes designed for each situation, and utilizing crowd support.

"If we're behind at home, our late-game strategy is focused on gaining crowd involvement," she points out. "We will run plays that will excite the crowd, like 3-point shots and alley-oop plays." Getting vocal crowd support has a positive

In summarizing Coach Bracker's thoughts on mental preparation, she believes that mental preparation is similar to motivation in that it requires a desire to perform well.

Mentally preparing the players for the season includes a number of strategies. For the grind of pre-season practices, she establishes short-term personal goals, developes player progress charts and begins emphasizing the importance of team unity.

Non-conference games are approached as a time to prepare for conference games. A variety of game strategies are used, different player combinations are experimented with, players try out new positions, and all team members get playing time. Bracker is quick to point out that a competitive non-conference schedule is very advantageous, and that over-preparation for non-conference games should be avoided.

Conference games are the focal point of the season. Game plans are specific and preparation is thorough. It is important for the players to be confident and in total control during these games. Bracker and her staff also utilize different motivational themes for each game.

The key of late-game strategy to overcome a deficit is changing traditional patterns in both offense and defense, she says. Changes will be specific and include assigning specific responsibilities to players. It is important to utilize crowd support late in a game, so Bracker will implement 3-point shot and alley-oop plays to gain the support of the crowd and motivate her players.

* * * * * * * * * *

...on Mental Toughness

Mental toughness is a trait found in all successful student-athletes. Coach Bracker stresses mental toughness with her players and believes an individual can become mentally tougher with practice.

"I think a mentally tough individual is very self-disciplined," she says. "Someone who is always in control emotionally."

Bracker is quick to list her traits associated with mental toughness.

"As I mentioned before, a mentally tough individual is always emotionally in control," she states. "There are no sudden outbursts."

Consistency in performance and a competitive nature are also mental toughness traits in Bracker's book.

"The player must be consistent in her performance. As coaches, we want to know that we will be getting the same solid performance from a player all the time," she says.

A player who thrives on competition is a mentally tough individual.

"I appreciate a player who is highly competitive and thrives on challenges," she says, noting, "and a mentally tough player plays best when she is challenged."

In addition, Bracker believes a mentally tough individual is committed to excellence in all aspects of life, not just athletics. A mentally tough individual is also extremely confident in her abilities.

A mentally tough individual has a mature outlook on life and is relaxed and comfortable with herself, she states.

In summary, Bracker believes mental toughness is comparable to self-discipline and emotional control. Mental toughness traits include emotional control, consistency in performance, and a competitive nature that thrives on challenges.

Finally, a mentally tough individual is committed to excellence, conveys an air of confidence, and is mature and relaxed in her outlook on life.

* * * * * * * * * *

...on Communication

Communication with the players and staff and effectively dealing with adversity are important psychological factors for the success of any program. Coach Bracker understands these matters and has her own way of dealing with them.

"There is no screaming or yelling during halftime in the locker room if we're behind," she says. "We take the approach of simply changing strategy or substituting in new players."

Bracker states that there is no place for emotional outbursts late in a close game.

"During those time-outs, we try to build the confidence of the players by redefining responsibilities, stressing goals and adjusting our game plan," she says.

Post-game comments after a disappointing loss or a poor performance by the team are always positive in nature.

"I try to key on the positive accomplishments of the game rather than dwell on poor performance factors," she says.

This kind of approach helps to solidify team unity, Bracker believes.

"We also discuss ways we can avoid any disappointing performances in the future," she states.

The post-game comments usually end with a challenge to the team for the next game.

"I like to give them something to anticipate during preparations for our next opponent," she concludes.

In summary, Coach Bracker believes that communication is an important psychological factor concerning team success. Halftime talks and late-game timeouts take on a business-like approach. Changes in strategy and player substitutions are implemented to change negative momentum.

Bracker tries to build player confidence by redefining player responsibilities, stressing team goals and adjusting the game plan.

In her post-game comments following a disappointing loss or an underachieving team performance, the tone is upbeat. Positive accomplishments are reviewed instead of poor performance factors.

Finally, she ends her post-game comments with a challenge to the players to get them thinking with anticipation to the next opponent.

* * * * * * * * * *

DALE BROWN

Louisiana State University

Position
Head Men's Basketball Coach

Career Record
340-202   (18 seasons)

Education
B.A. 1958 Minot (N.D.) State College
M.S. 1965 University of Oregon

Team and Personal Highlights

*   Tied with legendary Harry Rabenhorst for winningest coach in LSU history with 340 wins.

*   Head Coach of South team in 1990 U.S. Olympic Festival.

*   Fourteen consecutive winning seasons.

*   Twelve straight post-season tournament appearances.

*   Ten NCAA tournament appearances, seven in a row.

*   Four NCAA Tournament Regional Championship Game appearances.

*   Two NCAA Final Four appearances.

*   Most consecutive games coached at LSU - 542.

*   Recipient of numerous coaching and civic honors.

Dale Brown

Introduction...

Dale Brown arrived in Baton Rouge, Louisiana, in March of 1972 with a dream of making Tiger basketball a fan favorite throughout the football-dominated Cajun state. After completing the 1989-90 season, his 18th at LSU, Coach Brown has not only seen that dream come true, but has solidly established the Fighting Tiger basketball program as a perennial national power.

Building winning teams is a challenge that Dale Brown cherishes, and no greater challenge was evident than during the 1988-89 season.

Despite the loss of three prominent freshmen due to Proposition 48 and a team that was left with one senior and no juniors, the Tigers started shakily as Brown and his staff molded the team into a cohesive unit that contended for the Southeastern Conference title until the final week of the regular season.

Brown, one of the most colorful and out-spoken personalities in college athletics, has been a basketball coach for 33 years. Before taking the LSU job in 1972, his other coaching stops included high school coaching in North Dakota and junior high and high school coaching in California.

A brief coaching stint with the U. S. Army preceded an assistant coaching position at Utah State from 1966-71. He was also an assistant at Washington State University for one year before taking the LSU job.

An outstanding athlete at St. Leo's High School in Minot, North Dakota, Brown was the leading scorer in both football and basketball. As a senior, he was the state scoring leader in basketball and also set a school record in the 440-yard dash.

Brown continued his athletic career at Minot State College (now the University of North Dakota-Minot) and earned 12 letters in basketball, football and track, making him the school's only athlete to achieve that honor.

A fiery competitor who is emotionally attached to every endeavor he embarks upon, Brown's teams play with the same intensity, tenacity and aggressiveness that exemplifies their leader's approach to life.

A superb motivator, Brown makes hundreds of speeches annually to various audiences around the world. His wife, Vonnie, is recognized as one of the nation's leading folk dance instructors and daughter Robyn, a 1985 LSU graduate, is associated with Dale Brown Enterprises in Baton Rouge.

The highly-energized coach is eager to talk about meeting challenges and building winning organizations. Let's begin this journey toward successful team building with Dale Brown's thoughts...

...on Motivation

Opposing coaches have been heard to say, "If there's one thing that Dale

Brown can do, it's motivate his players." Brown's entire life has been built around the concept of motivation: for himself, his family and his players.

Motivation encompasses several components in Coach Brown's philosophy: responsibility, belief in oneself, maximum effort and coachability.

Motivation, he says, first begins with a person's thinking.

"You are what you think, you attract what you think, your life is a product of your thoughts and belief and nothing in the world can change this fact," he states. "To alter your life, the only single course open is to alter your thinking."

Brown says responsibility plays a major role in motivation.

"You and you alone are responsible for your future," he states. "You are really free the moment you do not look outside yourself for someone to solve your problems. You will know that you are free when you no longer blame anyone or anything, but realize you control yourself and your destiny."

Belief in one's abilities is paramount in the motivation process.

"If you don't have confidence in yourself, others will not rely or trust in you when the going gets tough," he concludes.

A third element in the motivation process revolves around maximum effort at all times.

"If you truly do your best, and only you will really know, then you are successful and the actual score is immaterial, whether it was favorable or unfavorable," he points out. "However, when you fail to do your best, you have failed even though the score might have been to your liking. Doing the best you are capable of doing is victory in itself, and less than that is defeat."

A final element in the motivation process according to Coach Brown is the athlete's receptivity to the coaching process.

"A motivated athlete must also recognize that one of the most consistent findings in relation to the emotional qualities of men who are labeled as extraordinary athletes is that they have been coachable," he states. "There have been so few exceptions to this observation that it is concluded that coachability is one of the most essential qualities for truly great athletic effort."

In summary, motivation is a combination of elements as far as Coach Brown is concerned. Those elements include responsibility, belief in oneself, maximum effort and coachability. Brown best sums up his ideas on motivation in these words, "All of us should recognize that the best potential of me is we."

Finally, he believes that effective motivation techniques involve activities that build confidence and self-esteem in the athlete while strengthening the team concept.

* * * * * * * * * *

...on Team Cohesion

The philosophy of the LSU basketball program is one of a family unit, and the responsibility for developing and maintaining team chemistry rests on the shoulders of only one person.

"The head coach is the role model for the team," he says. "My motto is 'Don't do what I say, do what I do'."

Actions speak louder than words in Coach Brown's program.

"Actions talk around here, so my interactions with my staff is essential in giving the right impression to the players," he points out. "If the players see that the head coach and the staff have good cohesion, then the team will fall in line, also."

Team cohesion is a vital ingredient for ultimate team success. Coach Brown says that it is absolutely impossible for a basketball team to be successful without team unity and teamwork.

"To live by relying on one another implies a risk, but without some trust in humanity, life would be unliveable," he says.

As many of the other master teacher-coaches in this book divulge, espousing the "family" philosophy is also a part of Brown's recruiting presentation.

"Our recruiting philosophy is that we recruit human beings first and basketball players second," he says. "We tell our recruits that college is not just a place to play basketball. It is an opportunity to prepare yourself as a student-athlete so you can secure a college degree and lead a successful and happy life long after your playing days are over, and I will do everything I can to help him reach that goal."

He points to the statistic that 76% of all basketball players that stayed at LSU for four years received their college degrees.

Even though he considers the head coach the ultimate role model for his players, he also emphasizes that each person must show respect to one another.

"As I've stated before, the greatest potential of me is we," he says. "Each player must respect one another and give of himself for the good of the team."

The family atmosphere also builds loyalty, devotion and dedication, he says.

"We must be loyal and supportive of one another. Unity involves a devotion and dedication to a cause which puts everyone closer together. When an individual loses oneself in something they think is bigger than they are, they instantly become a winner," he states.

In summarizing Brown's thoughts on team cohesion, he believes that developing a "family" atmosphere is essential in promoting team chemistry and he strongly asserts that it is the responsibility of the head coach to be the role model in this endeavor.

Self-respect and respect for each person in the organization is also important in developing and maintaining team unity. Loyalty, devotion and dedication are all by-products of a close-knit organization, he adds.

Finally, successful methods of building team cohesion are the examples set by the head coach in his dealings with every member of the basketball program on a daily basis.

* * * * * * * * * *

...on Discipline

Discipline is a trait of the championship team and individual, and Coach Brown is adamant in his philosophy concerning team discipline.

"The only true discipline is discipline with love, " he says.

It is Brown's belief that when disciplinary action must be invoked against a player, that the player understands that the only reason he is being disciplined is because Coach Brown cares and loves him and that the disciplinary action is proof of that love.

"It may sound corny in this day and age of sophistication, but when I discipline a young man, it's because I love him and I don't want to see him fail, " he says.

He points out that the easy way to handle the situation is to ignore it.

"If a parent allows his child to do things that are not right without any kind of disciplinary action, then that parent is not doing his job, and that's to teach the child what is right and what is wrong," he states.

He continues the example by utilizing basketball analogy.

"The same thing goes within our program. If I allow a player to break team rules and in the process put a dark cloud over our program and then do nothing about it, then I'm not doing my job as head coach," he states.

He once again emphasizes the importance of taking action with his players.

"I love my players and that's why they must be disciplined when it is appropriate. If I don't discipline them, then they think I don't love them, and that's even worse," he says.

Least effective disciplinary methods involve any kind of penalties.

"I've found that taking what can be considered short-term remedies, like running penalty miles or extra conditioning, are not effective in the long run," he says.

He has found one disciplinary procedure to be most effective.

"The only really effective disciplinary method is suspension from the team," he says.

By taking the individual away from an environment that he enjoys makes the biggest impression, Coach Brown states.

In summary, Brown believes that the only true form of discipline is "discipline with love." It is the responsibility of the head coach, he adds, to explain the definition of "discipline with love" to his players and then enforce that rule when it is appropriate.

Finally, the least effective disciplinary method involves penalties in the form of extra running or conditioning, while the most effective disciplinary method involves suspension from the team for a game, games or indefinitely.

* * * * * * * * * *

...on Mental Preparation

Mental preparation has been an important element in the development of successful teams at LSU over the years, and Coach Brown again takes the forefront in teaching the players the way he wants the skill to be learned.

"We believe that mental preparation involves teaching mental imagery to the players," he says. "The unique aspect of it is that we teach imagery for two distinct reasons."

Those two reasons are teaching imagery for improving self-image and teaching imagery in a basketball-oriented setting.

"I want the players to know that imagery is a powerful skill that can be useful to them not only in the basketball setting, but also applies to real life," he states

Establishing a strong self-image is extremely important to Brown.

"Without a strong self-image, the player has self-doubt and lacks the confidence needed to be successful in life," he concludes.

After working on imagery for self-image, Coach Brown proceeds to teach imagery skills that are basketball-specific in nature.

"We teach mental imagery that includes late-game situations and other basketball-related topics," he says.

The other mental imagery topics that he covers with the players include the correct reaction to what he considers to be a bad call by an official during a game, the correct reaction to the distracting actions of an opponent's fans, correct reaction to a bad foul committed against the player, and the correct reaction to an unsportsmanlike foul against the player.

"The players know how powerful the mind is, so if we can teach them the correct way to handle a difficult situation, and they can play it over and over in their minds, then when the situation actually occurs, the player will react in a positive fashion," he states.

Where does all this teaching take place?

"We teach it in the locker room before practice, at private meetings with players and at team meetings. The players utilize it on the court, and then we develop the skill for non-sport settings as well," he says.

Mental preparation techniques are utilized throughout the season for the Tiger basketball players. The mental approach to each part of the season is different, however.

"The players know that they need to meet certain expectations of the coaches when pre-season practice begins," he says.

Those expectations include arriving in excellent physical condition as a result of running and lifting weights, and most importantly, "being mentally ready for what lies ahead in early practices."

Coach Brown's philosophy from a mental standpoint concerning non-conference games is similar to the pre-season approach.

"We basically feel that non-conference games are an extension of practice," he says. "This means that we want the players to enjoy the games and have fun and play in a relaxed manner."

Even though the general rule of Coach Brown is not to scout non-conference opponents, there is always an exception.

"We will scout an opponent if the game is important and of national stature", meaning that the opponent is a national power.

Coach Brown reiterates that the season is divided into four mini-seasons and that the players must be mentally prepared for all four.

"As I've mentioned, pre-season practice is the first season we must mentally prepare for, and then our non-conference schedule is really an extension of pre-season practice," he states. "But when the SEC schedule begins, we must be playing some of our best ball."

Playing competitively throughout the conference schedule is important, but to a lesser degree for the Tigers.

Brown says their goal is and always will be to win the conference tournament and thus qualify for the NCAA championship tournament.

The fourth and final mini-season is post-season NCAA tournament competition.

"We must be razor-sharp mentally at this time of the season," he says. "Hopefully all our mental preparation during the season will pay off for us during this time."

Late-game strategy is taught through mental imagery throughout the year and then is reinforced by physical practice on a daily basis, he states.

"We have been successful in the majority of our late-game strategy over the years because the kids have played those situations over and over in their minds every day of the season," he states. "So when we actually find ourselves in that predicament, the kids have the utmost confidence in their abilities to do what is necessary to win."

In summarizing Coach Brown's approach to mental preparation, he is quick to mention that teaching mental imagery skills to the players on a daily basis is the key to being ready for all phases of the season. He also addresses the need to teach imagery skills to the players as they relate to non-athletic settings.

Mental preparation is needed for pre-season practices, non-conference games, conference games and post-season tournaments, he says.

Non-conference games are approached mentally as an extension of practice and no non-conference opponent is scouted unless the game is of national importance and stature.

The key time of the season mentally is during the conference portion of the schedule, climaxing with the post-season tournament. NCAA tournament games is the time when Coach Brown wants his teams to "peak" mentally.

Finally, late-game strategy is taught through mental imagery sessions on a daily basis, in the belief that the team will be successful in an actual game setting because they have played the game "in their mind" and have the confidence to execute the proper game movements when necessary.

* * * * * * * * * *

...on Mental Toughness

Mental toughness is a trait found in all highly-skilled athletes, and Brown is a living example of the results of mental toughness.

"When I was growing up in North Dakota, life was very tough for my family," he says. "If you weren't mentally tough, you couldn't survive."

That is why the subject of mental toughness can always be found in the daily conversations of Dale Brown and his players.

Coach Brown defines mental toughness in a distinct manner.

"Mental toughness is a combination of traits, and these are the traits we try to imbed in our athletes," he says.

The first trait involves the ability to not fear failure.

"The mentally tough individual is not afraid to fail," he says. "If we can instill that lack of fear of failure in our playrs, then we're on the right track."

A second trait is the ability to react in a positive way to failure.

"The mentally tough individual gets back up instantly after experiencing failure," he says, reinforcing the adage that "it's not how many times you stumble and fall, it's how many times you stumble and fall and get back up again."

A third trait of mental toughness concerns intimidaiton.

"The mentally tough person can not be intimidated," he says.

He adds that a fourth mental toughness trait involves the element of pain.

"I mean not only playing with the physical pain, but playing with the emotional and mental pain that acompanies the physical pain," he states.

Finally, Brown believes that concentration is imperative when discussing mental toughness.

"Concentration is the supreme art," he begins, "because no art can be achieved without it. While with it, anything can be achieved."

He goes on to say that the masters all have the ability to discipline themselves to eliminate everything except what they are trying to accomplish.

In summary, mental toughness is a combination of traits found in all highly-skilled and motivated athletes. Those traits are the ability to not be afraid of failure and the ability to bounce back in a positive way after experiencing a failing moment.

Finally, other traits include the ability to disregard intimidation by anyone or anything, the ability to play with pain, and the ability to concentrate completely on the task at hand without being affected by distractions.

* * * * * * * * * *

...on Communication

Coach Brown has been called "The Great Communicator" over the years because of his ability to get the maximum effort from his players and inspire them to reach goals they perhaps didn't believe they could reach.

He also possesses the special ability to touch people's lives with his spoken words. If the spoken word carries a psychological punch, Coach Brown knows how to utilize its powers.

It is somewhat ironic that you will not find Brown exhorting his team during timeouts or at halftime with an impassioned speech if the team is losing.

"Hey, we've been preparing the kids during practices and pre-season to be ready for these kinds of situations," he says. "So I really don't have the time during games to 'inspire' them. They better be inspired when that game started."

He does use specific methods for communicating important messages to the players during practices, however, and it is his hope that these messages stick in the minds of his players throughout the season.

"We use lots of videotapes showing past game successes," he says. "We like to visually show the kids how successful they have been against certain opponents, so that if there is some kind of a fear factor present, we might be able to change that fear to confidence."

Another method of inspiring his players is to bring in motivational speakers to talk to the players at practice. He uses the speaker's message as the focal point of importance, he says, and often he will mention that message to the players during games when it is needed.

The most effective method he has used over the years is to bring to practice sessions a person who has beaten the odds in life.

"I like to bring in extraordinary persons who have beaten the odds," he says. " We've brought in individuals who have licked cancer and muscular dystrophy and other life-threatening diseases.

"I tell you, they give me goose bumps with their stories and I've cried more than once at the remarkable resilience they show."

He says that if the team needs some kind of inspirational punch at halftime or late in the game, he will quickly remind them of the videotapes or speakers or extraordinary person they have met. The reference will not be a long one because game situations don't merit those. Just mentioning a name or action will cue the player's mind, he says.

Post-game comments to the players are very brief, whether the results were victory or defeat, he states.

"I pretty much say the same thing for a tough loss as for a good win," he says. " I always tell them that it's not the I.Q. of a person I'm interested in, but the F.Q., failure quotient of a person."

The failure quotient of an individual , he points out, is the ability of that person to bounce back from adversity.

"So if the player has a high F.Q., he was able to handle any adversity in the game and come out successfully, " he says. "If we lost, then we'll see how quickly they bounce back for the next game."

In summary, communication skills are extremely important in Coach Brown's program. He does not utilize impassioned speeches with players during games to inspire them to better execution or effort.

All inspirational methods are utilized during practice sessions in the form of highlight videotapes, motivational speakers and extraordinary individuals who have beaten high odds of survival in life. Brown will use these examples during games to give the players a psychological boost, but the reference will be brief in nature.

Finally, post-game comments are always brief whether the game has been won or lost, and the general comments to the players usually entail Brown's "I.Q./ F.Q." comparison. He says the importance of the game lies not in a person's intelligence quotient, but his failure quotient, the ability to successfully bounce back from adversity.

* * * * * * * * * *

DENNY CRUM
University of Louisville

Position
Head Men's Basketball Coach

Career Record
463-156   (19 seasons)

Education
B.A. 1958 UCLA

Team and Personal Highlights

* 1990   Became winningest basketball coach in Louisville history.
* 1987   Coach of the USA Pan-American Games Team.
* 1986   *The Sporting News* Coach of the Year Award.
* 1983   Metro Conference Coach of the Year Award.
* 1980   *Basketball Weekly* Coach of the Year Award.
* 1979   Metro Conference Coach of the Year Award.
* 1978   Coach of the ABA/USA National Sports Festival.
* 1977   Coach of the USA World University Games Team.
* 1974   *Kentucky Sports World* Coach of the Year Award.
* 1973   Missouri Valley Conference Co-Coach of the Year.
*   Two NCAA Championship Teams (1980, 1986).
*   Six NCAA Final Four Teams (1972, 1975, 1980, 1982, 1983, 1986)
*   Twenty or more victories in 17 of 19 seasons.
*   Second earliest coach to gain 200th, 300th, and 400th career coaching victories.
*   Fifteen NCAA tournament appearances, including 12 of last 14 seasons.
*   Ten regular season Metro Conference titles and eight Metro Conference Tournament Championships.

Denny Crum

Introduction...

Just mentioning the name of Denny Crum conjures up images of basketball, championships, and competitive excellence. Since his arrival at Louisville in 1971, Coach Crum's accomplishments have been astonishing and of legendary proportions.

Denny Crum is surely the "Coach of the Decade" in the 1980's. Six times he has guided the Cardinals into the NCAA Final Four, including four in the last decade. Only John Wooden at UCLA and Dean Smith at North Carolina have coached more Final Four teams.

He has achieved the ultimate goal of all college coaches by directing Louisville to the 1980 and 1986 NCAA Championships, becoming only the eighth coach in NCAA history to win two or more titles.

Even more amazing, Crum has engineered the Cardinals to 20 or more victories in 17 of his 19 seasons at the school. His teams have won an average of over 24 games per season while losing just eight games a year. If Crum were to go winless over the next three years, he still would maintain an average of 20 wins per season.

Being a player in Denny Crum's program is also special. All but one four-year player (Larry Williams, 1975-79) has reached the NCAA Final Four during his playing career.

The 53-year-old native of San Fernando, California, attended Pierce Junior College and went on to play for John Wooden at UCLA. He received the Irv Pohlmeyer Memorial Trophy, an award presented annually to the outstanding first year varsity player. Denny was honored the following year with the Bruin Bench Award, presented annually for the most improved player.

Following his graduation in 1958 from UCLA, Crum stayed with the Bruins as the freshman coach before eventually returning to Pierce College in 1961. He became head coach at Pierce in 1964.

After four successful years at Pierce, he returned to UCLA in 1967 where he served as John Wooden's top assistant coach until his move to Louisville in 1971.

Coach Crum has a proven success formula for his teams. The Cardinals concentrate on fundamentals early in pre-season without intense conditioning and play a rugged schedule that has consistently ranked among the nations's toughest. This type of squad development has Denny's teams playing its best at season's end.

An avid reader and collector of Louis L'Amour westerns, Coach Crum spends time away from the hectic world of college basketball playing golf and fishing. He, his wife Joyce and their son Robert Scott live on a farm in Jeffersontown, Kentucky.

One of the most sincere and considerate persons you will meet, Crum enjoys sharing his ideas on successfull team building. Let's begin our look at competitive excellence by examining Coach Crum's thoughts...

...on Motivation

Motivation has always been an important ingredient in determining the success of Coach Crum's teams over the years, and he is quick to point out that all motivational factors must come from within the athlete himself.

"Motivation is the inner drive in an individual," he says. "This drive pushes the athlete into action and dictates the amount of time and effort a player is willing to put into the sport to be the best player he can be on the level he is performing."

It is idealistic to assume that a collegiate athlete can maintain motivation at all times, on or off the court. Therefore, it is extremely important that the head coach utilize motivational techniques that will be beneficial to the athlete.

"We don't do a whole lot," Crum says, "but what we do seems to work for our players."

Least effective motivational techniques are those involving fear or punishment, he says.

"You just can't use fear or intimidation with your players all the time and expect them to perform well," he states. "It just won't work and besides, it's not in my nature to create an element of fear or intimidate my players."

He says the most effective motivational technique is developing a system that nurtures self-motivation within the athlete.

"What's worked for us is developing a system in which the player sees for himself that what is being done is for his benefit," Coach Crum states. "When an athlete sees for himself that the activity he is performing is for his benefit, he will be far more likely to perform at his top level."

The specific technique Coach Crum utilizes within his system includes short-term goal setting and a reward system that emphasizes team strengths through individual delvelopment.

"We want the athlete to know that if he works hard and keeps improving and meeting his individual goals, that his overall development is going to benefit the team," he says.

"Plus, the player knows that he will play a lot if he is performing his role on the team."

In summary, Coach Crum defines motivation as an inner drive that pushes the athlete into action and dictates the amount of time and effort the athlete is willing to expend to become the best player he can be at his particualr level of competition.

Least effective motivation techniques include all forms of fear, punishment, or intimidation. The most effective form of motivation is the development of a system that helps the player benefit personally by working for team development.

Finally, some specific techniques include goal setting in addition to establishing a system that rewards the player for individual improvement and for successfully performing his role on the team.

* * * * * * * * * *

...on Team Cohesion

Team cohesion is a vital ingredient for ultimate team success and Coach Crum believes that role playing is at the heart of team chemistry.

"Team cohesion or chemistry occurs when the players know their role on the team and are willing to play that role for the good of the team," he says.

Developing team cohesion is not an easy task. The head coach must be able to fully explain each player's role and develop practice plans that allow each player to experiment with that role.

"To develop team chemistry, you must effectively explain what the roles on the team are going to be," he says. "Then you must develop or plan your practices so that the players know which of them play each role best."

Fairness is a big factor when players are adjusting to a new role, he points out.

"You must allow each player to have equal opportunities in practice so that he will accept his role on the team," he says.

There are several methods that Coach Crum utilizes to build team cohesion, including team social activities and study hall. But none play as important a function to building team cohesion as does daily practice sessions, he mentions.

"Your practice organization is very important in developing team chemistry," he states.

How must practices be planned in order to build team cohesion?

"Plan your practice so that everyone feels he is an important part of the team," he says. "Every player must know that every role on the team is important and that all roles must be played in order to have a good team."

In summarizing team cohesion, Crum equates team cohesion with the willingness of each player to play a designated role on the team. The importance of team development superceding individual glory is well ingrained in each player through meetings with Coach Crum.

Effective methods of building team cohesion include team social activities and team academic endeavors. Coach Crum also emphasizes the importance of the organization of daily practice sessions.

Finally, practice sessions must be designed to allow each player the opportunity to develop and strengthen his role on the team, he says. By giving each player time and opportunity during practices to execute their roles effectively, Denny believes that the players ultimately develop self-confidence in the role which helps build team cohesiveness.

* * * * * * * * * *

...on Discipline

Championships teams and highly successful individuals share the same trait: discipline. Crum's teams have been very successful over the years because of it, and he points out that there are no secret formulas concerning team discipline.

"The real key is to have very few rules," he begins. "The rules you do have should be those that the team believes are important."

Coach Crum is adament in his philosophy concerning team participation in setting the rules because "the more you can involve the team in setting the discipline code, the better chance you have in them following the rules."

Crum says there is really only one ineffective method of team discipline.

"The least effective discipline is to punish the whole team for the failure of one or two players," he says.

He follows this statement with his thoughts on the most effective method of handling discipline problems.

"You should really handle each case on an individual basis," he begins. "This is the best way I've found to handle any discipline problems that have arisen over the years."

Coach Crum is quick to reinforce his thoughts that mutual respect plays an important role in how successful your disciplinary procedures are received by the team.

"Treat the players as important members of your team and not as someone who has no say in team matters." he states. "By showing that kind of respect to all members of the team will have a very positive effect in establishing a discipline code."

In summary, Coach Crum believes that team discipline can be effective when there are very few rules and the rules that are established have been a result of all members participating in the rule-making process.

Least effective disciplinary methods, he says, involve punishing the entire team for the failure of one or two players.

The most effective method of dealing with disciplinary cases, he points out, is to handle each case on an individual basis.

Finally, Coach Crum believes that mutual respect among the players and coaching staff has a very positive impact on setting and enforcing the discipline code.

* * * * * * * * * *

...on Mental Preparation

Having been a part of the great UCLA teams of the past both as a player and a coach has left a strong impression on Coach Crum concerning mental preparation.

"Mental preparation is a 365-day job," he says. "It is getting yourself ready each day for the season."

Once the grind of pre-season practice begins, Coach Crum and his staff are quick to set the mental approach they want the team to follow.

"It's our job as coaches to convince the players that pre-season practices set the tone for the entire season," he states.

He also tells the team that once games start, there is not a lot of time for hard practices.

"The players are smart enough to understand that the most difficult time of the season as far as learning and conditioning are concerned is during pre-season," he says.

"Because of our schedule, once the season begins, we don't have many physically demanding practices. So the players know that they must establish good work habits during pre-season practice if they want the opportunity to play once the season begins."

The approach to preparing for non-conference and conference games is the same in Coach Crum's philosophy.

"We approach every game in the same manner," he states. "This helps us to eliminate the peaks and valleys from your play and has allowed our teams to be ready for all games."

Louisville teams in the past have been very successful in executing late-game strategy that leads to victory, and Crum explains the reasons behind that success.

"We've been fortunate over the years to win some games in the late stages," he says. "But we've prepared the players for those kinds of situations, and they've responded to the challenge."

Denny is quick to point out that the games are won and lost on the practice floor, not the game floor.

"Have situations in practice to cover your late-game strategy so that when they come up, it will be something the players have prepared for," he says.

This kind of preparation during practice will allow the players to perform under the pressure of game situations, he asserts.

In summarizing Coach Crum's philosophy on mental preparation, he strongly believes that mental preparation is a year-round process.

He claims that pre-season practices are extremely important in that these practices set the tone of the work ethic the players will follow for the remainder of the season.

Non-conference and conference games are approached in the same work-man-like fashion by the players and coaches. Coach Crum believes that this consistent approach to games eliminates the peaks and valleys asociated with team play.

Finally, practice preparation is the key to successful late-game strategy. He says that exposing the players to pressure situations during practice will assist them in performing under the pressure of actual game conditions.

* * * * * * * * * *

...on Mental Toughness

Denny Crum claims that every player has the ability to demonstrate mental toughness, but that same student-athletes do not always accept the challenge.

"Mental toughness," he begins, "is the ability of the players to accept the challenges of practice and games."

These challenges, he says, include accepting the physical demands as well as the emotional and psychological aspects associated with a highly successful college basketball program.

Coach Crum also believes that mental toughness is the key element when adversity strikes a player, both on and off the court.

"A mentally tough player has the ability to lift his game to a higher level when it is necessary to get the job done," he states.

Mental toughness also assists the student-athlete in handling success and adversity, he says.

"When a player is mentally tough, he has the ability to handle the good and the bad when they come in practice, in games, and in life."

In summary, mental toughness is a player's ability to accept the challenges of practice, games and life. These challenges include accepting the physical demands in addition to the emotional and psychological aspects.

He also believes that mental toughness is the ability of the player to elevate his level of effort and execution when it is necessary to get the task accomplished.

Finally, Coach Crum advocates mental toughness as an important life skill for the student-athlete. He says that a mentally tough individual has the ability to accept both the good and the bad that life has to offer and to benefit from the experience.

* * * * * * * * * *

...on Communication

Coach Crum takes pride in the fact that his program has been consistently successful on the playing floor, that his student-athletes have become successful college graduates, and that his coaching staff has remained stable throughout the years.

He emphasizes the fact that communication skills among the coaching staff, players, and support staff throughout his coaching career has been the glue that keeps the parts together.

"Jerry (Jones, a long-time assistant) and Wade (Houston, now head coach at Tennessee) and I were together for so long that the players thought we were brothers," he says.

"But I can honestly tell you this. The rapport we had among ourselves, the way we communicated, had a big influence on the communcation skills within the entire program. And these communication skills have been the most consistent element of our program."

Inspirational messages to the players in times of adversity during games is not a part of Crum's philosophy.

"I very rarely try to inspire my team," he begins. "I try to make corrections and give them a new plan for how we can do better."

Motivational talks are never utilized during games, he says.

"I do not believe in motivational pep talks. I only use things in games that we practice and feel these show confidence to the players."

The practice floor, he points out, is where games are won and lost.

"Games are usually won or lost on the practice floor, not by pep talks," he says.

In his post-game comments to the team, Coach Crum is consistent with his evaluation, whether the game was won or lost.

"If we lost the game and played poorly in the process," he begins, "I go over the game and point out the areas of poor play so that they are aware of them and hopefully will learn from their mistakes."

Playing well and still losing the game brings a more empathetic response from Coach Crum.

"If we played well and lost, I say so and explain that they have nothing to be ashamed of," he says.

The game of life and the game of basketball both take funny bounces, he states.

"You can play well and still lose a game, just like you can prepare well for the job interview and still may not get the job. You have to be able to accept those results in life. The key is that you were prepared and gave it your best shot," he concludes.

In summary, communication skills have been the backbone of success in Coach Crum's program. Consistency in staff and rapport among the coaches, players and support staff are important factors in establising long-term success.

Inspiration from Coach Crum does not take the form of motivational pep talks during times of adversity. He is quick to establish the fact that games are won and lost on the practice floor, not from pep talks during games.

A consistent communication approach in evaluating losses from poor performance is necessary, he believes. Explaining errors in a low-key way is best when you want the players to learn from their mistakes.

Finally, Coach Crum tells his players that basketball and life both deal funny bounces, and that preparation, effort and attitude are the key elements of success.

* * * * * * * * * *

BILL FOSTER

Northwestern University

Position

Head Men's Basketball Coach

Career Record

445-348   (30 seasons)

Education

B.S.   1954   Elizabethtown (PA) College
M.S.   1957   Temple University

Team and Personal Highlights

* 1979   Inducted into Pennsylvania Sports Hall of Fame.
* 1978   National Association of Basketball Coaches
         National Coach of the Year Award.
* 1978   *The Sporting News* National Coach of the Year Award.
* 1978   Atlantic Coast Conference Coach of the Year Award.
* 1975   Charter Member of the Elizabethtown College Sports
         Hall of Fame.
* 1974   NCAA District VII Coach of the Year Award.
*   Listed in *Who's Who in America* publication.
*   Listed in *Who's Who in the World* publication.
*   Member of the Naismith Basketball Hall of Fame
         Board of Trustees.
*   Second Vice President, Naismith Hall of Fame Board.
*   Past President of the National Association of Basketball
         Coaches of the United States.
*   Only head coach to have won 20 games in a season at
         four different NCAA Division I schools.
*   Teams have participated in seven post-season tourna-
         ments: Three NCAA and four NIT tournaments.
*   The 1978 Duke University team competed in the Final
         Four, finishing second.

Bill Foster

Introduction...

When Bill Foster was hired as Northwestern's 20th head basketball coach on April 4, 1986, he brought with him a long list of impressive credentials and praise from his coaching peers.

"The selection of Bill Foster was an excellent one," commented Denny Crum, head coach at 1986 NCAA champion Louisville. "He has had success in every program he has been associated with. He is an outstanding game coach and recruiter, and his players play hard and enjoy playing for him. He is a class coach. He'll bring an exciting brand of basketball to Northwestern."

Indeed, he has! Just ask 1987 NCAA champion Indiana and perennial winner DePaul University. Indiana left Northwestern's Welsh-Ryan Arena in 1988 a 66-64 loser while the Blue Demons were handled, 78-64.

Playing in the Big Ten Conference, the toughest basketball conference in the nation, has forced Northwestern into playing one of the toughest schedules in college basketball.

The schedule two years ago was rated the second-toughest in the country according to *Basketball Times* magazine. Last year Northwestern faced the nation's 10th toughest opposition according to *Basketball Times*.

Building successful programs has been Bill Foster's forte since the beginning of his illustrious coaching career.

In 1981, he was named by nationally recognized sports commentator Billy Packer as the No. 1 builder of collegiate basketball programs in the country.

After serving two years in the United States Air Force (1951-52), the Norwood, Pennsylvania native graduated from Elizabethtown College in 1954. During high school coaching stops at Chichester and Abington High Schools in Pennsylvania from 1954-60, he was also busy earning a masters degree from Temple University in 1957.

Profiled in the *New York Times* as a "supercoach", the 58-year-old Foster began his collegiate coaching career at Bloomsburg State College in 1960, posting a three-year record of 45-11.

He them spent eight years at Rutgers University, winning 120 of 195 games and leading the Scarlet Knights to NIT tournaments in 1967 and 1969.

Foster then moved to the University of Utah for three seasons, compiling a 43-39 mark, including a 22-8 ledger in 1974 when the Utes reached the NIT.

From 1975-80, he headed the program at Duke University, guiding the Blue Devils to three Atlantic Coast Conference titles, three successive NCAA Championship appearances ((1978-1980), and a second-place finish in 1978. His overall record at the North Carolina school was 113-64.

Prior to arriving at Evanston in 1986, he served as head coach for six seasons at the University of South Carolina, where he compiled a 92-79 record, including the 1983 Gamecock squad that finished 22-9 with an NIT appearance.

Bill Foster is a fighter, and that was clearly in evidence when he was felled by a heart attack in 1982 while coaching at South Carolina. He has since fully recovered and enjoys the challenge of building the Wildcat basketball program into a Big Ten contender while upholding the high academic standards of the university.

Foster and his wife, Shirley, have four daughters: Vicki, Debra, Julia and Mary. They live in Evanston.

A warm-hearted individual and workaholic who likes country and western music, Bill Foster's infectious enthusiasm was never more apparent as he welcomed the opportunity to share his thoughts on successful team building. Here are Coach Foster's thoughts.....

...on Motivation

Motivation is a prime ingredient for success within every organization, and Bill Foster has been successfully motivating his student-athletes for over 30 years.

"Motivating players is a difficult process, I don't care how many years you've been associated with athletics," he begins. "I certainly don't consider myself an expert on the subject."

But after so many years, Coach Foster has no difficulty giving his definition of motivation.

"Motivation is the ability to get the individuals and the team to perform steadily at maximum potential," he says.

If each player is giving a consistent performance and playing up to his potential every time on the court, then Coach Foster believes that the student-athlete is highly motivated to succeed.

Bill doesn't think there are standard motivation techniques that work for all players all the time.

"It really depends upon the individual and the circumstance," he says.

Over the years, Foster has found some methods to be less effective than others.

"Threats really are not effective when you're trying to motivate someone," he states.

But he believes that some extra physical conditioning plus banishment from practices may be effective at times if used in the correct way.

"I guess I'm from the old school, but I still think that a little extra running proves to the players that we're serious in what we're trying to accomplish," he says.

Banishment or dismissal from practice is a method that Foster utilizes very infrequently, but he also thinks the long range effects are positive ones.

"Any time a player is not allowed to practice with the team, you're taking him out of an environment he enjoys," he states. "So even if the experience is a traumatic one initially for the player, in the long run he knows that he never wants that situation to happen again."

Another effective motivational technique is writing personal letters to each player, he says.

"I like sending letters to the players during the off season," he remarks. "I usually include sports articles of interest to our program, statistics for our players to beat for the coming year, and inspirational quotes from the motivational tapes I listen to all the time."

In summary, Foster defines motivation as the ability to get an individual or team to perform in a consistent fashion utilizing the maximum potential of the player.

Effective motivation techniques may include extra conditioning, with dismissal from practice also being an option. Writing personal letters to the players in also an effective motivation technique, Bill concludes.

Finally, least effective motivation techniques, he says, include threats of any kind.

* * * * * * * * * *

...on Team Cohesion

Team chemistry is a vital ingredient for ultimate team success, and Coach Foster knows the importance of blending the right individuals together.

"Team chemistry is the blending of players to get maximum potential," he begins.

He also thinks that inspiration and motivation must be self-directed.

"The players must have a good feeling about themselves and about the team," he states. "Each person must be self-motivated and inspired to be successful."

A cohesive team also has few distractions and internal problems, he says. The key to team cohesion, according to Foster, lies in the recruiting process.

"You recruit cohesive individuals," he says. "You have the players talk to the recruits and you talk to the players about the recruits. After all, it is the player's team, so they should have some input into the decision."

Coach Foster is always looking for "success" articles, articles from newspapers and magazines, that tell of successful organizations and teams who win because they get along with each other.

In summary, team cohesion is extremely important in building and sustaining successful organizations. He states that the players must feel good about themselves and the team before team chemistry can be established.

Coach Foster believes that recruiting is the key element to building team cohesion. He thinks that players need to evaluate the recruit in the areas of self-motivation and inspiration, and that present team members should have some input in the final selection of recruits.

Finally, a method of building team cohesion includes locating and distributing "success" articles to team members. These newspaper and magazine articles describe successful organizations, how they win and how they gained fame.

* * * * * * * * * *

...on Discipline

Discipline has been a success trait in all of Coach Foster's teams, and this is one area of coaching philosophy that has changed little over the years.

"Team discipline must come from the self-discipline of each player," he says. "As a coach, you must work toward the development of self-discipline in all your players."

As one would expect from Coach Foster's philosophy, the individual is responsible for his own actions.

"Each individual must demonstrate responsible behavior," he points out. "Without self-discipline, there can be no team discipline."

What discipline methods are most effective and least effective?

"The least effective discipline methods involve punishing the entire team for the indiscretions of one or two players," he says.

Effective disciplinary methods involve removal from the team in some aspect, he believes.

"If a player breaks a team rule for the first time, the penalty for such an infraction is usually removal from practice for a day," he states.

Foster says that continuous violations tend to carry heavier penalties.

"A second offense will carry at least a one game suspension with it," he points out. "Any prolonged violations will carry suspension from the team for a longer period of time."

In summary, Coach Foster's philosophy concerning team discipline is that each individual is reponsible for his acitons and that self-discipline should be the ultimate goal of each student-athlete.

Least effective disciplinary methods are team punishment for individual indiscretions. Finally, effective disciplinary methods include dismissal from practice for a day for a first offense or suspension from the team for continued violation of team rules.

* * * * * * * * * *

...on Mental Preparation

Mental preparation is essential to team and individual success, and Foster considers it a very delicate process.

"I must constantly be watching the mental condition of my players," he says. "By that I mean that when they need a pat on the back, I give them one, and if they need a kick in the butt, I do that, too."

The process is a delicate one because he believes that mental preparation may differ from player to player.

"I must have a thorough understanding of the mental makeup of all my players," he says.

Mental preparation begins from the first day of pre-season practice, and

Coach Foster makes sure that perceptions of the players are focused in the right direction.

"We don't want the players to consider pre-season practice a mental grind," he begins. "We want them to perceive pre-season as a time of learning and improving."

He continues to establish the theme that pre-season practice is a time for accomplishment and team building.

"We want players believing that this is a time when they come together as a team," he says. "We stress individual fundamentals, and we tell the players that this is the time for them to establish themselves and to help make the team better."

Mental preparation is the same for non-conference games as it is for conference games.

"The goal is always to win 20 games--that will never change," he says. "So we believe that a habit of winning needs to be established from the first game on."

He is quick to assess the fact that since the Big Ten Conference is so competitive, that a major emphasis is not needed because the players and coaching staff know that each game is a big challenge to the program.

Late-game strategy that can lead to success is the combination of a number of factors in Coach Foster's mind.

"Conditioning, confidence and repetition are all needed to be present when late-game strategy can lead to victory," he states.

He thinks that if the players are in shape, if they have the confidence to know they can accomplish the task, and if they've practiced the late-game strategy to the effect that it is second-nature to them, then the team will be successful at game's end.

"But you must practice these situations all the time," he points out. "Without adequate practice time for late-game strategy, you will not be successful."

In summary, mental preparation is a delicate process in Coach Foster's estimation. It is also the responsibility of the coaches to understand the mental makeup of each athlete on the team so that mental preparation techniques can be enhanced.

Pre-season practice must be perceived by the players as the most important time of the season, he says. They must not view this time period as a grind, but as a period in which the team comes together and individual players establish themselves as important members of the team.

Non-conference games and conference games receive identical treatment from a mental preparation standpoint, he says.

Finally, success in late-game strategy is the result of conditioning, confidence and repetition. He states that these three factors are the result of practice sessions that teach the players how to be successful late in the game.

* * * * * * * * * *

...on Mental Toughness

Mental toughness is a trait that all coaches want their players to possess, including Bill Foster. But he has found that the majority of the student-athletes do not have it.

"It's too easy as an athlete to make excuses today," he says. "Society really makes it too easy to make excuses."

Even though mental toughness is a trait that most student-athletes do not possess, Coach Foster is quick to point out that the trait can be developed.

"Oh, yes, I think that mental toughness can be developed," he states. "But I also think it's the most difficult trait to develop."

Coach Foster defines mental toughness as a willingness to expend great effort all the time.

"Mental toughness," he begins, "is the ability, the willingness of a player to expend great effort when things aren't going well."

He reinforces his philosophy that the "mental" portion of mental toughness is the key element.

"If you're very physically tired, but your mental approach is still good, then eventually the physical part will come around, also," he says.

So what are the characteristics of a mentally tough person? Coach Foster can name them in rapid fashion.

"First, the person has to have a 'no-excuse' attitude," he begins. "That includes being able to work over obstacles and any kind of distractions."

Persistence is another characteristic of a mentally tough individual, he says.

"A mentally tough person does not let down in any degree of effort at any time," he claims. "That 'never-give-up' attitude is always present."

The ability to raise the level of effort when it is needed is another mental toughness trait, he adds.

"The mentally tough individual can raise his level of play when he needs to overcome extraordinary odds," he states.

Concentration and discipline are the final two elements of the mentally tough person, he concludes.

"Concentration and discipline really work together," he says. "You need the discipline to concentrate when things are happening quickly around you."

In summary, Foster believes that mental toughness is a very important trait to have as a player, but he insists that most student-athletes do not possess it.

Mental toughness is a trait that can be developed, he says, but the effort must be great in order to achieve it.

He defines mental toughness as the willingness to continue to expend great effort when things are not going well. He also stresses the point that the"mental" aspect of mental toughness is the key element in acquiring the trait.

Mental toughness traits include a "no-excuse" attitude and a persistence in effort that keeps the energy level high for the person.

Additional mental toughness traits include the ability to increase the level of intensity when the extra effort is needed and the ability to discipline oneself into concentrating on the task when numerous distractions are present.

* * * * * * * * *

...on Communication

Communication within the program is extremely important when dealing with staff members and players. It is also a critical psychological factor during times of adversity.

"If we're losing at halftime, I try not to get very emotional, he says. "But I do use the same methods most of the time in these kinds of situations."

Those methods include wrapping positive statements around any kind of occasional tongue-lashing the team may deserve.

"I must be positive because there is not much time to explain very many things to the players," he states. "Usually I say 'Let's try this against their defense' or something along those lines. The main point is telling the team that they can do better in the second half."

But if the team has played poorly because of a lack of effort, a firm reprimand is not out of the question.

"Sometimes you need to give them a little hell," he says.

Post-game comments include only positive statements whether the game was lost or won.

"If we lost, I tell them 'Our day will come' and I really mean that," he states. "I tell them that they did so many things right that they deserved to win."

There is also a lesson to be learned in times of adversity.

"You must tell them that it's important to fight back from the adversity. In addition, you tell them that fortunately they will be playing again very soon, that they don't have to wait a week in between games. Players are usually very resilient."

In summary, Coach Foster understands the psychological implications of effective communication with the players and staff, especially in times of adversity.

Halftime talks when the team is behind will include positive statements and suggestions for improving execution. He will also reprimand the team if he thinks it is needed.

Post-game comments after a loss will also include positive statements, he says. He also reminds the team that fighting back from adversity is important for both personal and team improvement.

* * * * * * * * *

JIM HARRICK

University of California-Los Angeles

Position
Head Men's Basketball Coach

Career Record
210-118 (11 seasons)

Education
B.A. 1960 Morris Harvey

Team and Personal Highlights

* Teams have won 542 games at the high school and collegiate levels over a 27-year coaching career.

* Only 10th head coach in history of UCLA basketball.

* Four-time West Coast Athletic Conference Coach of the Year Award.

* Teams have participated in 6 NCAA Tournaments and 2 NIT Tournaments.

* Teams have won 20 or more games six times.

* Pepperdine University teams won five West Coast Athletic Conference championships.

* His 1973 Inglewood Morningside High School team was voted America's top-ranked high school squad by *Basketball Weekly* magazine after compiling a 28-1 record.

Jim Harrick

Introduction...

When Jim Harrick was named the Bruin head coach on April 12, 1988, it climaxed a life-long dream to return to his beloved Westwood where he had begun his high shool coaching career in 1964 and was an assistant at UCLA in the late 1970's.

In only his first season as UCLA's head coach, Harrick led the Bruins back to the NCAA Tournament. The Bruins reached the second round of the Southeast Regional, finished the year with a record of 21-10 and tied for third in the Pacific-10 Conference with a 13-5 mark. Of the 10 losses, eight were to teams with 20 or more wins that played in the NCAA Tournament.

His 1990 team finished 22-11 and advanced to the "Sweet 16" round in the NCAA tournament, the first time since 1980 for a Bruin basketball team.

Harrick began his coaching career at Inglewood's Morningside High School in 1964. After serving as an assistant for five seasons, he became head coach prior to the 1969-70 season.

As the Monarch's head coach, Harrick compiled a record of 103-16 over the next four years. His 1973 team compiled a 28-1 mark and was voted America's top-ranked high school squad by *Basketball Weekly* magazine.

Following the 1973 season, Harrick became an assistaant coach at Utah State. During his four seasons in Logan, the Aggies were 66-40 and earned an NCAA Tournament bid in 1975 with a 21-6 record.

After his success at Utah State, Harrick moved to UCLA as an assistant under head coach Gary Cunningham. During his two seasons at Westwood, the Bruins won two Pac-10 titles, reached the NCAA West Regional title game in 1979 and the Regional semifinal in 1978, and compiled an overall record of 50-8. Like at Utah State, his coaching specialties as a Bruin included recruiting and scouting.

Following the 1978-79 season, Harrick moved to Malibu as head coach at Pepperdine University. He earned an NIT invitation in his first year and had the Waves winning 20 games and playing in the NCAA Tournament by his third season.

He had eight winning seasons during his nine years at Pepperdine, his best season being 1985-86, when the Waves went 25-5 en route to their fifth league crown in six years.

Jim and his effervesscent wife, the former Sally Marple, have three grown sons: Monte, Jim, and Glenn. The laid-back Bruin coach, a dry sense of humor always present, was eager to begin discussing the key elements of sucessful team building.

Here are Coach Harrick's thoughts.....

...on Motivation

"There is no magic formula for motivation," Jim Harrick says. To him, motivation entails several elements that both the coach and player must cultivate.

Trust and attention are at the core of the motivation process, he belives.

"First of all, to motivate someone you first must somehow gain the trust and attention of your players," he says. "And that's certainly no easy assignment."

He continues by stating that the players must be willing to learn and want to do what the coaches ask.

"If I can gain the trust of the players," he states, "then I'm pretty confident that I will be able to get the players to do what I want."

Harrick isn't sure that he's found the foolproof formula for motivating each of his student-athletes, but he's sure that each individual's needs must be met.

"The best method of motivating our players here at UCLA has been for me to be myself, and to treat everyone with respect and as an important member of our team," he states.

Coach Harrick also believes that motivation is a result of developing relationships with each player.

"If there is one thing I can't stress enough, it's the importance of developing a positive relationship with each player," he says.

Another method of motivating student-athletes is the ability to strive for voluntary cooperation, he says.

"The players must establish a mindset that whatever we accomplish as a team is a direct result of a voluntary team effort," he concludes.

In summary, Coach Harrick believes that motivation is the result of gaining the trust and attention of the players. He strongly asserts that there is no magic formula for motivating today's student-athletes, but that certain methods may be effective for coaches.

The methods he mentions for effective motivation include being yourself with the players, and not a different personality for each athlete.

He also thinks that developing relationships with each student-athlete is very important. Finally, all effective motivation techniques must be ones that strive to develop voluntary cooperation among the players and staff.

* * * * * * * * * *

...on Team Cohesion

Team cohesion is a vital ingredient for ultimate team success, and Harrick considers it the most important element of any team sport.

"Team cohesion is the most vital aspect of a team sport," he says. "Without it, nothing can be accomplished."

There are several methods a coach can utilize to build team chemistry, he states. But the basic factor is developing a sense of "oneness" within all team members, he concludes.

"We want our players to pull for one another," he begins. "We encourage our kids to cheer for one another all the time."

Coach Harrick devises practice drills that are fun for the players while subtlely encouraging team spirit and cohesion. He also addresses the team daily on the importance of getting along together.

"We want to develop some sense of team accomplishments whenever we can," he says.

Other methods of building team cohesion, he adds, include team social activities, study hall responsibilities and community involvement projects.

In summary, Coach Harrick believes that team cohesion is the most vital aspect of a team sport. He stresses with his players the importance of pulling for one another during practices as well as games.

Finally, he devises practice drills that are fun, but also help build team cohesion. In addition, he says, team cohesion can be built through team social activities, study hall responsibilities and civic involvement.

* * * * * * * * * *

...on Discipline

Throughout Harrick's coaching career, opposing coaches have always commented on the disciplined style of play his teams exhibited. These comments are not surprising when you listen to his philosoophy concerning discipline.

"Discipline is an absolute within our program." he begins. "There are no grey areas."

As many of the other coaches have expressed in this book, Coach Harrick agrees that all team rules should be established by team members. As long as each player has had his imput into the rules-making process, he says, the players are most likely to abide by the rules.

Effective and ineffective discipline methods involve the same concept in Jim's mind.

"Consistency." he states. "Consistency is the most effective method and the key to any disciplinary situation."

Just as consistency is the most effective method of discipline, lack of consistency causes the most problems.

"If you are not consistent in dealing with discipline problems on your team, the resulting behavior of other team members will deteriorate into additional discipline problems," he concludes.

In summary, Coach Harrick believes that discipline is an absolute factor in every successful organization. He also affirms his belief that team rules should be established by all team members.

Finally, there should be no grey areas concerning discipline, he says, and the most effective way of handling discipline problems is to act consistently. Least effective methods of discipline involve lack of consistency in handling discipline problems on the team, he concludes.

* * * * * * * * * *

...*on Mental Preparation*

Mental preparation is an essential element for team and individual success. Coach Harrick believes mental preparation is a result of being focused in the right direction.

"Mental preparation," he states, "means being focused on your objectives and your responsibilities. We always want our group to be focused on their jobs. At our pre-game meal on the day of games, the horse play stops. We demand a quiet atmosphere to encourage our players to think about the game."

Mentally preparing for pre-season practices is extremely important for Harrick's teams.

"When our pre-season practices begin, we want the players to understand that this is the most important time of the year," he says. "This is the time period when the players must be focused and concentrating on everything we're teaching them."

Mental preparation for non-conference games are approached in the same way, Jim states.

"We really can't justify to ourselves that we need to prepare differently for non-conference games," he says. "All games are important to us. We feel that preparing the same way for all opponents gives us a consistent approach that the players feel comfortable with."

Late-game strategy that can lead to victory is another aspect of preparation that Coach Harrick does not leave to chance.

"We strongly believe that all games are won on the practice floor," he states. "There really isn't enough time during games to explain something new to the players. It would only confuse them. So it's very important that we prepare our team for anything that can happen during games at practice, and then hope that the preparation pays off."

In summary, Coach Harrick defines mental preparation as the ability to focus on objectives and responsibilities. Pre-season practice is the most important time of the year for teaching mental preparation skills, he says.

UCLA players mentally prepare themselves the same way for non-conference and conference games, Jim points out. He believes this consistent approach helps both the players and the coaching staff.

Finally, late-game strategy needs to be taught to the players every day at practice. Since Coach Harrick believes that games are won and lost on the practice floor, it is imperative that all late-game strategy is taught during practice so that players will become confident in the strategy and can execute it correctly during game situations.

* * * * * * * * * *

...on Mental Toughness

Mental toughness is a trait in student-athletes that can ultimately spell the difference between winning and losing. Coach Harrick enthusiastically addresses the topic of mental toughness in his players.

"Mental toughness is the combination of enthusiasm, competitiveness, and the undying will to win," he says.

When the student-athlete can combine all of these traits, Harrick knows that he's got a hard-nosed player that will do what needs to be done to be successful.

"I really like the hard-nosed player," he says. "Players who are soft and accept losing as a way of life are not mentally tough."

Coach Harrick wants his players to be mentally tough, on and off the court.

"The mentally tough person is going to be successful in every endeavor in life," he says. "It's important to us as coaches that we prepare our players not just for basketball games, but for life in general."

In summary, Coach Harrick defines mental toughness as a combination of traits, including enthusiasm, competitiveness, and the undying will to win.

These traits, when combined, make for a hard-nosed competitor, which is the type Harrick wants in his program.

Finally, Coach Harrick believes that mental toughness is a life skill that will assist the student-athlete in all aspects of life once he leaves the UCLA campus.

* * * * * * * * * *

...on Communication

Coach Harrick prides himself in the fact that throughtout his coaching career, communication among his assistant coaches, players, and support staff has always been good. He believes this communication process is instrumental in the success of his program.

"There is no doubt in his mind that communicating effectively within the program can have an impact on how successful you can be," he states.

Herrick does not believe in "Win-one-for-the-Gipper" type speeches during the game to inspire his players.

"Hey, if we didn't prepare well to play, nothing I can say is going to have any impact during the game," he says.

But he thinks it is important to create an atmosphere of open communication within your program.

"We are pretty positive with our players," he says. "The atmosphere we try to keep here at UCLA is one of being positive with the players at all times. We encourage them to come to us to discuss anything that's on their minds."

In post-game comments to the players, whether the game resulted in a win or loss, Jim takes the same positive approach.

"Regardless of who we played and regardless of what the outcome was, we still discuss our strengths and weaknesses from the game," he states. "But one aspect of evaluation we always use is this: we follow all criticism with praise."

In summary, Coach Harrick believes that open, honest communication among assistant coaches, players, and support staff is important in developing a winning atmosphere within his program.

Positive statements are utilized continually within the Bruin program to develop an atmosphere of confidence and comradery.

Finally, Coach Harrick follows all critical comments to players with praise. He believes this type of balanced communication is the most effective when dealing with young student-athletes.

* * * * * * * * *

MARY HIGGINS
Creighton University

Position
Women's Athletic Director
Head Softball Coach

Career Record
562-245 (14 seasons)

Education
B.S.   1973 Creighton University
M.S.   1975 University of Nebraska - Omaha

Team and Personal Highlights

* First woman inducted into the Creighton University
  Athletic Hall of Fame.

* Inducted into the 500 Victory Club by the National
  Softball Coaches Association.

* Teams have ranked in the Top 20 nationally since Creighton
  softball became Division I in 1982.

* Four team appearances in the College World Series.

* Six NCAA post-season tournament appearances.

* Two High Country Athletic Conference championships.

* Four team appearances in the College World Series is
  unprecedented by any other private institution.

* One of only four active softball coaches at the collegiate level
  with more than 400 wins.

* Past chairperson of the NCAA Softball Committee.

Mary Higgins

Introduction...

Creighton University head softball coach Mary Higgins is a landmark in the history of Creighton University athletics.

As a student in 1973, Higgins went to the University administration with the purpose of initiating a women's athletic program. Four years later, she returned as head softball coach, and the Lady Jay softball program quickly established itself as a top team in Nebraska, winning two consecutive state titles.

In 1980, the Lady Jays gained national attention by placing second in their first regional tournament and qualified for the Women's College World Series. Their four appearances there are the most by any private institution.

Serving in a dual role as Women's Athletic Director, Mary has an endless list of accomplishments in her tenure. In 1989, she was inducted into the 500 Victory Club by her softball coaching peers. In 1987, she was the first woman inducted into the Creighton University Athletic Hall of Fame.

A 1973 graduate of Creighton, she was instrumental in bringing the Women's College World Series to Omaha from 1982-87. She is also a past chairperson of the NCAA Softball Committee.

Higgins is married to Pat Kennison, a corporate litigation lawyer, and they have two children, David and Julie Kathleen.

The 14-year head coach is a ball of energy, constantly on the move, looking for ways to improve Creighton women's athletics and her softball team. She is a perfect candidate to discuss successful team building, having been the architect behind the formation of women's athletics at the Omaha Jesuit-affiliated institution.

Mary Higgins is very enthused to begin discussing her ideas on successful team building. Here are Coach Higgin's thoughts...

...on Motivation

Motivation is a prime ingredient for success within every organization and Mary Higgins regards it as one of the most important aspects in the Creighton softball program.

"Motivation," she begins, "is an enthusiastic willingness to put forth effort." Intrinsic motivation, competing for just the thrill of competition, is the best kind of motivation, she says.

From her experiences as a coach for many years, Mary would be the first to admit that she doesn't have all the answers concerning motivation of her athletes, but she also asserts that some motivation techniques are better than others.

"I can tell you what doesn't work with my student-athletes," she says. "All of them are associated with some kind of negative behavior on my part."

Coach Higgins lists four motivation techniques she has found to be most ineffective when utilized with her players.

"The first ineffective technique surrounds any regular display of anger on my part," she states. "Any time I start to puff up to blow off steam, I immediately back off because I know it's not going to have any positive effect on the team."

Public criticism of a player is another terrible motivational technique.

"You just can't expect to get a positive response from a student-athlete after you've humiliated her in front of her peers," she says.

A third ineffective motivational technique is the use of constant criticism.

"Constantly harping on a player or the team is only going to harm the players psychologically," she states. "Every athlete knows she is going to receive some aspect of constructive criticism once in a while, but constantly being harrassed simply because the coach thinks it's motivating the athlete is wrong."

The final technique that Mary believes is not an effective motivational tool is the use of the negative challenge.

"Now I know that some coaches use this type of challenge with their student-athletes all the time and it works for some of them," she says. "But any time I tell the team or a player 'There's no way you can do that', I'm defeating myself and it's deflating to the athlete, also."

Higgins lists four techniques she has found to be most effective in motivating her student-athletes.

"Without a doubt, positive goal setting is one method that has worked well with our players," she says. "We are always setting goals for the team and individual."

A second motivation method involves building group confidence.

"We try to be realistic at all times with our players," she begins. "But it is also very important that as coaches, we positively build up the confidence of not only individuals, but the team, too."

She believes that individual and team confidence can be strengthened by having the coaching staff take a personal interest in the development of each player.

"Taking a personal interest in each student-athlete is the best way I know to help build confidence," she says.

The third technique Coach Higgins uses to motivate her players is the "Us-versus-them" approach.

"When we were just building this program, struggling along, we had to inspire the players when our opponent was a big-name school," she states.

"The best way I thought was to circle the wagons and establish the mentality that it was us against the world. It worked at that time and it's still working today," she says.

The fourth and final motivation technique that Coach Higgins has found effective surrounds individual challenges, she says.

"I believe that an occasional private, individual challenge can be effective," she says, quickly noting that this private challenge is not related to any negative challenge that she mentioned before.

"This private challenge is usually associated with a goal the player and I have set," she concludes.

In summary, motivating today's student-athlete is a big challenge for all coaches. Mary believes that motivated players possess an enthusiastic willingness to put forth effort.

Ineffective motivation techniques include a regular display of anger and public criticism of the player in front of other teammates. Constant criticism and negative challenges are also ineffective motivational techniques, she says.

Finally, positive goal setting and group confidence building are two effective motivational techniques, Mary states. Two additional effective techniques are creating the "us versus the majority" mentality and the utilization of an occasional private, individual challenge.

* * * * * * * * * *

...on Team Cohesion

Team cohesion is a vital ingredient for ultimate team success, and Higgins ranks it as one of the most important elements of any organization.

Building team chemistry, she says, is a combination of accepting roles and having a feeling of togetherness.

"Team cohesion is a willingness for individuals on the team to genuinely care about group results more than individual results," she says. "The players need to understand and play their roles, but I want them to genuinely have fun to gether and pull for each other."

There is no hesitation on Coach Higgin's part when the discussion of successful methods of building team cohesion begins.

"Many organizations are successful because the people in them have a mentality that the group is bigger than the individual," she states. "We try to develop that same kind of mentality here at Creighton."

She believes there are a number of ways to establish a "team mentality."

"To build team cohesion, the team must physically and mentally survive some difficult situations together," she says. "Those situations can be athletics-related or can be personal. The key element is that the team has experienced and survived the ordeal together."

Communication between the players and coaching staff is another crucial aspect of building team cohesion, she says.

"I must communicate to the players, as head coach, that I genuinely like them as people, which hopefully encourages them to do the same with each other."

Mary stresses the point that she also needs to be "relaxed and confident" around the players to again demonstrate to them the feeling of togetherness.

Creating the appropriate mentality in the players' minds is evident in three additional scenarios, she relates.

"We strongly build on the idea that 'all we have is each other'," she says. "We build the family atmosphere by telling the players that no one on campus knows what it's like within our group except us."

The second scenario utilizes "the concept of need" as the building blocks for team cohesion.

Higgins tells us that it is her responsibility "to create a mentality that we truly need each other to be successful, that we can't do the job alone."

The third scenario centers around the theme of "specialness."

"We believe that every person we recruit to Creighton is special," she states. "Therefore, we build on that idea by creating and reinforcing the mentality that this group of student-athletes is a special group in a special situation."

In summarizing Coach Higgins' thoughts on building team chemistry, she believes that team cohesion can be established if there is a willingness of the players to genuinely care about group results more than individual accolades.

Methods for building successful team cohesion revolve around the concept of establishing a specific mentality, she says. Those specific mentalities include building and reinforcing a feeling of specialness within the group and a feeling that the group cannot be successful unless they pull together as a whole, not as individuals.

Communicating a feeling of genuinely liking the players as people is also important in building team cohesion, she asserts.

Finally, the mentality that "all we have is each other" assists in building successful team chemistry.

* * * * * * * * * *

...on Discipline

Higgins believes that since Creighton University is a small, Catholic institution, that the student-athletes who choose to attend the school have some degree of self-discipline when they arrive on campus. But she still doesn't take anything for granted.

"My philosophy concerning discipline is pretty simple because we have few team rules," she states.

Coach Higgins believes that the key aspect of discipline lies not in how many rules a team has, but how the head coach enforces those rules.

"I think you need to establish a minimal number of rules," she says. But you must be very clear as to what those rules are."

The head coach needs to act quickly when a violation occurs, she asserts, and the punishment must fit the crime.

"If a violation occurs, the head coach must deal with it quickly, with the penalty being appropriate to the violation," she says.

Coach Higgins believes that idle threats, negative reforcement and physical penalties are the least effective methods of discipline.

"I hate idle, scary threats that ultimately could not be enforced," she says.

Mary states that those idle threats can take the form of "You'll be kicked off the team if..." or I'll reduce your scholarship if... ."

Threats mean nothing unless you really intend to carry them out, she says.

Negative punishments are also ineffective, Mary points out, and can be the most damaging method a coach can use.

"Negative punishments, like not talking to a player or giving the impression that a player is in your doghouse, are really very damaging psychologically," she states. "It's important for the head coach to <u>not</u> be in a punishment mentality. The coach needs to realize that a season is a <u>process</u> in human growth, just as is an individual career that the student-athlete is pursuing."

Finally, Higgins has discovered that any form of physical punishment is not effective when disciplining a player.

"Physical penalties, like running laps or extra sprints or putting the equipment away just hasn't been effective for us," she states.

Mary believes that effective discipline methods can be as creative as the head coach envisions, but that expectations should be clearly defined at the outset.

"Clearly state your expectations to the players," she says. "Ultimately, the payers <u>want</u> to please you, but they must know specifically what you want from them."

Mary also utilizes a rare, occasional display of anger to shake up the troops.

"I guess this really isn't a disciplinary method," she laughs. "But to the players, any time I display anger, which is very rarely, it shocks them a bit and helps me get their focus of attention on what needs to be accomplished."

Coach Higgins enjoys substituting extrinsic rewards for a job well done instead of negative behavior for goals not achieved.

"Again, this is what I've found to be effective. I'd rather reward than punish, so I'm not sure this would be considered "disciplinary" in context," she says.

The example she uses to illustrate this point involves incentives for off-season conditioning.

"We give a 100% Club Award to the players meeting all goals in the off-season conditioning program," she states. "This type of reward system reinforces the family philosophy that we have established, and is more effective than any form of punishment would be."

In summary, discipline is a trait evident in all championship teams, and Coach Higgins believes that most student-athletes arrive on the Creighton campus with some degree of self-discipline.

Her philosophy concerning team discipline states that few rules should be established. However, the rules need to be clearly explained, along with the penalties for violating team rules.

It is also important that the head coach act quickly once a violation occurs, and that the punishment is appropriate for the violation.

Least effective discipline methods include idle threats that can not be enforced, negative punishment involving player-coach relationships, and physical punishment in the form of extra running, she says.

Effective discipline methods include communicating player expectations in a clear fashion, exhibiting an unexpected display of anger, and substituting rewards for punishment for meeting off-season goals.

* * * * * * * * * *

...on Mental Preparation

Mental preparation is an essential element for team and individual success, and Higgins has been a proponent of the mental approach throughout her coaching career.

"Mental preparation means different things to different people," she says. "But it's still a matter of having confidence and being in the right frame of mind.

"I define mental preparation as being in an aggressive, yet relaxed frame of mind to prepare for competition as in practice or to prepare to compete in an actual game. The players must be relaxed while they're mentally preparing themselves, and hopefully mental preparation will build their confidence level."

Coach Higgins has developed a system of mentally preparing her players for pre-season practices, non-conference and conference games, and late-game strategy.

"During pre-season practice, we coaches make sure that the player's minds are always focused on a task. We make sure that no two practices are the same, so we use a variety of drills to keep things fresh."

During the pre-season, Mary and her staff set specific goals for each practice, for each week, and for the entire pre-season.

Another method used during pre-season is the development of positive talk among the players and coaches.

"We talk a lot about positive self-talk and talk positively with each other," she states.

Organization and practice length are also important during pre-season mental training.

"I think a coach needs to be incredibly organized," she says, noting that the players appreciate organized practices. "We also keep practices short, less than two hours as a rule."

Mary says that mental preparation for non-conference games takes on a little different approach.

"We generate respect for our opponents right away," she begins. "We also emphasize to the players that what the opponents do doesn't matter. What matters is what we do."

Non-conference games also bring an emphasis on national recognition.

"We will re-emphasize our bigger goals, for example national rankings and improving our execution."

Hopefully by the time the team enters the conference portion of their schedule, she states, the mental preparation techniques have sunk in and the players are confident.

"During conference games, we stress the ideas that we want the players to be relaxed, yet confident," Higgins says. "We also utilize visualization techniques, winning the games in our minds and experiencing success."

Late-game strategy is simple as long as you have a plan.

"We practice strategy situations all the time, but the most important aspect of strategy is that you have a plan, you practice that plan, and the players are confident in your plan," she says.

Mary adds a footnote to the effect that "I must be relaxed during strategy time and I must always stress the positive to the players...'you can do it!'."

In summary, mental preparation is an integral part of the success system Mary Higgins has established at Creighton. She defines mental preparation as being in an aggressive, yet relaxed frame of mind when mental practice begins.

Pre-season mental preparation techniques include varying practice routines, setting specific goals, talking positive at all times, being organized and keeping practices short in length.

Mental preparation techniques utilized during non-conference games include generating respect for the opponents, concentrating on team strategy and not opponent strategy, and re-emphasizing larger goals, such as national rankings and improving execution.

Emphasizing relaxation and visualization techniques to build confidence are the mental preparation elements utilized during conference games.

Finally, late-game strategy methods include developing a plan, practicing the plan, and building confidence in the plan through repetition.

* * * * * * * * * *

...on Mental Toughness

All coaches want mentally tough individuals because they know the mentally tough player will be productive in times of adversity. Higgins believes mental toughness can be found in the student-athlete who perseveres.

"Mental toughness is the ability of the student-athlete to have the confidence to persevere in difficult situations," she says. "The person who continues to work hard despite setbacks and disappointments will be successful in the long run."

Coach Higgins discusses the traits of a mentally tough player in her own characteristically wide-eyed, enthusiastic way.

"A mentally tough person never loses confidence in her abilities," she points out. "The confidence is still intact even when mistakes are made."

"The mentally tough person always focuses on the positive aspect of every situation. For example, at practice, the mentally tough individual does not pout or get down on herself when things aren't going well for her. She simply continues to focus on practice and on how she can improve."

Emotional stability and long-term enthusiasm are the final two traits of a mentally tough person, Higgins says.

"Mental toughness means that a player always exhibits a very stable emotional exterior. She is never moody; she is always on an even keel, emotionally."

"Finally," she concludes, "the mentally tough person has the ability to be positive and enthusiastic over the long haul, not just occasionally."

In summary, Coach Higgins defines mental toughness as the ability of a person to persevere in difficult situations.

Mental toughness traits include showing confidence after mistakes have been made and keeping a focus of attention on the task at hand during distractions.

Additional mental toughness traits include the ability to keep a positive and enthusiastic attitude present at all times plus the ability to stay emotionally stable during times of duress.

* * * * * * * * * *

...on Communication

Communicating effectively with your assistant coaches, support staff and players is a very important element in all successful organizations. In times of adversity during games, Coach Higgins' communication skills are selective, depending upon the effort being exerted.

"My response to difficult game situations really varies depending upon the effort being exerted by the players," she states. "If the effort was good, regardless of outcome, I positively reinforce their confidence levels."

Unsatisfactory effort brings a different response from Higgins.

"If the effort was not there, then I'll chew them out, but only after telling them what was done right," she says.

Reacting to a disappointing loss when the effort shown by the players should have resulted in a win is a very delicate situation, Coach Higgins assures us.

"After a tough loss, we emphasize to the players what was done correctly, how we improved and got better as a team, and how close we are to winning games in the late innings."

In summary, communication skills are very important within all organizations, and Mary Higgins makes sure that the lines of communication are always open with her student-athletes.

The only aspect of competition that Mary expects from her players is a consistent effort and the visible sign of trying their best.

When the effort is lacking, Mary usually reacts with a form of castigation, but only after telling the players what they did correctly.

In reacting to a difficult, unpredictable loss, as long as the effort was good, Coach Higgins will praise the effort of the players.

When the effort is not satisfactory, the team can expect some fired-up response from their head coach. However, Coach Higgins is quick to balance the stinging remarks with praise in the areas that showed improvement during the game.

* * * * * * * * * *

KELLY HILL

Western Illinois University

Position
Head Women's Basketball Coach

Career Record
62-128 (7 seasons)

Education
B.A.   1980 University of Southern California
M.Ed.   1987 University of Nebraska-Lincoln

Team and Personal Highlights

* Graduated magna cum laude from the University of Southern California.

* Captain of Southern Cal women's basketball team during her senior year.

* Assistant coach of women's gold medal-winning South team in 1986 U.S. Olympic Festival

* Invited speaker at the Colorado Educators for Athletic Equity and Leadership Conference in 1987 and 1988.

* Officer of the Council of Administrative Personnel at Western Illinois University.

* Chairperson for the Affirmative Action Council at Western Illinois University.

* Member of the Council of Collegiate Women Athletic Administrators (CCWA).

* Member of the Women's Basketball Coaches Association (WBCA) Legislative Committee in 1985.

* Member of the Women's Basketball Coaches Association Wade Trophy Committee in 1983-84.

Kelly Hill

Introduction...

Kelly Hill was a scholar-athlete during her days at the University of Southern California, and she has built the Western Illinois Westerwinds women's basketball program into a respected, competitive force again by mixing brains with athleticism.

Coach Hill believes in education first and actively recruits those persons who show a strong desire to be a complete student as well as a competent athlete.

"The success a person feels in the classroom gives them confidence," she states. "If you feel good about academics, you can't help but feel positive about life. In particular, we pay a lot of attention to a player's first semester on campus. We really try to open the channels of communication between the student-athlete, coaches and faculty."

The vivacious, high-energy coach who likes pasta, back-packing and Paris, France, has seen her philosophy pay off well, not only for the program, but more importantly for the students.

In her three previous years at Western Illinois, Coach Hill has had each of her seven seniors in her program graduate. Two are furthering their education in graduate school. Three are coaching basketball at the collegiate level, and one is enjoying her chosen career in law enforcement.

More of the same can be expected of the current team. In total, the returners to the 1989-90 squad posted a team cumulative grade point average of 3.0 on a 4.0 scale. This is an indication of the success of the team, both academically and athletically.

Hill herself has lived what she expects from her players: a focused drive to be the best student and athlete possible.

Kelly's initial year of collegiate basketball was as a player at California State-Fullerton under the guidance of 1976 U.S. Olympic coach Billie Moore, who now heads the UCLA women's program.

With a transfer to Southern Cal, she competed three years under the direction of Linda Sharp, who has coached two NCAA champion teams in 1983 and 1984. She was captain of the team her senior year.

A native of Colorado, Hill traveled to the Midwest to begin her coaching career at Big Eight Nebraska. After three years as an assistant coach at Nebraska, Hill was appointed head coach in 1984. She held that post for three years before moving to Western Illinois for the 1986-87 season.

A strong admirer of the late Martin Luther King, Kelly is very active in campus activities and very vocal on issues of equal rights and leadership opportunities for women.

A naturally-positive individual who espouses integrity and loyalty to her staff and players, Kelly was very flattered to be given the opportunity to discuss successful team building.

Here are Coach Hill's thoughts...

...on Motivation

To Coach Hill, motivation is a combination of momentum, excitement and personal challenges. But she says that one needs to be alert of any overarousal or underarousal.

"Motivation is the essence behind everything we do," she states. "But I've found out that too much or too little motivation gets in the way of our best performances."

She defines motivation as the ability to generate momentum and excitement within the person in order to accomplish a task.

"I believe that motivation is the ability to generate some kind of momentum, and possibly excitement, to meet and challenge the tasks or obstacles before us," she says.

What are some motivation techniques that have been successful for Coach Hill over the years?

"The most successful motivation techniques I utilize are those associated with goal setting," she begins. "Clear goal setting strategies along with high level communication and mutual interaction between the players and staff work best."

This proactive form of motivation, she remarks, "requires both parties to not only participate, but creates the need for both to be accountable and responsible for their behaviors and attitudes."

Kelly continues her thoughts on successful motivation techniques by concluding that "generally, my best motivation strategies have been to help the players see a need (goal), and to have me provide a means to achieve that need (goal)."

Least effective motivation techniques include any form of fear, threats, negative innuendos or punishment.

"You cannot expect student-athletes to perform at their best if they know you have a hammer over their heads all the time," Coach Hill says. "Negative reinforcements or fear tactics are highly ineffective if you want long-term positive results."

In summary, Hill defines motivation as the ability to generate momentum and excitement in the player to meet the challenges of any task.

Goal setting strategies are the best motivational techniques, she says, while least effective motivational techniques include fear tactics, threats, negative innuendos or any form of punishment.

* * * * * * * * * * *

...on Team Cohesion

Team cohesion is a vital ingredient for ultimate team success, and Coach Hill believes that the right environment can help in building team chemistry.

"I define team cohesion as a mutual trust, admiration, appreciation and conviction that each player has in working toward a common goal," she begins.

Coach Hill also states that "chemistry" in a team can't be manufactured, but the optimal atmosphere can be established.

"Chemistry is a delicate balance that can't be created from the wrong 'chemicals'," she says. "You can't make chemistry, but you can provide an environment from which it may develop."

Effective methods of building team cohesion vary greatly depending upon the team members' backgrounds and other variables, she says. But one common theme is apparent.

"It is not a mandate and there is no simple recipe," Coach Hill says. "However, open and honest lines of communication are integral for every member of a team."

Cohesion can be developed if each person believes she "belongs" and it is up to the coaching staff to make each player feel wanted.

"Cohesion develops when people invest and commit to each other," Kelly states. "Understanding one another's strengths, weaknesses, attitudes, family backgrounds and goals helps open those lines of communication."

One method Coach Hill has found very effective in building team cohesion is the utilization of a retreat for the players.

"A retreat away from the classroom and gymnasium provides an optimum chance for these informal associations to develop, she concludes.

"Structuring frequent meetings, both team and one on one,is vital to further developing habitual communication patterns."

Kelly ends her thoughts on building team cohesion by concluding that "cohesion develops as people build upon their experiences together and invest more and more of themselves in the process."

In summary, Coach Hill states that team cohesion can't be created artificially, but that chemistry can be developed by making the environment conducive for team cohesion.

Effective methods for building team chemistry include the use of open, honest communication between the players and coaching staff and the use of retreats away from the campus atmosphere. Frequent team and individual meetings also foster a communal feeling among the players, she says.

But in the final analysis, Kelly states it is the responsibility of the head coach to make sure that team members feel comfortable in their environment and that ample opportunities are given to have the players interact and converse among themselves on topics of common interest.

** ** ** ** ** **

...on Discipline

Discipline is a matter of accountability for behaviors, Kelly asserts, but there are some instances when a college coach has no control over the actions of the players.

"I believe you discipline people by making them accountable and responsible for their attitudes and behaviors," she states.

But there are times when coaches words carry no weight with the student-athlete, she says.

"I do not feel the college coach can change the patterns of a 17 or 18-year-old if they are not open and willing to accept their responsibilities to the team."

Kelly emphasizes that "my tolerance level is exceedingly low for disrespectful, selfish players."

Coach Hill believes there are two effective methods of handling discipline issues with the team.

"I have the players discuss what team rules we should have and what punishments they will have if those rules are broken," she remarks.

Peer pressure plays a big role in the success of this self-enforcement process, Kelly states.

"I have found that peer pressure far outweighs a list of mimeographed 'team rules' passed out by the coach in September," she says. "Generally speaking, their rules are stricter and carry a heavier penalty than I would have required."

The second effective method concerning discipline is the coach's reaction to team rules.

"Being a good role model for the players is important,"she says. "Practicing what I preach can have a very positive effect on the team."

Kelly emphasizes that "if dressing nicely, not swearing excessively and being considerate of others are things the team feels are important, then I, too, will try to demonstrate those exemplary qualities to the players."

Least effective disciplinary methods involve the coach making and enforcing the rules, she concludes.

"Passing out team rules, playing watchdog or baby sitter is not the way to handle discipline."

In summary, Coach Hill reinforces her philosophy that discipline is the result of making people responsible and accountable for their attitudes and behaviors.

She believes the most effective methods concerning discipline revolve around the concept of player participation in the rules-making and enforcement process. She also stresses the fact that peer pressure is the best method of team rules enforcement.

Being a positive role model to the players is another effective method of curbing discipline problems, she says.

Finally, the least effective methods of discipline are those in which the coach makes the rules and enforces them without player input.

* * * * * * * * * *

...on Mental Preparation

Mental preparation is essential to team and individual success, and Coach Hill knows the importance of teaching mental preparation skills to her student-athletes.

"We believe that mental preparation gives us a feeling of confidence when we know that we are in every way prepared for any challenge we are likely to meet," she concludes.

Variety of drills is the best way to mentally prepare for the grind of pre-season practices, she relates.

"You need to make things interesting, not only for the players, but for the coaches as well," she says.   "We are always incorporating difficult and easy, new and familiar drills with the players."

Non-conference games are utilized as a teaching period for the team, but the emphasis is on daily improvement, Kelly says.

"As coaches, we must make the players understand that this is the time when we learn how to play our game together. Constant feedback and communication with the players is essential during this time."

Once games begin in the tough Gateway Conference, Hill tells the team that now is the time to put things together.

Goal setting and constant evaluation are two key elements for success during league play, she says.

"We want the players challenging each other daily in practice," Kelly says. "We set goals for each game and we evaluate the outcome and reassess the direction we're going as a result of that assessment process."

Late-game strategy is practiced daily, according to Coach Hill.

"We work on concentration cues," she says. "We talk about different scenarios and give the players options and then allow them to figure out the best call for that situation."

Hill reiterates the belief that late-game strategy success is the result of "evaluate, evaluate...relate, share, communicate and teach!"

In summary, mental preparation is an important element for team and individual success. Coach Hill believes that mental preparation builds confidence in the players because it prepares them to meet all challenges that come their way.

Mental preparation techniques for pre-season practices include utilizing a variety of drills, mixing in the old with the new to keep the teaching approach interesting and fun.

Non-conference games are used as a teaching period to prepare the players for the Gateway Conference schedule.

Conference games are the focal point of the season because the results can lead to post-season tournament participation.

Finally, late-game strategy is taught during practice sessions. The players use concentration cues and practice various scenarios with success options for each situation.

Kelly concludes that mental preparation is the result of constant evaluation, relating to the player's needs, sharing and communicating information, and teaching the skills that will build player confidence.

* * * * * * * * * *

...on Mental Toughness

Mental toughness is a trait that all successful persons possess, and Coach Hill believes it's a part of a competitive spirit in the individual.

"Mental toughness," she begins, "is believing in your competitive spirit and trusting it will never let you down."

She continues her thoughts on mental toughness by saying "you won't allow yourself to be stopped...your effort, attitude and perspective is simply relentless."

Consistency, commitment, poise and resistance are some characteristics of a mentally tough person, Kelly says.

"A mentally tough person has no excuses at any time because she always believes in herself, her coaches and her teammates.

"A mentally tough person always looks for a challenge and never walks away from one."

Finally, she says, a mentally tough person "is in control, poised and unwilling to seek refuge from imposing obstacles."

In summary, Coach Hill defines mental toughness as a belief in one's competitive spirit and a relentless attitude toward personal challenges.

Mental toughness traits include belief in oneself, a consistency of effort, accepting challenges, commitment to a goal, resisting outside influences, control of emotions, poise under pressure and an unwillingness to seek refuge from imposing obstacles.

* * * * * * * * * *

...on Communication

Throughout this chapter on successful team building, effective communication has been a recurring theme for Kelly Hill. She understands the importance of effectively communicating with players and staff during times of adversity.

"If we're behind at halftime or late in the game, my procedure for 'inspiring' the team is to refocus the player's attention on three elements: belief in the game plan, their preparation method for the game, and their pride in themselves," she says. "You must develop this base to communicate to your team and expect them to respond."

Spontaneous improvisation on the part of the head coach can prove to be more harmful than helpful, she concludes.

"You can't make something up and expect a reaction that can withstand adversity," Kelly states.

"The players must be prepared and confident to continue the fight against the odds. They must know and believe in what you tell them."

She emphasizes that "mentally tough teams will always react positively to this challenge."

Post-game comments after a disappointing loss or a poor performance take a "team-oriented" approach, she says, focusing the comments on game preparation, concentration, and belief in the game plan.

"I try to focus on where our practice and pre-game preparation was lacking," she begins. "If we did not practice hard, concentrate well, or believe in the game plan, we probably didn't execute very successfully."

After commenting on practice preparation, she immediately refocuses her comments on the team.

"Immediately afterward, I try to refocus us into a team, not as a group of individuals who performed inconsistently or ineffectively," she says.

The "team" theme is the most important aspect of post-game remarks, she believes.

"The team has 'weight', far greater than any individual who did not perform well, she states.

Kelly also likes to leave her players with a closing message.

"I usually end my comments with something I want the players to think about," she states. "I try to make it positive, but it is always something to contemplate, something they all must sleep on."

In summary, communication skills are extremely important in Coach Hill's program. Without effective communication, she says, a team will not be able to perform up to its potential.

Procedures for dealing with adversity during games are similar in all circumstances. Kelly refocuses the attention of the players to three key elements: belief in the game plan, player preparation for the the game and pride in themselves.

She is quick to address the misconception that players react positively to coaching improvisation during games. She believes that a coach can't draw up a new strategy that the players have never seen before and expect successful execution.

Post-game comments center around game preparation and team commitment if the game resulted in a loss or poor performance on the part of the players, she states.

Finally, she closes her post-game comments with a challenge to the team for the upcoming game or practice.

* * * * * * * * *

DON JAMES
University of Washington

Position
Head Football Coach

Career Record
147-71-3 (19 seasons)

Education
B.A. 1954 University of Miami (Florida)

Team and Personal Highlights

* 1989 President, American Football Coaches Association;
         Freedom Bowl Champions.
* 1988 Became Pacific-10 Conference All-Time Winningest Coach.
* 1987 Independence Bowl Champions; Coach in East/West Shrine Game.
* 1986 Coach/Sun Bowl.
* 1985 Freedom Bowl Champions.
* 1984 Orange Bowl Champions; Columbus (Ohio) Touchdown Club Coach
         of the Year Award; Seattle Gold Helmet Coach of the Year Award.
* 1983 Coach/Aloha Bowl.
* 1982 Aloha Bowl Champions; Coach/Hula Bowl; *Playboy* Magazine Pre-
         Season National Coach of the Year.
* 1981 Pacific-10 Conference Champions; Rose Bowl Champions; *Athlon
         Publications* Coach of the Year Award; *Seattle-Post Intelligencer* Man
         of the Year in Sports Award.
* 1980 Pacific-10 Conference Champions; Coach/Rose Bowl; Pacific-10
         Coach of the Year Award; District IX Coach of the Year Award.
* 1979 Sun Bowl Champions.
* 1978 Coach/East-West Shrine Game; Coach/Japan Bowl.
* 1977 Pacific-8 Conference Champions; Rose Bowl Champions; UPI
         National Coach of the Year Award; AFCA National Coach of the
         Year Award.
* 1976 Coach/American Bowl.
* 1975 Pacific-8 Conference Co-Coach of the Year Award.

Don James

Introduction...

Could it be mere historical coincidence? Washington head football coach Don James served as president of the American Football Coaches Association in 1989, coinciding with the 100th year of Husky football. Washington football followers saw this as no surprise. James has been making history since coming to Seattle in 1975.

The James Gang legacy is well documented. James, the dean of Pacific-10 Conference football coaches, has a list of accomplishments that is blazing a trail for him toward the Hall of Fame.

The veteran coach owns the most victories in school history with 121 over 15 seasons. James also collected his 71st conference win during the 1988 season, allowing him to surpass former conference leader John McKay, who accumulated 70 wins in 16 seasons at the University of Southern California.

James' Husky teams have averaged better than eight wins per year, and the University of Washington owns a string of 13 consecutive winning seasons.

Washington has experienced just one losing season (5-6 in 1976) during James' career. Under James, the Huskies have finished in the upper division of the conference standings 14 times and 10 of the teams have finished either first or second in the league. All of those wins have added up to bowl games.

James and the Huskies set a conference record by appearing in nine consecutive bowl games from 1979 through 1987. The University of Washington has gone bowling 11 times in the last 13 years of the James era.

Washington has won three conference titles (1977, 1980, 1981) and trips to the Rose Bowl with James at the helm. He is 7-4 in bowl games, including a Tangerine Bowl appearance while coaching at Kent State University in 1972.

Often referred to as one of the best coaches in college football, James has garnered several significant coaching awards. The Seattle-based Gold Helmet Banquet and the Columbus (Ohio) Touchdown Club both named James the college Coach of the Year in 1984. He has also been voted District Coach of the Year, West Coast Coach of the Year, Pacific-10 Conference Coach of the Year, and Seattle's Sports Star of the Year.

Aside from having carried out his duties as AFCA President, James is also a member of the NCAA Rules and Recruiting Committees, as well as a member of the Pacific-10 Officials and Rules Committees.

Before joining the Huskies, James was the head coach at Kent State University from 1971-74 where he built a record of 25-19-1 and led the Golden Flashes to their first-ever bowl game.

James developed his coaching expertise while serving as an assistant at

Florida State University (1959-65), the University of Michigan (1966-67), and the University of Colorado (1968-70).

The 57-year-old James grew up in the football hotbed of Massillon, Ohio, where he played quarterback and defensive back for two state championship teams at Washington High School. He later accepted a scholarship to Miami (FL), where he set five school passing records, and graduated in 1954.

Don and his wife, Carol, both have roots in Massillon and attended the University of Miami together. They have three children, Jeff, Jill and Jeni and five grandchildren.

An avid reader who likes to run and play golf, Don James is the consummate team builder. He was most pleased to have the opportunity to share his ideas on this timely subject.

Here are Coach Don James' thoughts...

...on Motivation

Motivation is certainly one of the most important ingredients within all successful organizations, and James believes motivation and productivity go hand in hand.

"Motivation is just getting the most out of the people in your organization," Coach James says. "How they produce for you, their productivity level, is a result of how motivated they are."

There are several methods that Coach James has found to be effective in motivating his Husky players, but anger is not one of them.

"You just can't use anger, fear or intimidation to get positive responses from the players," he says. "Those types of motivation methods can no longer be used with athletes because the players won't tolerate it, and I'm in their corner on this one."

The most effective motivation techniques, he says, are centered around a family atmosphere.

"We truly believe that everything we want to accomplish as a team can be accomplished if we treat each player as a family member."

Members of Coach James' Husky family are required to show respect to each person in the organization, and exhibit self-discipline at all times.

"Each person needs to show great respect for one another," he states. "Self-discipline helps build a commitment of excellence in a person."

Building confidence in each player and treating all individuals the same are two additional motivation techniques that James has found to be effective.

"We keep communication positive with the players," he says. "That's a big plus for building self-confidence and self-esteem."

You also won't find Coach James making any special deals with his more-talented players.

"Make no special arrangements or deals with players," he begins. "Star treatment or favoritism can really kill team morale. Besides, with college football trying to recover from scandals and improprieties, a coach would be very foolish to attempt this kind of arrangement."

In summary, Coach James believes that motivation is the ability to get the most from your players. He also states that the productivity level of each person is indicative of the person's motivation for the task.

Effective motivation techniques include establishing and nurturing a family atmosphere within the organization. Treating each individual with great respect is also an important technique.

Administering a program that is built on discipline is an effective motivational technique, as is building self-confidence in the players.

Another effective motivation method is refusing to show preference to star performers. It is crucial to treat all team members in the same way, he says.

Finally, Coach James lists anger, fear and intimidation tactics as the least effective motivation methods.

* * * * * * * * * *

...on Team Cohesion

James reiterates his belief that developing a family atmosphere not only motivates his players, but is the essential element when building team cohesion.

"Team chemistry or team cohesion, whatever you wish to call it, means that a team will give a 100% effort because they believe everyone on the team is interested in team goals," he states.

Coach James points out that there is a hierarchy of leadership within all family units, and his Husky teams are successful when the senior-class players are effective leaders.

"There is no doubt that our leadership among the players must come from the seniors," he says.

In utilizing senior leadership, Coach James provides an open forum for team input concerning goals and rules. This forum is one of the best methods of building team cohesion, he concludes.

"We have team meetings and we also have senior-only meetings," he says. "During the senior meetings, we ask the players their ideas on how the squad can be improved. Also at this time, the coaching staff will discuss team rules with the seniors to get their feedback."

Team meetings during the week of games are used to not just prepare for the upcoming opponent, but to be used as an arena to award special performance awards from the previous game.

"We like to give credit and exposure to players who did great things for us during the last game," Don says. "We might pick out the best offensive and defensive play of the game, or something from our kicking game. It's something positive and the players really seem to enjoy it."

Since football players and staff continually scrutinize game films, Coach James says it is important that each film session is positive in approach and that learning takes place.

"The players put in many hours of film study with their respective position coaches, so it is extremely important that this time is well spent," he says. "If the player understands that each film session is going to focus on each player's strengths and not turn into a horror show with the coach screaming at him, then we have accomplished a lot that day."

In summary, team cohesion is defined by Coach James as the ability of the team to give maximum effort at all times because the players believe that everyone on the team is interested in only team-oriented goals.

Effective methods of building team cohesion include the use of senior leadership in formulating team rules and the utilization of awards days during weekly practice sessions.

Team meetings are also organized so that all players have an opportunity to give their ideas on improving the team.

Finally, the entire concept of the team being a family unit is constantly reinforced by the players, coaches and all support staff within the organization.

* * * * * * * * * *

...on Discipline

Discipline and team success go hand in hand within the University of Washington football program, and Coach James believes that you can't win championships without it.

"My philosophy concerning discipline has been the same since I started coaching," he says. "A team would have a very difficult time reaching its potential if it wasn't disciplined."

Over the years, Coach James has discovered disciplinary methods that have been effective and some methods that have not been effective. He elaborates on those methods.

"The least effective disciplinary methods involve having a list of infractions and penalties," he begins. "It's almost like a 'fine' system. When an athlete breaks a rule, he must pay the penalty for that infraction. I have found that this method is not a satisfactory one if you are trying to establish a successful long-term discipline policy."

The most effective method of discipline, Don says, is a policy of fairness, consistency and compassion.

"Every student-athlete must be given the opportunity to have his story heard," he states. "Every case is different and every player is different. So in all fairness, every player should be treated equally when team rules are compromised.

"I must also be consistent in my dealings with the players. The punishment must fit the infraction and there should be no favoritism shown when the penalty is given."

Coach James also concedes that an element of compassion is needed when disciplinary problems occur.

"These are my players," he says. "I brought them to campus, and I'm responsible for them. I must make sure that I am giving them my complete attention and that I care about them. Sometimes I must give them the benefit of the doubt. But the players understand that I will not compromise my standards."

Finally, Coach James says that his most serious penalties occur when crimes have been committed against teammates.

"I do my best to be fair and consistent and compassionate," he states. "But I have absolutely no tolerance when a player has committed an indiscretion against a teammate. I will react to the problem with quick disciplinary action."

In summary, James believes that a team cannot reach its potential if it has no sense of discipline.

The most effective disciplinary method involves the coach being fair, consistent and compassionate in his dealings with the players. He believes that every student-athlete must have his story heard before disciplinary action is taken.

Coach James states that his most serious penalties are given when a player has committed a crime against a teammate.

Finally, least effective disciplinary procedures involve listing detailed infractions with a penalty to go with it.

* * * * * * * * * *

...on Mental Preparation

All successful coaches say that mental preparation is essential to team and individual success and James is very vocal in singing praises of mental preparation.

"Over the years, we've found that we were most successful in games in which we knew our mental preparation had been at its best," he says.

Coach James believes that mental preparation is a combination of knowledge and motivation.

"We continually tell all of our players that learning their game assignments builds confidence and confidence helps build motivation," Don states. "If the players know what they're doing and they 'get up' for each game, then we think our chances for success that day are very good."

Mental preparation is an on-going process, he says, and that preparation is in full force during the fall camp.

"The coaching staff is constantly emphasizing the importance of fall camp to the players," he states. "We want the players to have good practices and begin developing a strong work ethic that will carry over the entire season."

The seniors on the Husky team also play a major role in mental preparation, Coach James concedes.

"Our seniors talk to the team about a practice attitude," he says. "They mention how important the practice attitude is in preparing for a new opponent.

We have the seniors do this once a week throughout the entire season."

Non-conference games take on a special emphasis during the season, Don says, noting that national rankings and bowl possibilities are the focal point.

"Non-conference games are important for a number of reasons," he begins. "Our first priority is always an emphasis on getting better, improving with each game. That never changes.

"A second approach to improving is to state that we are really playing ourselves and not an opponent. If we prepare totally, then no matter what the opponent does will have any negative effect on the team.

"Third, the team understands that national rankings, national prominence are gained through successful non-conference games. They also understand that a successful non-conference schedule will benefit us at bowl-decision time."

Non-conference away games hold a special place in Don's coaching psyche.

"Our team really enjoys playing away from home," he says. "The players also have a tremendous amount of pride in knowing they can quiet a large, noisy crowd by playing well."

Pacific-10 Conference games are the most important time of the season as far as Coach James is concerned.

"We tell the players that the league race changes each week," James says. "We have to make sure that we're always ready for each game because you never know who is going to beat whom."

It is also extremely important not to look beyond the next game, Don says.

"We always stress the point of playing a game one at a time and not looking ahead," he states. "Looking beyond an opponent can be disastrous."

The importance of each game is reviewed and new ideas to motivate the team are implemented, he says.

"We constantly remind the players that any team can beat any other team on any given day," he states. "We also look for any new motivational angles to utilize with the players."

Late-game strategy, the two minute plan, is practiced every day during the season, Don says.

"Offensively and defensively, we practice late-game situations. We practice when we're ahead and need to waste time, and we practice when we're behind and have to conserve time."

All late-game strategy is written in each player's playbook, Don says, and then that information must be transformed on to the playing field.

"We have every situation written up in the playbook," he says. "But the strategy isn't worthwhile if the players can't make it happen on the field during games."

In summary, mental preparation is an on-going process for each Husky player. Coach James believes that mental preparation is the result of knowing assignments and being motivated to perform.

Fall camp is treated as a special time, crucial to the development of the team and individuals. Senior players are utilizes during this time period to talk to team members about practice attitudes.

Non-conference games are used as team development periods, with national rankings and constant improvement being the goals.

Conference games are the most important games of the season. Special emphasis is put on playing one game at a time and not overlooking an opponent.

Finally, late-game strategy is practiced daily with all the information stored in each person's playbook.

* * * * * * * *

...on Mental Toughness

Coach James believes that mental toughness is a trait found in all highly skilled athletes, but he also thinks that all athletes, regardless of ability level, can develop the trait if they wish.

"Most great athletes are blessed with mental toughness." he says. "But then again, there are some great athletes who have to work like the devil to get mentally tough. So I think all athletes, regardless of ability, can develop mental toughness if they work at it."

James defines a mentally tough individual as a person who has the ability to handle adversity.

"The mentally tough person not only handles adversity better than others, he also has the ability to get better in the process," he says.

Adversity, James states, can be found in three areas: defeat, not playing and injury.

"A mentally tough person will set goals and stick with a plan to reach those goals," he begins. "He must be able to handle defeat and bounce back for the next game with renewed enthusiasm."

Coach James continues by saying that mentally tough individuals will play through injuries.

"Not major injuries, but the usual hard hits that come in a game."

Major injuries also test the mental toughness in the individual, he adds.

"I've seen good players quit trying when they've been struck with a career-ending injury," he states. "A mentally tough player will take this kind of injury as a personal challenge and try to make the best of the situation."

Working hard in spite of less or no playing time is a true test of mental toughness, Don says.

"A mentally tough person continues to work hard to improve, even if he's on the third or fourth team," he states. "We'll find a spot for that individual when we see that kind of attitude."

In summary, Coach James defines mental toughness as the ability of a person to handle adversity. Adversity, he says, can manifest itself in team defeat, lack of playing time, and personal injury.

Mentally tough individuals set goals to overcome adversity, he says. Don concludes that accepting the challenge of overcoming any adversity in life is the mark of a mentally tough person.

* * * * * * * * * *

...on Communication

Communication with staff and players during times of adversity is an important psychological factor in maintaining a successful program. Coach James goes so far as to script his comments to deal with such occassions.

"We discuss this long before it happens," he says.

Halftime procedures are handled the same way whether the Huskies are winning or losing, Don states.

"At halftime, our goal is simply to help the players," James says. "We'll make the needed technical adjustments for offense and defense, but mostly we try to keep the atmosphere positive so that the players are mentally ready for the second half."

Don asserts his belief that his attitude on the sideline during the course of the game remains positive at all times.

"I'm not saying that the coaches won't get a little upset by some aspect of the game," he begins. "But overall, we try to keep every player thinking positively at all times on the sidelines."

Coach James gives credit to the late Paul "Bear" Bryant, the legendary football coach at the University of Alabama, for his post-game comments to the team.

"Before we play a game, I have already written down ideas to cover victory or defeat," he says. "I simply add thoughts about how the game was actually played to the ideas I had written out.

"Many years ago I heard Coach 'Bear' Bryant give this tip at a coaching clinic and I have never forgotten it. He also advised to always give credit to the team if you win and the coach to take the blame if you lose. That advise has truly helped me over the years."

In summary, Coach James believes that communication is vital during times of adversity. Halftime talks are handled in the same manner whether the Huskies are winning or losing. Technical adjustments are made offensively and defensively, with the coaching staff keeping the atmosphere positive in nature.

Coach James prepares his post-game comments to the team long before the game is actually played. He then complements his scripted thoughts with the actual conditions of the game.

During his post-game comments to the team, Don also utilizes some coachings tips he gained from Coach Bear Bryant of Alabama. That coaching advice includes giving credit to the team during victory and the coach accepting the blame during defeat. He says that this advice has worked extremely well for him throughout his coaching career.

* * * * * * * * * *

GENE KEADY
Purdue University

Position
Head Basketball Coach

Career Record
253-112 (12 seasons)

Education
B.A. 1958 Kansas State University
M.A. 1964 Kansas State University

Team and Personal Highlights

* 1990   Inducted into National Junior College Basketball Hall of Fame.
* 1990   Named a member of the Board of Directors of the National Association of Basketball Coaches.
* 1990   Big Ten Conference Coach of the Year Award.
*   Overall winning percentage (.693) one of the best among active NCAA Division I head coaches.
*   Teams have participated in eight NCAA and two NIT post -season tournaments, including six consecutive NCAA tournament appearances from 1982-88.
*   Teams have won or tied for league championship four times.
*   No team has finished lower than fifth place in league play.
*   Overall head coaching record, including high school and junior college; 542-207 in 28 seasons.
*   Hutchinson (KS) Junior College teams participated in six national tournaments, finishing second during 1972-73 season.
*   Beloit (KS) High School teams participated in three state tournaments, finishing third during the 1962-63 season.

Gene Keady

Introduction...

Gene Keady would appear to possess the classic Type A personality: high-strung, competitive, driven, a perfectionist. His coaching style, intense in practice and games and thorough in preparation, has served him well since his coaching career began in 1957.

The 54-year-old native of Larned, Kansas, is highly respected among his peers because he has reached a high level of success the old-fashioned way: he earned it. He has taken the blue-collar route to a major Division I coaching position: high school coach, assistant and head junior college coach, Division I assistant coach, and head coach at a smaller Division I school.

Kansas will always remain special to Keady because it was here, in this state drenched in rich basketball tradition, that he started his illustrious coaching career.

After graduating from Kansas State University in 1958, Keady took the head boy's basketball position at tiny Beloit High School. Despite losing records in the first three seasons, his teams won 77 games during his last four years at the school. His 102-47 overall record still ranks as one of the best in Beloit basketball history.

Keady's sparkling prep coaching record earned him an assistant coaching position at tradition-rich Hutchinson (KS) Junior College in 1964. One year later, he assumed the head coaching responsibilities, leading the Dragons to six junior college post-season tournament appearances in nine years at the school. A 187-48 record during his tenure at Hutchinson whetted his appetite for the challenge of Division I coaching.

His dreams of coaching Division I basketball were realized in 1974 when he became an assistant coach at Arkansas. During his four-year stay as a Razorback assistant, the Southwest Conference basketball power won or tied for two league championships and participated in two NCAA tournaments, including a visit to the Final Four during the 1977-78 season where the team finished third.

Riding the wave of success at Arkansas, Western Kentucky courted Keady to become its next head coach. He eagerly accepted the lure to the Sun Belt Conference school, moving to Bowling Green in 1978 to build the Hilltoppers program into a national power.

He won 38 games during his two years at Western Kentucky, winning the Sun Belt Conference league championship in his last year and taking the team to the NCAA Tournament.

Truly appreciative of the opportunities he was given at Western Kentucky, Keady, nevertheless, could not deny himself a chance to explore coaching in one of college basketball's premier leagues, the Big Ten Conference.

Purdue University was searching for a strong advocate of academics and athletics to lead its basketball program into the 1980's. They found that combination in Gene Keady.

Taking the helm in West Lafayette in 1980, Boilermaker basketball has been on the rise ever since. His Purdue teams have won 215 games during his tenure at the school.

A string of six consecutive NCAA tournament appearances was snapped during the 1988-89 season when the team finished under .500 with a 15-16 record, the only losing record during Keady's 10 years at the school. The Boilermakers began a new string by participating in the 1989-90 NCAA Tournament.

Astoundingly, the 15-16 record in 1988-89 marked the first losing season for a Keady-coached team since his days at Beloit High School, when his 1959-60 team finished 8-11.

In tribute to his outstanding coaching accomplishments, Coach Keady was honored in 1990 by being inducted into the National Junior College Basketball Hall of Fame. Additional honors in 1990 included the Big Ten Conference Coach of the Year Award and his selection to the Board of Directors of the National Association of Basketball Coaches.

Blessed with explosive energy and a blue-collar work ethic, Keady possesses a heart of gold. He and his wife Patricia are active in many civic projects within the Purdue University community. They live in West Lafayette.

Always willing to help others, Coach Keady addressed the topic of successful team building with his customary bursts of verbal intensity.

Here are Coach Keady's reflections...

...on Motivation

Not surprisingly, Gene Keady connotes motivation to action. If a person is truly motivated, he says, their actions speak for that motivation.

"To me, a motivated person is an action-oriented person," he says. "By that, I mean the person must visibly indicate his or her motivation through his or her actions."

In other words, by Coach Keady's definition, a motivated person does not take a passive approach to life.

"When my players make good grades, I know they're motivated to be good students," he states. "When the players practice and play hard, I know they're motivated to be good athletes.

"You become successful by working hard for everything you get in life. Nothing comes easy. So it's important that you take action to become the best you can be. You indicate your willingness to become great through your actions.

"Hey, you can yell and scream at some kids because you've found through experience that this is the best kind of technique to use to motivate that kind of person," he states. "But that kind of approach doesn't work for every athlete."

A softer approach is needed for some individuals, and Keady works hard to meet that need in his players.

"I am by nature a very intense person," he says. "I talk loud and I'm very emphatic in my actions when teaching on the court.

"But I have been able to soften my approach over the years when the most effective motivation technique calls for me to be calm and fatherly in my dealings with an athlete. It hasn't been easy, but that's the way you have to deal with athletes today."

In summary, motivation means action in Coach Keady's definition of the word. A motivated person is an action-oriented person, someone who aggressively approaches life and its offerings.

Success in the classroom and on the court comes from hard work, he says. You are motivated when your actions speak for your intentions.

Coach Keady utilizes motivation techniques that are specific to each individual. Through experience and knowing his athletes, he has found which techniques work better than others.

Finally, he says it is important to quickly discern the most appropriate motivation approach for each athlete. The sooner you discover the most effective technique, the sooner the athlete begins to perform at his best, he concludes.

* * * * * * * * * *

...on Team Cohesion

Team chemistry is vital for team success, and Keady strongly believes that this is a key element to the success of his program over the years.

"Team chemistry is really about attitudes," he says. "Team cohesion is built upon the positive attitudes of the players. They need to be positive about themselves and positive about their teammates and coaches. Team cohesion means that each player is willing to put the team first before any individual honors."

Team cohesion is also built through positive leadership, mutual respect and total honesty, he says.

"Leadership must start at the top, so it is very important that the coaching staff gain the respect of the players," he points out. "Once that respect becomes a two-way affair, meaning the players respect the coaches and each other and the coaches respect the players, you have the seeds of team chemistry beginning to grow."

Total honesty with the players not only builds mutual respect, it also builds team cohesion, Gene says.

"We are always honest, brutally honest in fact, with our players when discussing their contributions to the team," he states. "Sometimes the players don't like to hear the honest appraisal you give them, but they know I'm shooting straight with them, and they respect that. We pull no punches. We tell it like it is."

What methods has Coach Keady found to be effective when building team cohesion?

"First of all, we try to do everything as a team. Team meetings and team meals where everyone is present and participating are very effective.

"We also like to bring in outside speakers to discuss important issues with the players. We've bought in speakers to address the topics of drugs and gambling, to mention just two.

"Finally, we conduct seminars with the players to help them develop the poise they need when speaking with the media. The players appreciate these kinds of opportunities to better themselves, and it helps build team unity in the process."

In summary, Coach Keady believes that team cohesion is a result of the positive attitudes of the players. The players are positive about themselves and others, he says, and they espouse the conviction that the concept of team is more important than individual honors.

Team cohesion is also built through positive leadership, mutual respect, and total honesty, he says. The head coach is responsible for establishing an environment where mutual respect can be cultivated, and it is the responsibility of the head coach to honestly communicate his thoughts with the players at all times.

Effective methods for building team cohesion include team meetings and team meals. Additional methods for building team cohesion, Coach Keady says, are bringing in outside speakers to discuss topics of interest to the player, and conducting seminars with media personnel to assist the players in developing the skills and poise needed to effectively handle media-related situations during the season.

* * * * * * * * * *

...on Discipline

The topic of discipline brings a twinkle to the eye of Coach Keady. Many coaches do not feel comfortable with the task of disciplining a player, so they allow a transgression to slide by in some instances. Don't count Keady in that group of coaches.

"Discipline is extremely important to a team," he says. "Without it, a team slowly destroys itself."

Coach Keady's philosophy concerning team discipline involves answering a set of questions.

"First you answer the question 'What is the discipline for?' In other words, what rule has been compromised in order for the discipline to be invoked?

"Next, how is the discipline going to be administered? Is it a suspension for a game or extra conditioning or disqualification from the team? How is it going to be done?

"The next element involves being consistent and doing things the right way. As head coach, I make the decisions concerning discipline. I must be fair, but I can't start setting precedents for each new problem that arises. So handling things consistently is very important.

"Finally, discipline should be a learning experience for the player. Therefore, all discipline should be administered with goals in mind. What should the athlete be learning from this? Is he learning anything from this?

"So as you can tell, my view on discipline may be a little different from anyone else's," he says.

As he stated in his thoughts on motivation, Keady does not possess a one-method-fits-all kind of discipline method.

"You can't have blanket discipline," he says. "Every situation needs to be dealt with on an individual basis. That's why it's important to listen to each athlete before jumping to any conclusions."

In summary, Coach Keady believes that discipline is an extremely important element of team building. The entire process of disciplinary action needs to be discussed thoroughly by the staff and athlete before actions are taken, he says.

Finally, Keady says he has no totally effective blanket method of disciplining an athlete. He says that each case needs to be viewed on its own individual merits.

* * * * * * * * * *

...on Mental Preparation

All successful coaches say that mental preparation is essential to team and individual success. Coach Keady concurs, defining mental preparation as a combination of self-discipline, concentration, and consistency of effort.

"The team that is mentally prepared is a very self-disciplined team," says Keady. "They have the ability to concentrate totally at every practice on what needs to be done.

"Most importantly, I believe, is that each player has the will to practice to win. Remember, the will to win is not as important as the will to prepare to win. There's a big difference.

"Finally, mental preparation means being able to give the same consistent effort day in and day out at practice and during games."

Techniques for mentally preparing a team for the grind of pre-season practice involve physical conditioning and another important element, he points out.

"How an athlete prepares himself for the grind of a long season really has a lot to do with the kind of person you recruited in the first place.

"If you recruited kids with character, then you don't have to worry about their preparation methods because you know they'll do what they're supposed to do to get ready."

Coach Keady stresses the point that each athlete must report for pre-season practice in excellent physical condition.

"You know the kind of beating our players take by playing in the Big Ten," he says. "So they must be physically strong to begin with, and then we can mentally prepare them after that, we hope," he says.

Non-conference games are approached like a big tournament, Gene says. The challenge is to win as many games as possible, knowing that these games help determine post-season tournament appearances in either the NCAA or NIT.

Conference games are the most important games of the year in Coach Keady's estimation.

"Our goal is always winning the Big Ten Conference championship," he states. "National championships will follow if we can take care of business in the Big Ten."

Late-game strategy is practiced daily, Keady says, but he again returns to the subject of recruiting when talking about the success or lack of success late in a game.

"Kids with character can accept the pressure late in a game," he begins. "Kids with a lack of character will not handle the pressure for you in the end. It simply comes down to recruiting the right kids for your program."

He concludes his thoughts by saying that "the more experience a player with character gets, the more wins you will get late in a game when the game is on the line."

In summary, Keady believes that mental preparation is important when preparing a team for a long, competitive season.

He defines mental preparation as the ability to be self-disciplined, to concentrate totally at every practice, have the will to prepare to win, and display a consistent effort at all times on the court.

Recruiting players with character is the only way to be successful in any kind of program, he says. The quality athlete will be more conducive to preparing himself for pre-season practice and the player with character will be the person who can handle the late-game pressure situations, he states.

Winning the Big Ten Conference championship is the goal of the team every year, and that's where the bulk of mental preparation is directed.

Finally, non-conference games are considered a big, pre-conference tournament, with the goal of winning as many non-conference games as possible in order to better position the team for post season NCAA or NIT tournament consideration.

* * * * * * * * * *

...on Mental Toughness

Coach Keady believes that mental toughness can be found in all athletes. The difference lies in the ability to develop that trait to its fullest.

"Mental toughness is really self-discipline," he says. "It's the ability to live within and without yourself."

He further explains his thoughts on mental toughness by saying that "living 'within' yourself means living with the skills you have and developing them to the fullest."

"Living 'without' yourself means having the self-discipline to play within the physical and mental boundaries you've established for yourself," he concludes.

What are some traits of a mentally tough individual? Keady believes a positive attitude and pride top the list.

"A mentally tough person is someone that is positive with himself and positive with the people around him," he says. "But most of all, a mentally tough person has a tremendous amount of pride in his abilities."

In summary, Coach Keady defines mental toughness as the ability to self-discipline yourself, and to be able to live within and without the limitations you have set.

Mental toughness traits, he says, include self discipline, a positive attitude with himself and others, high self-esteem, and tremendous pride in his abilities.

* * * * * * * * * *

... on Communication

Throughout this essay, Coach Keady has stressed the importance of communication with his staff, the players and the support personnel. He has stated that it is the responsibility of the head coach to be totally honest in all communications with the athletes.

Half-time communication procedures, as a rule, do not include fire-and-brimstone speeches, he says.

"At halftime, we make technical adjustments only," he says. "I really don't like to go into a tirade with the players because I'm wasting by breath if I do. The players are smart enough to understand that all motivation preparations had to precede the game. Halftime is too late to raise your voice to motivate the players."

Post-game comments take on a different approach, he states.

"If we win, and it's a big win, I'll blend in a little chewing out around the accolades if I think the players are cocky about the win.

"If it was a tough loss, chewing out is not a good thing to do. You can always bring up negatives during practice or during film review later. I usually try to leave the kids with something positive.

"We have 11 goals for each game. I will mention the ones we met and stress those positive results," he says.

In summary, communication skills cloaked in total honesty are essential in every organization, Keady says. Without effective communication, the entire program can be harmed.

Halftime talks are utilized for technical game adjustments only, he states. He rarely raises his voice to motivate the players, believing that it is a waste of energy.

Post-game comments will differ, depending upon the results of the game. If the players exhibit a cockiness after a big win, he most likely will blend some chewing out with the accolades during his talk with the players.

If the game resulted in a tough loss, his comments will be more soothing and positive in nature. Negative remarks, he says, can be directed to the players at practice the next day or during film review the day after the game. The game goals that were met are accentuated with the players during this time, also.

* * * * * * * * * *

JERRY KINDALL
University of Arizona

Position
Head Baseball Coach

Career Record
706-392-4 (18 seasons)

Education
B.S.   1959   University of Minnesota
M.A.   1968   University of Minnesota

Team and Personal Highlights

*	1991	Assistant Coach of USA Team in 1991 Pan American Games.
*	1990	Chosen for induction into American Baseball Coaches Association Hall of Fame.
*	1989	Pacific-10 Conference Southern Division Coach of the Year Award.
*	1986	National Coach of the Year Award from American Baseball Coaches Association.
*	1980	Pacific-10 Conference Coach of the Year Award; *The Sporting News* Coach of the Year Award; ABCA Coach of the Year Award.
*	1976	ABCA National Coach of the Year Award; *The Sporting News* Coach of the Year Award.
*		College World Series champions in 1976, 1980, and 1986.
*		Two Pacific-10 Conference championships.
*		Teams have played in 10 NCAA post-season tournaments.
*		Coached 15 All-America players and sent 91 players into the professional ranks.
*		Only coach to play for a national championship team (1956, University of Minnesota) and coach a national championship team (1976, 1980, 1986, University of Arizona).
*		All-America baseball player at the University of Minnesota in 1956.
*		Member of the 1965 American League Champion Minnesota Twins.
*		Eight-year major league playing career with Chicago Cubs, Cleveland Indians and Minnesota Twins.
*		Active member in the Fellowship of Christian Athletes and Young Life campaign.

Jerry Kindall

Introduction...

The box score in the life of Jerry Kindall is loaded with statistics of personal and team successes: devoted husband and father, published author, national television baseball analyst, award-winning collegiate coach, All-Star Major League infielder, Hall of Famer. If you want to know how to build winning teams, Jerry Kindall is the architect you want to contact.

The 55-year-old native of St. Paul, Minnesota, has taken his Midwestern work ethic to the Valley of the Sun and infused blue-collar pride into the University of Arizona baseball program.

"Our three national championships mean we've had succession of wonderful ball players at Arizona," is Coach Kindall's modest way of describing success.

For Kindall, success did not come easily.

"It's such hard work. You can't win the championship with karma, nor with destiny. You get some young men with talent together, you get them to work hard and you get them to shoot for the top," he says.

Kindall has earned a reputation for excellence among his coaching peers. Only one other college baseball coach, retired Rod Dedeaux of the University of Southern California with 10, has won more NCAA titles than Kindall, who shares his niche with his former coach Dick Siebert of Minnesota and Bobby Winkles, then at Arizona State. All three have won three national championships. To honor his achievements, the American Baseball Coaches Association will induct Kindall into it's Hall of Fame in January, 1991.

As a player, Kindall excelled on both the collegiate and professional levels. In 1956, the talented shortstop led Dick Siebert's Minnesota team to a 33-9 record and the NCAA title. The team that the Golden Gophers beat for the championship in 1956 ironically, was the University of Arizona. The coach of the Wildcats then was Frank Sancet, the man Kindall succeeded in 1973.

After gaining All-America status in 1956, Jerry signed a bonus contract with the Chicago Cubs. He played eight years as one of the major leagues top-fielding infielders with the Cubs, Cleveland Indians and Minnesota Twins. He was a member of the American League Champion Minnesota Twins when he retired from professional baseball in 1965.

Kindall joined the University of Minnesota coaching staff in 1966 as an assistant basketball coach, and in 1968 assumed a dual role as assistant baseball coach. Kindall held those positions until taking the reins of the Wildcat baseball program in 1973.

Kindall is most proud of the fact that he has sent two assistant coaches, Jim Lawler and Mark Johnson, on to head coaching positions.

A man with a firm grasp on life's priorities, Kindall is an active member of the Fellowship of Christian Athletes and also finds time to assist Young Life campaign in Arizona. Widowed in 1987 after 30 years of marriage, he married

Diane Sargent of Colorado Springs, Colorado, on November 25, 1988. Kindall has four adult children.

A very soft-spoken and sincere individual, Kindall was appreciative to have the opportunity to share his ideas on successful team building. A man with the E.F. Hutton image, when he speaks about building successful organizations, people listen.

Here are Coach Jerry Kindall's thoughts...

...on Motivation

Coach Kindall considers himself a supporter, an encourager and a motivator. Those are traits he believes are vital when trying to build successful organizations.

"Perhaps the most important role played by the coach today is that of the motivator," he states.

Motivation is not a haphazard, gung-ho type of activity to Kindall. In order to motivate, you need to define the term and then find qualities that will be effective with your players. And that is no easy chore, he says.

"Every coach needs a frame of reference within which to operate as he seeks to bring out the best in his team and players," he states. "I need to determine my theory of motivation, decide what qualities I think are important to a winner, and then direct my motivation toward the specific ways of developing those qualities. This cannot be a haphazard thing. It takes planning and a system."

Jerry says that defining and redefining motivation is an on-going process. But through experience, he feels he has found three qualities, or "constants" as he calls them, that are at the foundation of motivation.

"There are three principles that have, in my mind, become constants and I recognize them now as essential as I seek to motivate my players to their best effort," he says.

The three qualities for building motivation within the framework of a team include organization and careful preparation, building trust, and being knowledgeable of your field of expertise, he states.

"Let's face it, baseball permits wasted time," Kindall says. "I don't blame youngsters for becoming bored with baseball when they are forced to stand in the outfield for an hour shagging and then are 'rewarded' with 2 bunts, 5 swings and more shagging.

"We must overcome those long, tedious hours on the practice field by planning in advance ways to stimulate the players with the desire, as well as tools, to improve.

"Therefore, it is incumbent on me to organize practices that will create that desire."

Jerry believes that posting the daily practice schedule is an excellent motivational tool as is an organized way of keeping player records and statistics.

"Post a practice plan in the lockerroom and on the field," he begins.

"The players will respond if they know what is in store for them that day."

Kindall also relates that specific information should be included on the practice plan.

"Include on the plan time allotments, player's names, coaches responsibilities, equipment needs, and statements of goals for that day," he says. "It's also a good idea to conclude the practice plan with a challenge or thought for the day or week."

Record keeping is another motivational tool, and Kindall believes that this may be the best motivation tool to utilize with players.

"The players need to know the coach is basing his evaluation of them on objective standards as much as possible," he says. "If a player is cut or benched, he deserves to see some objective, relative measurement of his performance as reasons, not merely the coach's hunch."

The second key principle for motivation concerns the development of trust between coach and players. Jerry tells of learning the importance of trust.

"I learned a great deal about the importance of trust in the coach-player relationship when my own children, two sons and two daughters, began competing on teams in baseball, basketball, football, swimming and cheerleading.

"During dinner-table talk, I gained much insight into coaching by measure of the trust my children put in their coaches. It is no accident that the winning teams on which they played were coached by persons they trusted implicitly."

Some methods to develop trust, he says, are punctuality ("No group of people likes to be kept waiting,") academic responsibility ("The most effective coaches I know were widely regarded as their school's best teachers."), and personal behavior ("We can't expect to motivate our teams to their best effort if they snicker and laugh at our personal conduct.").

The final principle of motivation that Kindall utilizes is the need for the coach to be knowledgeable in his field of expertise.

In a study by Dr. Lewis E. La Grand of State University of New York at Potsdam called "What the Athletes Look for in their Coaches," he found that players rank 'knowledge of coach' as a very important trait.

"I believe the ultimate compliment a player can pay his coach concerning on-the-field activities is 'our coach knows what he is talking about'," he states.

In summary, Kindall believes that motivation is an on-going process and that learning to motivate is a continual learning experience.

He has formulated his motivational philosophy around the concepts of organization, trust and knowledge. He is a strong proponent that if a coach is organized, has earned the trust of his players, and is knowledgeable in his sport, that these three principles make a strong foundation for motivating any athlete.

Finally, Coach Kindall mentions numerous methods that can be utilized within the team structure that can help build motivation for the athlete.

* * * * * * * * * *

...on Team Cohesion

Team cohesion is a vital ingredient for ultimate team success. Coach Kindall believes that team cohesion can be developed easier if the athlete has a positive self concept of himself and if the head coach makes the atmosphere around the program conducive to building team chemistry.

"When a player has self esteem and a good image of himself and those around him, he's free to play his best," he says. "When the entire team is experiencing this kind of feeling, the cohesion is tremendous."

Coach Kindall is quick to add the atmosphere within the program must be comfortable and enjoyable for the student-athlete, and that the head coach is responsible for creating and maintaining that comfort zone.

"As coaches, we must help the players feel important, heighten their self-image, and be kind and compassionate so that we can build up a lasting trust in each other," he points out.

"It's true that a coach takes on a father role for most of his players. It is also true that young men and women long to see truth, honesty, fairness and compassion in the adult world.

"If we can provide an atmosphere that builds on those qualities, then I think that team cohesion will be very strong."

Some techniques to build team cohesion, Jerry says, are simple activities in which all players participate.

Team meals and activities are important, as are the weekly Captains/Coaches meetings.

"The players elect our co-captains at Arizona, so everyone has some input as to who they want their leaders to be," Jerry states. "The coaches regard the captains as crucial links to our understanding the collective and personal need of our team."

Kindall says that the coaches have learned much about the players through the captains.

"In all the years we have had these meetings, our captains have found that we treat their comments and observations with respect and in confidence.

"In fact, they sense more quickly than the coaches where methods and relationships can be improved. It may well be a humbling experience for a coach to read the players' psyches through the captains, but I recommend it strongly as a needful means to improve the coach-player relationship," he comments.

In summary, Coach Kindall believes that team cohesion can be developed and nourished when each player has a strong self-image and when the head coach encourages a family atmosphere.

Effective techniques and methods used to build team cohesion involve team meals, team social activities, team selection of captains, and Captains/Coaches weekly meetings. Coach Kindall also stresses the point that mutual respect and trust among team members and coaching staff establishes a solid foundation for team cohesion.

* * * * * * * * * *

...on Discipline

Coach Kindall believes that discipline is a trait of championship teams, and he is a strong advocate of having a written policy on team discipline.

"It is essential that you not only have team policy on discipline, it is essential that you enforce that policy," he states.

He says that team discipline policy needs to include on the field and off the field behavior, and that the policy needs to be stated very clearly.

"Our team policy on discipline is always written down in clear, understandable terms," he says. "No doubts are left in the player's mind after reading the policy."

Even though the final decision on team discipline policy is the responsibility of the head coach, Kindall points out that player input is requested and received before the final version is implemented.

"Don't get me wrong," he says. "It's not total democracy around here. But we want the feedback of the players before we come up with a final version, and we can get that information from the players during our captain's meetings.

"The official policy is a reflection of the coaches, but much credit must be given to the players."

A copy of the discipline policy is given to each player at the beginning of the year. Having a written policy, Coach Kindall says, makes enforcement a much more accurate and fair procedure.

"Discipline can be implemented accurately when you have a written policy because everything is spelled out for the player," he states. "You don't have to worry about negotiating the penalities. It's all right there in front of you."

Jerry is very adament concerning his thoughts on most effective and least effective discipline methods.

"There's no doubt in my mind that suspension is the least effective discipline method," he begins.

"The reason is that it is not helpful to the team at all. I rarely suspend a player, but when I do, I've got the welfare of the player at heart.

"But I have to think about the good of the team, also. And that's the most difficult aspect, where do you cross the line from individual player to team?"

Coach Kindall quickly answers his own rhetorical question by explaining what he considers to be the most effective discipline method.

"I constantly remind the players that they are accountable to not only the coaches, but to the entire team as well. Therefore, when the actions of one player calls for disciplinary measures, the entire team pays for the offense of the one individual," he states. "So if one person has to run extra sprints, the entire team runs with him."

Coach Kindall asserts that peer pressure acts as the best discipline method "because players respect what other players have to say."

In summary, Kindall believes in having a written policy on team discipline.

The contents include behavior off the field as well as on the field and the consequences associated with those behaviors.

It is important to have player feedback concerning team discipline, and he receives that input from his captain's meetings. However, the final decision concerning team discipline policy, he contends, is the responsibility of the head coach.

Kindall mentions suspension as the least effective discipline method, and he favors team discipline as the most effective method of discipline. He also strongly believes that peer pressure makes each player accountable to the team.

* * * * * * * * *

...on Mental Preparation

Baseball may look simple, Kindall contends, but it really is a highly complex sport from a player and coach's perspective. That is why mental preparation is so important to the Wildcat program.

"I define mental preparation as a process in which I draw my player's minds into my own," he begins.

"I want them to understand my thought processes for every situation we find ourselves in," he says. "I want them to know why we can't make the third out at third base or why we need to be aggressive on the base paths and not reckless or why we lift weights at six in the morning instead of the afternoon.

"I don't want a robotic response from them, but I do want them to have an understanding of the way I think."

The University of Arizona players utilize relaxation and visualization techniques to prepare themselves for a long season and to stay sharp in critical situations, Jerry says.

"Over the years, we've used a sport psychologist from the university to assist the players with relaxation and visualization skills," he points out. "Even though I have not been totally satisfied with some of the sport psychologists we've used, I am committed to the belief that these skills are very necessary to the overall development of the players."

In summary, mental preparation is essential to team and individual success at the University of Arizona.

Coach Kindall defines mental preparation as the process by which he takes the mind's of his players into his mind. He believes that his players are mentally prepared when they understand the reasoning behind coaching decisions. He does not want his players reacting like robots, but he does insist that they understand his thought processes.

Finally, the most effective ways of preparing the team mentally, he says, are developing relaxation and visualization skills. He utilizes the services of a sport psychologist from the university for these purposes.

* * * * * * * * *

...on Mental Toughness

Mental toughness is a trait found in most highly-skilled athletes. As other coaches in the book contend, Coach Kindall agrees that the trait is not an inherent quality in all humans, but rather a trait that can be learned.

"I think that mental toughness is not necessarily a human emotion, but that it is a personality strength," he says. "You sharpen it, focus it, in order to use it."

Jerry defines mental toughness as "the ability to respond well in high pressure situations." He also claims that mental toughness "separates the good teams from the ordinary ones."

He says the mentally tough individual has certain characteristics.

"I think the mentally tough person concentrates very deeply when he needs to," he states. "I also think that dependability is the mark of a mentally tough player."

Coach Kindall also lists "being a competitor" and being "goal-oriented" as mental toughness traits. He also points out that he utilizes a John Wooden coaching approach to help develop mental toughness in his players.

"I create as many pressure situations in practice as I can," he says. "Hopefully the players will react correctly in games because they've already been through the same pressure situations during practice."

In summary, Coach Kindall believes that mental toughness separates the good teams from the ordinary ones. He defines mental toughness as the ability to respond well in high pressure situations.

Whereas he doesn't think mental toughness is an inherent human trait, he nevertheless believes that a person can develop the characteristics.

Mental toughness traits include the ability to concentrate, dependability, setting goals, and being highly competitive.

Finally, he orchestrates the practice environment into a pressure-filled scenario, conditioning his players to react correctly in game situations from the pressure situations they've experienced in practice.

* * * * * * * * * *

...on Communication

Kindall ranks effective communication as a key component when building successful programs, whether it's an athletic team or a corporate team.

"You've got to keep the door open for the athletes at all times," he says, "or you may lose them forever."

Kindall uses a story from his playing days to illustrate the importance of communication with the players.

"I recall a manager in the minor leagues who was one of the best hitting and fielding instructors I have met," he says. "But he languished for many years as a minor league coach and manager because the players were generally mad at him for his abrasive personality and thus seemed to lack confidence in his leadership."

Kindall relates that communication problems has also cost major league managers their jobs.

"A well-known big league manager quit his job following several unsuccessful seasons because he felt he could not 'reach his players and understand them'."

Coach Kindall gives much credit for his coaching success to the philosophy of his former college coach and mentor, Dick Siebert of the University of Minnesota. And the one coaching practice he has carried with him since his days at Minnesota is the "open door" policy for his players.

"Our 'open door' policy has not only kept the lines of communication open between coaches and players, it has also in the past headed off many problems and player's anxieties."

Kindall likes to illustrate this concept with another story, this one from his playing days in high school and college.

"As a young athlete, I was reluctant to approach my coach's office. It seemed he was always busy and I was imposing on his time in the midst of that hectic schedule most coaches keep.

"Later, I discovered that these men welcomed me as a visitor, and my regard for them grew even more.

"Remembering my cautiousness as a player, I now frequently encourage the players to come by the office. I tell them they are more important than anyone, except family, that I may have in my office at that time and they will get priority," he states. "They can also call me at home anytime."

In summary, communication is the life-line to success in all organizations, and Kindall is quick to point out its importance.

He believes that job security can be affected by lack of communication skills, and illustrates those thoughts with actual experiences during his playing days.

The most effective communication method is to set an "open door" policy with the team, stating that the athlete is welcome, and even encouraged, to stop by the coach's office at any time or call him at any time.

Coach Kindall says that developing this "open door" policy will greatly improve not only any communication barriers that may be arise, but also build the element of trust between coach and player.

* * * * * * * * * * *

MARILYN McREAVY
University of Florida

Position
Head Volleyball Coach

Career Record
514-178-6 (17 seasons)

Education
B.S.   1966   Southwest Texas State
M.Ed. 1970   Sul Ross State

Team and Personal Highlights

*   1989   Earned 500th coaching victory with win over University of South Alabama.
*   1987   Lady Gators cracked national Top 20 and received invitation to NCAA tournament.
*   1986   Coach of gold-medal winning East team at Olympic Sports Festival.
*   1985   Assistant coach of USA team at World University Games in Kobe, Japan.
*   1983   As coach at University of Kentucky, team was ranked among the nation's top five teams.
*   1978   Guided her Utah State team to the national championship of the AIAW (Association of Intercollegiate Athletics for Women).
*   1978   Inducted in Women's Sports Foundation Hall of Fame.
*   1970- Teams were undefeated on the way to
     1971   consecutive DGWS National Championships (Division of Girls' and Women's Sports).
*   1970   Member of USA World Games team.
*   1968   Member of USA Olympic team.
*   1967   Member of USA Pan American Games team.
*   Coach of more than 30 All-America players.

Marilyn McReavy

Introduction...

Marilyn McReavy has been associated with volleyball and winning since her playing days at Sul Ross State University in the late 1960's. With national and international experience as both a player and coach, Marilyn has built an impeccable reputation as a successful team builder.

When her Lady Gator squad defeated the University of South Alabama during the Lady Tiger Cup tournament at Memphis State University on September 1, 1989, Coach McReavy earned her 500th coaching victory and became only the fifth coach of NCAA Division I women's volleyball teams to join the prestigious 500 Club.

Among her 514 career victories are three national titles. McReavy's other accomplishments include induction into the Women's Sports Hall of Fame, and playing honors as a member of the USA Olympic, Pan American and World Games teams.

The 45-year-old native of Big Lake, Texas, began her collegiate coaching career at Sul Ross State University in 1969. Her Lady Lobos teams did not lose a single match during her two-year stay at the Alpine, Texas school, recording a 72-0 mark while winning consecutive DGWS National Championships. The Division of Girls' and Women's Sports championships were the predecessor to AIAW and NCAA national championships.

From 1972-74, Marilyn taught in the Public School Districts of Houston and Brazosport, Texas. She also played for and coached the top amateur team in the nation, which was made up primarily of Sul Ross players. This team was named the national training team and was the nucleus of the 1980 and 1984 Olympic volleyball teams.

Marilyn returned to collegiate coaching in 1975 at New Mexico State University, leading the Roadrunners volleyball program to a 27-7 record.

In 1976, Utah State came calling to McReavy, offering her the challenge to build a fledgling Aggies volleyball program. She accepted the challenge, and except for her first season at the Logan, Utah school, her teams never finished lower than 10th in the nation. Her six-year record at Utah State was 210-64-6.

Before moving to Florida, McReavy made a two-year stop at Southeastern Conference rival Kentucky, beginning in 1982. During her stay in Lexington, she took a nationally unknown Wildcat volleyball program to national prominence, as it ranked among the nation's top five teams in 1983.

Coach McReavy assumed the leadership of the Lady Gators in 1984, when volleyball was reinstated to varsity status at Florida for the first time since the 1978 season. Inheriting no players and building from scratch, she recruited junior college players and transfers from four-year universities to add experience and stability to her team, and added several freshmen to develop for the future.

With a goal to develop a nationally prominent team within five years, she made it in four. The 1987 Lady Gators cracked the national Top 20 and received an invitation to the NCAA tournament, where they reached the Final 16. In her six seasons at Florida, McReavy has accumulated a 141-84 record.

As a result of her sterling collegiate coaching resume, Coach McReavy has been tabbed several times for national and international coaching assignments.

She coached the East team to the gold medal at the 1986 Olympic Sports Festival and served as an assistant coach at the 1985 World University Games in Kobe, Japan, where the USA team finished in the top four, the highest finish ever for an American team.

As a player, Marilyn earned international notoriety. She was a member of the gold medal-winning USA team that competed in the 1967 Pan American Games. She was also a member of the 1968 Olympics and the 1970 World Games teams.

Long active in the advancement of women's volleyball, McReavy is a member of the board of directors of the United State Volleyball Association and the Florida Regional Board of Directors. She has also served as a past vice-president of the American Volleyball Coaches Association. She is married to Randy Nolan, a United States Navy chaplain.

A dynamic leader and builder of winning teams, Marilyn welcomed the chance to share her thoughts on successful team building. Very articulate and highly organized, she quickly delved into the first topic of discussion.

Here are Coach McReavy's thoughts...

...on Motivation

Coach McReavy believes that motivation is a blending of several key ingredients: goal setting, persistence and self-discipline. She says that these elements typify the state of mind of the high achievers in life.

"Motivation is establishing lofty, progressive goals and maintaining the energy to persist in attaining those goals," she says. "Motivation also requires the union of desire to achieve with the satisfaction in the daily process. I think it's important to enjoy the daily process of setting and attaining goals."

In order to stay motivated, Marilyn says, you need to have a high level of energy and also some self-discipline.

"Sustaining a high level of motivation takes a lot of energy," she states. "It requires a high physical metabolic state along with a sense of fulfillment along the way, which is a typical state of high achievers.

"But it also requires determination and self-discipline when the physical metabolic state is low or when training overloading is high."

Coach McReavy lists twelve techniques she believes are most effective in motivating student-athletes.

"It's imperative to have good communication with the players," she begins. "It all starts there.

"You need objective criteria when evaluating the players. You must have concrete information in hand to justify why a player is or is not playing. A player will stay motivated when she can see where improvement in a specific area will increase her chances of playing more."

McReavy thinks that top athletes can inspire others to greatness.

"We'll bring in a top athlete, from the university or outside, to help inspire the players," she says. "I like to use my former players, the All-America players, to talk with the team. The Florida players seem impressed when we do this."

Teaching self-management skills have been helpful to all players, "especially time management techniques," Marilyn says.

As many of the other coaches in this book have stated, Marilyn agrees that recruiting the right student-athlete for your program is extremely important.

"If you recruit the highly motivated high school player, that motivation usually carries over to college," she says.

Praise is always a motivator, Marilyn concludes, "especially if it is honest and sincere."

Demonstrating insights into player's problems can be very motivational to a player, Marilyn adds.

"If I can relate a player's problem to one I've also experienced, it really makes an impression on the player," she says. "So I try to keep every conversation as personalized as I can."

An eighth motivational technique involves encouragement when a player seems demoralized because of a bad game.

"I build on the positive," she points out. "If a player has had a really bad game, I encourage her through input involving objective criteria from the game. If her kills weren't as sharp as usual, then I'll mention good defense at the net or her hitting percentage. I'll find something positive out of a bad situation as far as the player is concerned."

Setting up the proper practice atmosphere and training environment is very effective, as is teaching human relation skills to the players, she says.

Coach McReavy says making expectations clear to the player is very motivational is some instances.

"I need to make my expectations very clear to the player, beginning during the recruitment process and then on through the player's college career."

The final motivational technique that is most effective for Coach McReavy involves helping her athletes to be happy and to enjoy success in achieving their goals.

"I want the players to be happy that they've decided to come to the University of Florida to get an education and to play volleyball," she states. "Therefore, I need to be as open and approachable as possible, as should my assistants. If the players feel good about themselves and feel good about me and the program, then the motivational level should remain high."

Over the years, Marilyn has found some motivational methods to be very ineffective, and they usually center around poor relations with the coaches and poor relations with fellow teammates.

"Poor communication among staff and players and players and players is very detrimental to motivation," she begins.

"Abusive, derogatory, demoralizing or degrading treatment of the players by coaches or between players is also very harmful to motivation."

Finally, inconsistency, confusion and double standards all contribute to lowering the motivation level of the players, she states.

"Any indication of double standards or inconsistency in handling problems with players can harm motivation and cause much player confusion," she concludes.

In summary, Coach McReavy believes that motivation is a prime ingredient for success in any organization. She defines motivation as a blend of key elements: goal setting, persistence and self-discipline. She also asserts that a <u>desire to achieve</u> is needed for motivation, as is a <u>feeling of enjoyment</u> in the daily process of setting goals.

She lists twelve methods of effectively motivating an athlete. The list includes active communication among staff and players, honest and sincere praise and setting the proper environment for the organization, to mention a few.

Least effective motivational techniques are poor relations with coaches and team members, inconsistency, confusion, double standards, and derogatory treatment of players by the coaching staff and other team members.

* * * * * * * * * *

...on Team Cohesion

Team chemistry is a vital ingredient for success in any organization, and Coach McReavy believes that it is the responsibility of the staff and players to make things work.

"On the court, I define 'team cohesion' as a team rhythm and decisive play, especially in the setting position," she says. "Off the court, I think team chemistry is a love of playing the game, and a respect and appreciation of teammates and staff. It certainly involves a love of the challenge."

Building team cohesion begins during the recruiting process, Marilyn says.

"A lot of building team chemistry is in recruiting correctly," she states. "A lot comes from within the staff, and other elements come from strong skills, precise execution, great communication, and lots of pride and fun."

Coach McReavy mentions five elements that she utilizes to build team cohesion.

"First of all, your staff must be compatible philosophically. The entire staff must believe in the same goals and be role models for team chemistry. If the players see the coaches getting along, they will also see the importance of getting along with each other.

"Next, the environment must be supportive and consistent in dealing with the players. The players should enjoy coming into the office to talk with coaches or support staff and know that they have someone in their corner all the time."

Developing individual and team confidence is another effective method.

"Helping the players learn to make decisions and then act freely on those decisions helps build team morale," she says.

Being organized is very helpful in building team chemistry, she believes.

"The players appreciate a highly organized environment in all aspects of the program," she says. "But you can't be a fanatic about it."

Finally, communication and praise build team chemistry, she asserts.

"Let the players know what you are trying to build, what you are trying to accomplish. When those expectations are being met, show enthusiasm and express pleasure when they start reaching those goals," she concludes.

In summary, Coach McReavy contends that team cohesion is evident during games and off the court. She asserts that team chemistry on the court is apparent when the team is in rhythm and when decisive play is evident, especially from the setter.

Team chemistry is visible off the court, she says, when players demonstrate a love of playing, show respect and appreciation of teammates and staff, and accept all challenges.

Coach McReavy believes that building team cohesion begins during the recruiting process. Bringing in the right student-athlete who blends in well with the other players is extremely important. She also thinks that team cohesion is built through the players' strong fundamental skills, precise execution on the court, great communication among teammates, and pride and fun in being a part of the team.

Effective methods of building team cohesion include a number of elements.

The staff needs to be philosophically compatible, she says, and coaches need to be role models of cohesion.

The environment surrounding the program needs to be consistent and supportive, she asserts, and it is important to develop decision-making abilities with the players.

Finally, being organized in all aspects of the program builds team cohesion, as does communicating team and individual expectations and then praising the players when those expectations are beginning to be met.

* * * * * * * * * *

...on Discipline

Discipline is a trait of the championship team and individual, and Coach McReavy says experience is the best teacher for the coach.

"At my age, discipline is a snap," she says.

McReavy stresses that the spontaneous chuckle does not indicate a lackadaisical attitude on her part.

"Some coaches find discipline so difficult to implement," she states. "I've been around long enough to understand that if you are organized and fair, the process will help you immensely."

Marilyn's philosophy concerning discipline is straightforward and clearcut, and that is the reason why she has few discipline problems with her athletes.

"Set up clear expectations, especially behavioral expectations," she points out. "Reiterate these expectations often and reward and be positive when these expectations are met."

Coach McReavy claims that the most effective disciplinary methods involve a positive approach with the person.

"Respect each participant, and help them feel important. That takes away much of any problem."

She believes that discipline problems are a result of frustration or unhappiness on the part of the player, but the duration of that frustration or unhappiness is the key element concerning the severity of the problem.

"Most discipline stems from being unhappy or frustrated, either momentarily or throughout the lifestyle," she says. "The second situation is serious."

That is why it is most important for the coach to listen to each individual case and act appropriately when administering any punishment, she says.

"Talk to the player first and find out their side and why the incident occurred," she states. "Then be clear when explaining what behavioral patterns you think they are developing. Let them know what is not O.K. Players are very sensitive toward what their coaches have to say."

Marilyn reiterates her procedures for handling discipline problems with players.

"Monitor, evaluate, make clear, reinforce and be caring, but not overbearing in any aspect unless there's a real recurring problem. Take action when necessary and early, so that the behaviors do not become habitual."

In summary, Coach McReavy believes that discipline can be handled most efficiently when behavioral expectations are clearly defined with the players.

She states that it is important to listen to each case individually, and to administer team rules appropriately and consistently.

Taking a positive approach with each athlete is the most effective way of dealing with discipline problems, she says. Monitor, evaluate, and reinforce good behavior at all times, she adds, without being overbearing in any aspect.

Finally, take action early so that any frustration or unhappiness on the part of the athlete does not escalate into an habitual problem, she concludes.

* * * * * * * * * * *

...on Mental Preparation

Mental preparation is essential to team and individual success, and McReavy believes that mental preparation is a continual process involving roles, relaxation and visualization.

"I define mental preparation as having clear roles and expectations of each performer," she says. "Mental preparation also means planning certain outcomes, for example, set 40% to the middle."

Coach McReavy is a strong advocate of the powers of relaxation and visualization when preparing players to reach their ideal performing state.

"I think it's very important to have a period of time to relax and rest before competition," she begins. "At this time we also like the players to visualize desired outcomes for individual performances. We believe that each person needs to work on relaxation and visualization skills in order to reach their best individual state of mind for each performance."

Mentally preparing the team for the grind of a long season has its roots in daily practice sessions, she states.

"You have to vary practices to the state of the performance level of the team," she says. "You need to mix in exhaustive drills with less intense drills. You need to practice appropriately, doing the things that will help each player improve, not do drills that makes the coach feel good.

"You must have fun with the team, and make things fun for the players. Finally, you need to give rest breaks during practice, and even cut practice early when you detect the players are getting overly-tired."

Mental preparation also means pushing the players to their physical and mental limits at times, she concludes.

"If the players are lazy or quitting during practice, you then intensify the drills, not necessarily lengthen the time of practice," she states. "At this critical moment, you need to emphasize the focus the player must take. When players get tired, the focus must fall on each individual doing her job well. This is how great teams and players are formed."

As every coach in this book has mentioned, McReavy agrees that late-game strategy is developed and perfected during practice sessions. But she thinks that lack of composure may be a result of some additional variables.

"Lack of composure late in games or during big games is probably from lack of experience or a need for more leadership," she states. "At this time, keep communication high between the players, and keep appraising the situation, with the focus on ways to overcome the problem and ways in which to cope best with the circumstances."

In summary, mental preparation is a very important element in the success process for University of Florida players.

Coach McReavy defines mental preparation as a process in which clear roles and expectations are set for each individual, certain game goals are planned, and relaxation and visualization skills are practiced on a regular basis.

Varying practice sessions, practicing appropriate drills, giving plenty of rest breaks, stopping practice early when the team is mentally and physicaly exhausted and making the environment fun are methods of mentally preparing a team for a long season.

Finally, late-game strategy is practiced daily, but lack of composure in an important match may be caused by lack of experience or lack of leadership on the court. You can help the athlete over come lack of composure by insisting on constant communication among the players, keeping an objective appraisal of the situation, and making suggestions on the most effective ways to cope with the situation.

* * * * * * * * * *

...on Mental Toughness

From her experience as a coach of national and international teams, Coach McReavy knows when she sees a mentally tough individual.

"The mentally tough player loves a challenge," she says. "She wants to play with and against the best."

McReavy insists that mentally tough players are not born with the trait, but have the type of personality that allows a person to develop those traits.

"The mentally tough individual usually spends as much extra time as necessary to be totally prepared," she states.

What are the traits of a mentally tough person? Marilyn has a list of characteristics she is eager to share.

"First of all, a mentally tough person has tremendous composure," she says. "She keeps her emotions under control at all times.

"Consistency is also a trait of a mentally tough person. You can count on the same top effort day in and day out, during practice and during matches.

"Rebounding from failure in a moment is also a characteristic. The ability to bounce back from adversity is the true mark of a champion.

"The mentally tough person is strategic and is always seeking self improvement. She is always thinking how she can beat her opponent, and will work hard to perfect a new move she thinks will help the team."

The last three character traits are quiet determination, the ability to cope, and a love of winning.

"Quiet determination is a trait," she states. "You see that in a person who doesn't stop working until the job is done the right way.

"The ability to cope means that a person is never flustered by anything," she points out. "She always reacts in a positive way to a negative situation.

"Finally, a love of winning is evident, she says. "But the win has to come by overcoming resistance, not through a forfeit or by beating an easy team."

In summary, mental toughness is a trait that all highly-motivated athletes possess. Coach McReavy believes that all athletes can become mentally tough if they work at it.

She lists a number of characteristics which the mentally tough person possesses. Composure, consistency, and loving a challenge begin the list.

The ability to rebound quickly from failure, the ability to cope, and wanting to play with the best are additional examples.

Finally, quiet determination, putting in extra time to become better, being strategic, and loving to win in the right context conclude the list of mental toughness traits.

* * * * * * * * * *

...on Communication

Effective communication has been a dominant theme throughout this conversation with Coach McReavy. She is a true believer that communicating effectively with players, staff and support personnel is essential to the overall success of every program in which she has been associated.

Communicating effectively during adverse times on the court is critical during volleyball competition. The coach does not have the luxury of taking the team into the locker room for a halftime strategy session. All strategy and communication must take place as the match progresses.

Marilyn and her assistant coaches must take a very active part in the communication process during critical periods in the match, she says.

"We must be realistic in our evaluation of the action, we must offer encouragement, and we need facts and statistics to justify any strategy moves we take," she says.

"The players must utilize coping methods for each adverse situation, we must have alternate game plans ready for implementation, we need to reevaluate goals, and we need to provide intelligent appraisal of what's happening on the floor."

New goals and areas of responsibility and accountability must also be considered during adverse times in a match, Marilyn asserts.

"There are times when we must set new goals and sights during a game," she says. "We also seek responsibility and accountability from each player.

"But we are very careful that the responsibility and accountability we are asking of a player matches the level, age and ability of the individuals involved."

In her post-game comments to players after a difficult loss, Marilyn is very careful in how she handles the situation, she says.

"We deal with specific problems, like poor communication or bad fundamentals, and not the overall loss," she states.

"We point out successes as well as weaknesses. It's very important to maintain strong communication ties and rapport with the players.

"Finally, we ask the players to regroup for action the next time. The key is to keep plugging away," she says.

In summary, communication skills are one of the most critical elements when building successful organizations. Communication skills are even more critical, Coach McReavy asserts, during adverse times during competition.

The coaching staff is responsible for establishing effective communication patterns during matches. Those responsibilities include realistic observation, encouragement, gathering facts and statistics, reviewing coping strategies, implementing alternate game plans, previewing new goals, and providing intelligent appraisal.

Post-game comments after a loss are handled cautiously by Coach McReavy and her staff. She deals with specific problem areas and not the overall loss. She reviews successes in addition to weaknesses of the game.

Ultimately, she says, it is vital that communication and rapport are maintained after a difficult setback, and that the team needs to regroup and focus on the next game.

* * * * * * * * * *

DANNY NEE
University of Nebraska

Position
Head Men's Basketball Coach

Career Record
168-131   (10 seasons)

Education
B.S.   1971 St. Mary of the Plains College
M.P.E.   1972 Kansas State University

Team and Personal Highlights

* 1986-87   His Nebraska team finished third in the post-season
             National Invitation Tournament.
* 1985-86   Mid-American Conference Coach of the Year
             Award; NIT post-season appearance by Ohio
             University team.
* 1984-85   NCAA Tournament appearance.
* 1982-83   Mid-American Conference Coach of the Year
             Award; NCAA Tournament appearance.
* 1970-71   President of student body as a senior at St. Mary of
             the Plains College; Dean's List; listed in *Who's
             Who Among American Colleges and Universities*.
* 1968   U.S. Marine Corps Honorable Discharge; Combat
             Air Insignia Medals, Vietnam tour of duty.
* 1964-65   Captain of Marquette University freshman
             basketball team.
* 1963-64   Teammate of Lew Alcindor at Power
             Memorial High School in Brooklyn.

Danny Nee

Introduction...

Danny Nee has experienced the war in Vietnam and the battles in collegiate basketball. The former toughened him mentally and spiritually, and the latter has established him as a dynamic team builder.

Danny Nee loves a challenge, and he found a big one awaiting him when he arrived at the University of Nebraska in 1986 after a highly-successful six-year stint at Ohio University.

Inheriting a senior-dominated team which, ironically, was short on game experience, he proceeded to lead the Cornhuskers to a 21-12 record, one victory short of a school record, and a third-place finish in the post-season National Invitation Tournament.

With five of the top seven players departing, Danny began a youth movement to Lincoln, Nebraska, to build a competive program in one of the country's premier basketball conferences, the Big Eight.

Playing with predominantly true freshmen players, the Huskers won 13 games during the 1987-88 season, including dramatic come-from-behind home victories over NCAA-bound Missouri and eventual national champion Kansas.

Nee established himself as a successful team builder by taking over a struggling Ohio University program in 1980 and turning it into a Mid-American Conference power in only three years.

Enduring losing records in his first two years at the Athens, Ohio, school, his last four Bobcat teams averaged over 20 wins a season. His Ohio teams participated in two NCAA tournaments and one NIT tournament and Danny was twice named Mid-American Conference Coach of the Year.

Coach Nee went to Ohio University after four years as an assistant under Digger Phelps at the University of Notre Dame. During that time, the Fighting Irish were 91-27 and went to the NCAA tournament all four years, making a Final Four appearance in 1978 and a Mideast Regional Final appearance in 1979.

The 43-year-old Nee has always been associated with winning teams. As a high school player, he was a part of the winning tradition at Power Memorial High School in Brooklyn. His teammate was a fellow by the name of Lew Alcindor, who later changed his name to Kareem Abdul-Jabbar, and became one of the best players in NBA history.

Recruited by Al McGuire to Marquette University, Danny captained the freshman basketball team in 1964-65 before leaving for a two-year tour of duty in Vietnam with the U.S. Marine Corps. He received Combat Air Insignia Medals and was honorably discharged in 1968.

Lured by the tranquil atmosphere of the Midwest, Danny returned to school at St. Mary of the Plains College in Dodge City, Kansas, and received a bachelor's degree in English and physical education in 1971.

While at St. Mary, he was on the Dean's List, was listed in *Who's Who Among American Colleges and Universities*, and was president of the student body as a senior. Nee received a master's degree in health, physical education and recreation from Kansas State University in 1972.

Nee's basketball coaching career began as a junior varsity coach at Red Bank, New Jersey, Regional High School in 1972-73. He left that position after one year to become head coach at Brick Township, New Jersey, High School, compiling a 38-35 record in three years. His Brick Township teams were 32-15 the last two years, winning a school-record 16 games each season. Digger Phelps then called from Notre Dame.

The highly-personable Husker coach has not lost his Brooklyn-ese sense of humor nor his love of the Midwest work ethic. He volunteers much time for civic and charitable organizations in Nebraska. He is married to the former Janet Scheib of Pittsburgh, Pennsylvania, and is the father of three children, Patrick, Nora and Kevin.

Ever-pleasant and hopeful that his comments would be helpful to others, Danny was excited to talk about the process of building winning teams and organizations.

Let's now begin this exploration into successful team building as Coach Danny Nee talks...

...on Motivation

Danny Nee understands the power of motivation within successful organizations. Without it, he says, you can't win life's littlest or biggest battles.

"Hey, you've got to be motivated to get up in the morning, to go to class, to come to practice and work hard," he says. "Life's not going to wait around for you to get your act together."

Coach Nee defines motivation as an inner desire to accept a challenge and do the best you can.

"We recruit the student-athlete who is challenged by the educational opportunities we offer and the challenge of playing basketball for a great state, in a great city, at an excellent educational institution with phenomenal facilities and in the best basketball conference in the country," he states. "If that scenario doesn't motivate you, then you don't belong here."

There is only one way to motivate, Nee asserts, and that is through a positive approach.

"We try to be as positive in our approach with the players as possible," he begins. "Being positive is always better than being negative."

Coach Nee also utilizes goal setting as a motivational technique.

"We do some goal setting, which we hope is motivating to our players," Nee states. "Setting and attaining goals can be very motivational for some, but not so helpful to others."

Nee is quick to point out that all athletes are different, thus motivational techniques need to be individualized.

"Players all have different personalities," he relates. "So the coach needs to learn the most effective way to motivate each player.

"You can be very verbal and animated with some athletes, but others prefer the low-key approach. The big point, though, is that you keep your approach positive in tone at all times."

In summary, Coach Nee defines motivation as an inner desire to accept a challenge and do the best you can. He states that the most effective motivation technique is to utilize a positive approach with the athletes at all times.

Goal setting procedures are also utilized for motivational purposes. And finally, it is the responsibility of the head coach to learn which motivation techniques work the best with the players.

* * * * * * * * * *

...on Team Cohesion

Team cohesion is a vital ingredient for ultimate team success. Nee believes team cohesion belongs at the top of a coach's priority list.

"I don't care how physically impressive your players are, " he says. "If they can't get along with each other and don't respect the coaches or each other, then the dissension will ultimately tear the team apart."

Coach Nee is a strong advocate of the theory that team cohesion is strengthened when the coaches and players know each other as human beings, and not just as athletes.

"As a team, we need to understand our strengths and weaknesses, not only as players, but as people as well," he says. "It's important that the players understand this."

Nee lists several methods he has used in the past to build team chemistry.

"The key element again is to build on strengths and take a positive approach," he says.

In order to establish team chemistry, all activities must involve all team members, he states.

"We have lots of team meetings, and the players even have their own team meetings without the coaches, if that's what they want," he says.

"We also have a lot of one-on-one communication with the players and we encourage them to talk with us about any problems they may be experiencing. We want them to feel comfortable in our environment."

Team meals are an important source of building team chemistry, he asserts, as are team study halls and other social activities, like going to football games together.

"We eat as a team on the road and we have a team lunch during recruiting weekends," Nee notes. "We learn a lot about ourselves as people during these meals."

Another morale-boosting technique that has a powerful effect on team members involves player participation in the rule-making process.

"We allow the players to make decisions concerning the program," he says. "These wouldn't be considered pivotal by the coaches, but they are important to the players."

Nebraska players, at times, he says, have input into practice times, team dress, eating locations, and most importantly, recruiting.

"Players have in the past made decisions on when we should practice, where we will eat on the road, how to dress, and even when study hall should be scheduled," Nee states.

But a critical area of involvement is in regard to recruiting, the coach points out.

"Our players have a deep commitment to recruiting the right person into our program," he begins. "It's extremely important that our players like the recruit and believe that he will fit into our system."

Nee says that player feedback regarding potential recruits carries a lot of clout with the coaching staff.

"I can honestly tell you that we have discontinued recruiting some outstanding student-athletes because, after the recruiting weekend, our players didn't feel he would fit in to our program."

In summary, Coach Nee believes that team cohesion is extremely important to the overall success of the program. He also asserts that team cohesion means understanding both the strengths and weaknesses of each person, and knowing the teammate outside the athletic environment.

Effective methods used to build team cohesion include building on strengths of the players and keeping a positive approach, he says.

Team activities are team meals, team study hall, and team meetings. The players also attend football games together.

Nee also states the importance of player feedback in the recruiting and decision-making processes. He says that team members have a big vote in which players are recruited into the program.

Finally, he says, players have a voice in deciding when practice will take place, where the team will eat on the road, how the team will dress and when study hall is to convene.

* * * * * * * * * *

...on Discipline

Discipline is a trait of championship teams and individuals, and Coach Nee understands the connection between discipline and being successful.

"If your players are undisciplined and you allow them to stay that way, then you're cutting down on your chances to be a truly successful team," he says.

Discipline policy needs to be kept simple, Nee states, so he has very few rules.

"We have only two rules," he says. "The first one is 'You do what is right' and the second one is 'Treat other people the way you want to be treated'."

Coach Nee believes that discipline should have an educational function in the life of his players.

"We are trying to teach our players to be responsible and live a proper lifestyle," he begins.

He continues his explanation of the educational value of discipline.

"If there is a player not following our rules, we first want the player to understand why some actions are wrong," Nee says. "We don't want to punish someone when they don't understand why they are being punished."

Disciplinary methods vary, Coach Nee asserts, because each player is different.

"Our disciplinary methods vary according to the individual," he begins. "These methods range from a one-on-one meeting to morning conditioning sessions to lack of playing time during games to suspension, if necessary. So we will do what is both best for the individual and in the best interest of the team."

In summary, Nee is a strong advocate of team discipline. He believes that rules should be kept to a minimum, and that all disciplinary action should have educational value for the athlete.

Finally, effective disciplinary methods vary according to the individual, he says. He lists player conferences, extra conditioning, lack of playing time and possible suspension as effective, educational disciplinary methods.

* * * * * * * * * *

...on Mental Preparation

Mental preparation ranks high on Coach Nee's list of successs skills for his players. But he also stresses the point that mental training is difficult to develop uniformly among the players.

"We put an extremely high emphasis on mental training skills," he says. "We've used a lot of time within our program to try to get the players to reach their peak, to get to that next level of competition.

"But, as hard as we try, some players develop the skills better than others, while some players never develop them at all."

Nee accepts the blame for some of those failings.

"I may be to blame for some of the problems," he admits. "Almost all of our mental training is done as a group. That's good to a point because all of the players are given the same techniques.

"What may be needed is more follow-up work with individual players. You never really get a good handle on the degree of development of those mental skills when players are together in a group.

"But taking them aside and finding out what they know or feel comfortable with in regard to mental training may be what is needed. And I'll do whatever is needed to help the players improve their mental skills."

Coach Nee has exposed his players to several mental training techniques. They include understanding how the mind works, positive self-talk, goal setting, stress management, improving attention and concentration and visualization.

"The players have a notebook just for mental training," he states. "But you just don't know how effectively they're utilizing it."

Nee brings in sport psychology consultants to handle most of the team mental training activities. He also includes resources for mental training within the basketball budget on a yearly basis.

"If I think this is important to the program, as I do, then I better have funds available to meet these needs," he concludes.

In addition to the formal mental training activities, Coach Nee and his staff utilize other methods to enhance the psychological state of the players.

"To help the players stay mentally sharp during pre-season practices, we run our practices in clips of four or five days and then have a day of rest," Nee says. "We have found this helps our players physically and mentally."

Mentally preparing for non-conference and conference games takes the same approach, he says, because all games are important, not just a few during the season.

"We try to approach every game as a step toward the NCAA tournament," he states. "So every game is special, and we prepare as well as we can for every opponent."

Mentally preparing his team for late-game strategy takes place during practice sessions, and Coach Nee takes pride in the fact that his teams seem to find a way to win when the outcome of the game is undecided.

"We have built a tradition here of winning the close games. We have won all but one overtime game."

"We just believe that we are a better team the longer the game or closer the game is," Nee states. "That's a mentality that you get by practicing late-game situations and then executing correctly when the situation arises during a game. We've been fortunate to have things happen the way they have for us."

In summary, mental training is a natural part of Coach Nee's program. He believes strongly in the powers of mental training, but admits the difficulty in producing a team with the same level of mental abilities.

He regularly exposes the players to mental training techniques and utilizes the services of outside sport psychology consultants. He includes funding for mental training in his yearly budgets.

The players are given mental training notebooks, but player use is not steadfastly monitored by the coaching staff. Nee admits the possibility that individual player consultation may be more effective than team mental training sessions that he has utilized in the past.

Coach Nee and his staff mentally prepare the players for the grind of pre-season practice by scheduling a day of rest after every five days of training. He believes this coaching concession keeps his players mentally and physically sharp.

Mental preparation for non-conference and conference games takes the identical approach. He states that every game is viewed as a step closer to the NCAA tournament. Therefore, maximum preparation is taken for each opponent.

Finally, late-game strategy is practiced daily. Coach Nee takes pride in the fact that his teams have been very successful in games when the outcome was in doubt until the very end. He concludes that combining physical execution with mental readiness has provided his teams with the "mental edge" at the end of close games.

* * * * * * * * * *

...on Mental Toughness

Coach Nee learned mental toughness as a Marine during his Vietnam duty, and he has been trying to teach that trait to every player that comes through his programs. But, he admits, it's easier said than done.

"Mental toughness is so important to being successful in anything you do," he says. "But it's one of those intangible qualities that some people have more of than others."

Coach Nee defines mental toughness as the ability to handle stressful events in a positive way. He also believes that mental toughness is a learnable skill and that emotional control is at the heart of the matter.

"We work towards showing no negative emotion on the floor during games," he begins. "We like to keep things positive with the players, and we continually stress the importance of keeping an emotional handle on themselves at all times."

Nee concedes that teaching the players emotional control is difficult at times, especially when the head coach is, by nature, an emotional person.

"As you can tell, I'm a very emotional person," Nee says. "I am very emotional during games with my players and the game officials.

"But the players have to understand that everyone must play their role. My role is to be their leader, and using emotion is one method I feel comfortable with.

"But the game is dictated not by my emotion, but by the players' emotions. That is why there is a delicate line concerning motivational emotion and out-of-control emotion.

"It's up to me to keep the motivational emotion high, and to teach the players to keep the out-of-control emotion low," he concludes.

Nee believes that emotion plays a pivotal role in the outcome of games.

"We believe negative emotion is a sign of weakness. If a player loses control emotionally during a game, it can have tremendous impact," he says. "The same goes for me. I must make sure that I never cross that line where my lack of emotional control has an impact on the game."

Coach Nee lists additional characteristics of mental toughness in addition to emotional control.

"The mentally tough individual knows his strengths and weaknesses and plays to his strengths.

"I think the mentally tough person sets goals and isn't satisfied until he meets those goals.

"I think the mentally tough player is a good listener, and I think a mentally tough person concentrates well.

"I think a mentally tough person consistently gives a top effort at all times. Consistency means reliability. If I know I can expect a player's top performance every day at practice and during every game, that is a tremendous lift for the coaches and players.

"Finally, you have to be resilient. You have to be able to get up after being knocked down. You have to be able to walk away from a situation, knowing you did the best you could do and leave it at that.

"But you have to learn from every misfortune. Mental toughness is the result of how you react to misfortune," he concludes.

In summary, Coach Nee believes that mental toughness is a trait that every person can learn, but it takes the right frame of mind to develop the concept fully.

He defines mental toughness as the ability to handle stressful situations in a positive way. He also believes that emotion plays a pivotal role in mental toughness.

Mental toughness traits include emotional control, knowing individual strengths and weaknesses, setting goals, being a good listener, having the ability to concentrate well, giving a consistent effort, and being resilient to misfortune.

* * * * * * * * * *

...on Communication

Nee has built a reputation as a great communicator. He believes strong communication is a key element within all successful organizations. He points out that his communication theme is the same at all times: keep a positive approach and things will work out.

Communication during halftime talks is critical, Nee states.

"Again, we like to be positive. We want our players to believe in themselves, in each other, and in our system and game plan.

"We don't get caught up with the score at halftime. Rather, we evaluate how we are performing, and then make technical adjustments.

"We tell the players that if the game is close at the end, that we will have the physical and mental edge because we've prepared well and we have a tradition of winning the close games."

Post-game comments will vary, depending upon the outcome, Nee states. But if the effort was good and the team still lost, he is quick to point out the positive aspects of the game.

"If we played well, but suffered a tough loss, I think despite the loss we can build and learn from the experience," he says. "It's important that I point that out to the players."

However, comments after a poor performance may draw some caustic remarks, he concedes.

"If we perform poorly from lack of effort, I tell them in no uncertain terms that that kind of attitude will not be tolerated.

"Don't get me wrong. I'm a very positive person by nature. But when I perceive a loss from a lack of effort, my Irish temper flares up.

"I don't chew the players out very often," he asserts. "But when I do, it's a doozy."

In summary, Nee takes pride in his ability to effectively communicate his thoughts within the program. He states that communication skills are a vital ingredient in all successful organizations.

Halftime talks stress technical adjustments and reassurances that the players believe in themselves, in each other and in the game plan, he says.

Post-game comments take on a naturally positive approach if the effort by the players was good, even if the outcome was a loss. Danny stresses the point that these kinds of games can be building blocks for future games, but that the players need to learn and benefit from the outcome.

Post-game comments to the players following a poor performance because of a lack of effort will draw a verbal assault from Coach Nee. He will vividly explain that lack of effort will not be tolerated, and that extra practice time may help cure poor efforts in the future.

* * * * * * * * * *

LUTE OLSON
University of Arizona

Position
Head Men's Basketball Coach

Career Record
353-155 (17 seasons)

Education
B.A. 1956 Augsburg College
M.A. 1964 Chapman College

Team and Personal Highlights

* 1990   Pacific-10 Conference Tournament title; Pacific-10 Conference regular season co-championship; NCAA West Regional.
* 1989   CBS-TV Coach of the Year Award; Pacific-10 Coach of the Year Award; NABC District 15 Coach of the Year Award; Pacific-10 title and tournament title; No. 1 national ranking; NCAA West Regional.
* 1988   *Basketball Times* and *Basketball Weekly* Coach of the Year Award; Pacific-10 Coach of the Year Award; District 8 Coach of the Year Award; Pacific-10 title and tournament title; NCAA West Region title; Final Four participant; No. 1 ranking.
* 1987   NCAA West Regional tournament.
* 1986   Pacific-10 Coach of the Year Award; Pacific-10 title; NCAA West Regional; Coach of gold medal-winning USA team in World Championships.
* 1985   NCAA West Regional tournament.
* 1984   Coach of USA team that won Jones Cup title.
* 1983   NCAA Midwest Regional tournament.
* 1982   NCAA West Regional tournament.
* 1981   NCAA Midwest Regional tournament.
* 1980   National Coach of the Year Award; NCAA East Regional title; Final Four participant while at the University of Iowa.
* 1979   NCAA Mideast Regional tournament.

Lute Olson

Introduction...

The folks back in tiny Mayville, North Dakota, always knew there was something special about little Luther Olson. The little boy worked hard on the family farm during the aftermath of The Great Depression in the 1930's.

So every time they hear the chant "LUTE, LUTE, LUTE" coming from the University of Arizona student body during television games these days, they remember with pride the hometown boy who has gone on to become a national symbol of successful team building.

His coaching record does most of the talking for Lute Olson, but the true worth of the man and his influence upon the lives of his players, staff and colleagues runs much deeper.

A man of deep loyalty, he has on more than a few occasions come to the aid of former colleagues who have felt the sting of a job firing or dismissal.

Olson believes in the concept of family. So it makes no difference if you worked a summer camp for him 10 years ago, or were his top assistant only last year, if you need his help, he is there to help you pick up the pieces. This conviction, plus the countless hours he has volunteered for charitable causes in Long Beach, Iowa City, and now Tucson, makes him most revered in the eyes of his fellow man.

Oh, yes. Now back to that coaching record.

From 1986-90, he has led the Arizona Wildcat teams to 130 victories. From 1985-90, his teams have won or shared four Pacific-10 Conference championships (1986, 1988, 1989, 1990) and finished within a game of the lead in the other two seasons. Three titles or co-titles are consecutive, in 1988, 1989, and 1990.

His notoriety for taking teams from nowhere and putting them in the national spotlight is legendary. He accomplished that feat while at Iowa and has continued the magic in the Valley of the Sun at Arizona.

For the past three years, no collegiate team has held the No. 1 ranking longer than the University of Arizona. The Wildcats were atop the polls for six weeks in 1988 and four weeks in 1989, including a first final No. 1 ranking in both Associated Press and United Press International polls in March 1989.

Olson's is an extraordinary rags-to-riches story. He took a program in ruins after a 1-17 league season in 1983 and spun it around 180 degrees to 17-1 league marks in 1988 and 1989. From a final record of 4-24 in 1983, Lute's teams recorded a glittering 35-3 mark in 1988, an equally-impressive 29-4 record in 1989, and a solid 25-7 record in 1990.

Together with athletics director Cedric Dempsey, Olson has put together one of the most competitive scheduling policies in Division I. The simple philosophy? In order to be the best, you must play the best.

In the 1988 and 1989 seasons, Arizona played regular season games against seven of the eight teams which advanced to the Final Four in 1988 and 1989.

Arizona was the eighth team in that span to make it to the Final Four.

There are numerous reasons why Olson's system works: hard work, excellent staff, good players, team chemistry, detailed recruiting, video review of opponents and his own squad, excellent practice organization, superb game coaching skills, first-class facilities, not to mention a gorgeous campus setting.

But there's one word that seems to symbolize a Lute Olson organization: class. The man is a class act by himself, and he makes sure his players are citizens and gentlemen off the court. His family atmosphere within the program is responsible for much of the team's success.

After graduating in 1956 with a degree in history and physical education from Augsburg College in Minneapolis, Lute began his coaching career at Mahnomen (MN) High School in 1957. One year later, he moved to Two Harbors (MN) High School, staying there from 1958-61.

From Minnesota, Olson and his family moved to the West Coast, where he resumed coaching in 1963 at Western High School in Anaheim, California. In 1964, he moved to Loara High School in Anaheim, again staying one year. From 1965-1969, he was the head basketball coach at Marina High School in Huntington Beach.

Bouyed by his success on the high school level and wishing to pursue collegiate coaching, Olson took the head job at Long Beach City College in 1970.

Despite enjoying tremendous success with his junior college program at Long Beach, he had aspirations of leading a major college basketball program.

That dream was realized in 1974 when Long Beach State University hired him. After posting a 24-2 record in his only year at the school, the Big Ten Conference came calling in 1975 in the guise of the Iowa Hawks.

Olson inherited a program that needed an infusion of self-esteem. Winning only 10 games in his first season in 1975, Olson's next eight Iowa teams won 157 games, participated in four NCAA tournaments and made a Final Four appearance in 1980.

Feeling suffocated from fan and alumni adulation and feeling that he had accomplished all his goals in Iowa City, Olson was lured by the challenge of the Pacific-10 Conference and the charm of Tucson. The 55-year-old Olson accepted the Wildcat's call in 1984, and University of Arizona boosters have been ecstatic ever since.

The silver-maned coach with the Hollywood tan and his beautiful wife, Bobbi, have five grown children: Vicki, Jodi, Christi, Greg and Steve, and eight grandchildren. They live in Tucson.

Always the gentleman, Olson was appreciative to have the opportunity to discuss his ideas surrounding successful team building.

Here are Coach Lute Olson's thoughts...

...on Motivation

Success breeds success, and Olson is quick to address the fact he feels fortunate that his teams have always been highly motivated.

"The players in our programs have always been highly motivated," he begins. "The credit must go to the players themselves and to my coaching staff. You recruit highly motivated young men, so you can see that my assistants have done a great job in that area over the years."

Lute defines motivation in terms of an inner drive that sparks a person to do his best.

"Motivation," he states, "involves a stimulus that is needed to obtain a maximum effort."

Coach Olson mentions that each player has his own reasons for being highly motivated.

"Some have high self-esteem and they love a challenge," he says. "Another's stimulus may be pride or ego or rising to the level of competitive spirit of their teammates.

"We have a good reputation with the players we recruit. Another stimulus may be a desire to a part of our program. You just can't pinpoint one reason that blankets everyone."

Olson agrees with the other coaches in this book when he mentions the most effective method of motivating players.

"The only way you're going to keep athletes motivated consistently is by giving positive encouragement," he states with conviction. "We make sure that the environment around the program is open, comfortable, and very positive."

Least effective motivation techniques surround negative behavior, he says.

"A negative approach will get you negative results," Lute asserts. "Studies concerning motivation have consistently proven that a positive approach to a situation will get you positive results and a negative approach brings negative results.

"I believe that all successful organizations have a philosophy of being positive with the members of their group, so that has been my philosophy since I started coaching," he concludes.

In summary, Coach Olson states that motivation is a prime ingredient for success in every organization, and he feels fortunate that his athletes have always been highly motivated.

He defines motivation as a stimulus needed to obtain a maximum effort. That stimulus can vary, he believes, because athletes are different and they have their own reasons for self-motivation.

Finally, Olson mentions positive encouragement as the most effective method of motivation, and lists a negative approach as the least effective motivation method.

* * * * * * * * * *

...on Team Cohesion

One comment that follows Lute Olson teams wherever he has coached concerns team cohesion. The comments may vary, but the idea is universal. You hear the statement, "You know, Lute's teams are like a family." That type of statement is at the heart of the success of the Olson-coached teams.

"Yes, I've heard those kinds of comments over the years, and they're very flattering," he admits. "But you have to make sure that the people around you in your program feel the same way."

Olson quickly mentions the fact that he has surrounded himself with personable, sincere and competent assistant coaches and excellent support staff.

"You're only as good as the people around you," he says. "And we've had the kind of people who fit in perfectly for the kind of atmosphere we want to establish in our program."

Coach Olson defines team cohesion as the ability of a diverse group of individuals to work together to realize a common goal.

"If every one believes in the same goals, then reaching those goals will be easier," he says. "If some individuals aren't sold on those goals, then problems arise."

Olson mentions that there are several effective methods of building team chemistry. Those methods include both team and individual meetings, but he says there's another element that brings the team together.

"We try to involve the players in the decision-making process," he states. "We want their input in a number of areas, but one area in particular."

That one particular area is recruiting.

"Even though the coaching staff is responsible for the recruiting process, we want each player to take an active part in helping select the players that will ultimately be in our program," he concludes.

A recruit on campus for his official visit will be scheduled for numerous activities and will be under observation by team members for much of that time. At the conclusion of the visit and after the recruit has departed, Arizona players are asked for feedback and recommendations as to the impression the recruit made upon them and if the players would want that person in the program.

"Again, the coaches make the ultimate decision," Olson states. "But the recommendations of the players are highly valued. Plus, they very rarely are incorrect in their impressions about the recruit. The thinking of the coaches and players are remarkably similar in most cases."

Coach Olson goes on to explain the importance of team and individual meetings with players.

"Our team meetings focus on team policy and many decisions are made during those meetings," he says.

Individual player meetings are a little different.

"During these sessions, we evaluate them and get them to understand their roles on the team. We discuss their strengths and also areas that need improvement," he states.

In summary, team cohesion is a trademark of Lute Olson teams.

Coming to the University of Arizona to obtain a college degree and play basketball for Olson is like joining an extended family. The environment is energetic, comfortable, and conducive to the player's home atmosphere.

He defines team cohesion as the ability of a group to work together to realize a common goal. How closely the group meshes concerning meeting those goals dictates how cohesive the team will be, he says.

Effective methods of building team chemistry include team and individual meetings plus an active part in the decision-making process.

Team policy is made during team meetings and player evaluation is discussed during individual meetings, Lute states. Player involvement in decision-making also includes recommendations concerning the continued recruitment of an athlete into the Arizona basketball program.

Player impressions are sought after a campus visit, and the coaching staff utilizes this feedback to come to a consensus to either continue recruiting the athlete or stop the process at that point. Coach Olson comments that very rarely do the coaches and players differ on their evaluation of the recruit.

* * * * * * * * * *

...on Discipline

Discipline is a trait of the championship team and individual. Olson believes that discipline and decision-making are closely related.

"Involving the players in making team rules makes the entire process so much more effective and easy to enforce," he says.

Coach Olson's philosophy concerning team discipline involves a working arrangement with the upperclassmen in the program.

"I meet with the upperclassmen, especially seniors, and we discuss things that I believe are important for our success," he begins. "The upperclassmen then will meet with the team to set team rules."

Olson proudly discusses rules set by the team.

"The players will set tougher standards than the coaches," he asserts. "And the players will be more inclined to follow the rules if they are their rules."

Coach Olson mentions individual meetings and peer pressure as the most effective methods when handling discipline.

"Sitting down with the individual and discussing the problem is always best," he says. "Team pressure is also very effective in preventing discipline problems."

Lute lists any form of negative behavior on the part of the coaching staff as least effective in handling discipline cases within the team.

"Screaming, yelling or threatening a player just won't work, at least for us," he states.

In summary, Coach Olson once again believes that giving players an active role in decision-making improves team discipline.

He mentions meetings with upperclassmen to discuss team needs as the first step in setting team rules. The upper-classmen then take those ideas to the team, ideas are gathered from all the players, and team rules are established through this democratic process.

Olson is happy with this policy because the players set tougher standards than coaches, and players are more inclined to follow rules which they have established.

Finally, he lists individual meetings with players and peer pressure as the two most effective methods of handling discipline. He also mentions negative coaching behavior (screaming, yelling, threatening) as least effective methods of disciplining athletes.

* * * * * * * * * *

...on Mental Preparation

All successful coaches mention mental preparation as essential to team and individual success. Coach Olson has long been a proponent of the mental aspect of the game, and has actively incorporated mental training into his program.

"In order to keep an edge on our opponents, the only edge is really the mental edge," he states. "Division I athletes are very similar physically and athletically. We believe that if they are mentally more alert than the opponent, then we have a better chance of winning."

He has utilized outside sport psychology consultants in addition to university professors versed in sport psychology techniques.

"We've had people come in to teach the players relaxation and visualization skills," he says. "We also have the players learn concentration techniques to help them during free throw situations."

Olson defines mental preparation as "being prepared to give your best effort." He says there are different ways to mentally prepare for a long season.

"During pre-season, we want the players to have fun, so we will change our practice routines and also change drills, just to keep the players mentally fresh," he states. "It's also good to keep teams evenly balanced talent-wise during practice so that the competition stays healthy."

Non-conference games are utilized as a means to an end.

"We understand the importance of all non-conference games, especially with our competitive schedule," he says. "But we also are striving for later goals...to win our league and advance to the NCAA tournament."

Mental preparation for conference games is not a problem, Olson asserts.

"Conference games need no big push from the coaches," he says. "The players understand that this is the most important time of the season for us."

Late-game strategy, he states, is a matter of practice organization and execution.

"We work on late-game situations in practice on a regular basis," he contends. "We want the players to gain confidence from the repetition and fully understand what they are going to do when that pressure situation arises late in a game."

In summary, Coach Olson strongly believes in the benefits surrounding mental preparation, and has incorporated mental training on a consistent basis within his programs.

He utilizes outside sport psychology consultants or university professors to teach mental training techniques. The skills taught include relaxation, visualization and concentration.

Lute defines mental preparation as being prepared to give your best effort. He uses various methods to mentally prepare his teams for the season, he says.

Pre-season practices are meant to be fun for the players. He often changes practice routines and drills so that the players do not become bored. He also stresses the importance of keeping teams balanced talent-wise during practice so that maximum effort and healthy competition exists.

Non-conference games are viewed as important stepping stones to league and NCAA tournament play. This is a time to learn and improve, both mentally and physically, he says.

The focal point of the season remains on conference games, Lute asserts. He also mentions that mental preparation for conference games becomes easier to implement because of the importance of league games.

Finally, he states that late-game strategy is simply a matter of practice organization and execution. Late-game situations are practiced regularly so that the players understand what they are supposed to do and establish the confidence needed to successfully execute the strategy during games.

* * * * * * * * * *

...on Mental Toughness

Olson agrees with the theory that mental toughness is not an inherent human characteristic, but rather a personality trait that can be acquired. He is also in agreement with the theory that all great competitors possess mental toughness to some degree.

"To me, mental toughness means having the ability to stay focused on your goals during difficult situations," he states.

Those difficult situations can be off the court as well as on the court, he says.

"You need to be mentally tough to prepare for semester finals or go through a job search," Olson contends. "So being mentally tough can help you in all aspects of your life."

Coach Olson lists four characteristics of mental toughness.

"There are probably a lot more than four," he states. "But these four seem to stick out with me."

"First, a mentally tough person is dedicated. It takes a tremendous amount of time to be a successful Division I athlete. I'm very pleased to see the NCAA taking action to shorten the basketball season.

"As a matter of fact, I've been pushing the idea of making basketball a strictly second semester sport. Begin practice on December 1 and begin play on January 1. That would give athletes the complete first semester to attend to their academics and not worry about athletics.

"There are not very many people who agree with me right now on that. But that is the way the NCAA President's Commission seems to be going, and I'm all for it," he says.

Determination is the next characteristic of a mentally tough person, Lute asserts.

"The mentally tough person is very determined. The-nose-to-the-grindstone kind of thing. The person who keeps bouncing back from adversity."

Self-confidence and a good work ethic are the final two characteristics of a mentally tough person, he says.

"The mentally tough person is very self-confident. I don't mean cocky or a braggart. But a person who quietly goes along, trying to do the right things.

"Finally, the mentally tough individual has a great work ethic," he states. "You know that he will be doing everything that's asked of him, plus a little bit more.

"Many of my teams have been called 'overachievers'," Olson recalls. "I think that's one of the nicest compliments anyone can receive."

In summary, Olson believes that mental toughness is a trait that can be developed by the athlete. He defines mental toughness as the ability to stay focused on goals in difficult situations.

He alludes to the fact that mental toughness is a life skill, one that will help any person in any career in life.

Finally, Coach Olson considers dedication, determination, self-confidence and a great work ethic to be the traits of the mentally tough person.

* * * * * * * * * *

...on Communication

Olson seems to be blessed with the complete package: good health, excellent physical condition, good looks, sharp mind, great family, and winning tradition. The key element in keeping it all together, he says, is the ability to communicate your thoughts clearly to those around you.

Critical situations demand appropriate communication, and two critical parts of a game occur at halftime and again at the end of the game.

"At halftime, we don't get into pep talks," he notes. "Halftime is a time to reflect on the successes and weaknesses of the first half and make the needed technical adjustments.

"We also give the players much positive reinforcement. If we're behind, we want to make sure they understand that we can still win the game. If the players keep hustling, we tell them that things will turn our way," he relates.

A tough loss calls for just the right words," he relates.

"Try never to criticize after a loss," he says. "Following a loss, the player's confidence level is down. Encouragement is needed at that time. The exception would be if there has been a lack of effort."

In summary, Coach Olson believes that communication skills are very important in building and maintaining successful teams.

At halftime, his talks focus on positive encouragement and technical adjustments. Post-game talks following a difficult loss are handled very gently. He makes it a point to keep comments positive and criticism mute during this delicate time period.

****

RICHARD "DIGGER" PHELPS
University of Notre Dame

Position
Head Men's Basketball Coach

Career Record
407-180 (20 seasons)

Education
B.A. 1963 Rider College

Team and Personal Highlights

* 1989-90 NCAA Southeast Regional tournament.
* 1988-89 NCAA East Regional tournament.
* 1987-88 NCAA East Regional tournament.
* 1986-87 NCAA East Regional, semifinalist; *Basketball Weekly* National Coach of the Year Award.
* 1985-86 NCAA Midwest Regional tournament.
* 1984-85 NCAA Southeast Regional tournament.
* 1983-84 National Invitation Tournament, runnerup.
* 1982-83 National Invitation Tournament.
* 1980-81 NCAA East Regional tournament, semi-finalist.
* 1979-80 NCAA Midwest Regional tournament.
* 1978-79 NCAA Midwest Regional tournament, runnerup.
* 1977-78 NCAA Midwest Regional Championship; Final Four participant.
* 1976-77 NCAA East Regional tournament, semi-finalist.
* 1975-76 NCAA Mideast Regional tournament, semi-finalist.
* 1974-75 NCAA Mideast Regional tournament.
* 1973-74 NCAA Mideast Regional; Coach of the Year Award from Metropolitan Basketball Writers Association, United Press International, *The Sporting News* and *Basketball Weekly*.
* 1972-73 National Invitation Tournament, runnerup.
* 1970-71 NCAA East Regional; Coach of the Year Award from the Metropolitan Basketball Writers Association.

Digger Phelps

Introduction...

Few people know him as Richard Phelps. It's just "Digger." The name is synonymous with Notre Dame athletics and academics, which to the knowledgeable person means excellence as a student and athlete, with the emphasis on "student."

Digger discusses his nickname.

"I got the nickname 'Digger' because my father was an undertaker and I worked for him part time," he says. "There were also other advantages to the job. For instance, while I was dating my wife I sent her flowers every day and she could never quite understand this."

Digger Phelps has been putting opponents "six feet under" ever since his arrival on the Irish campus in South Bend, Indiana, in 1971.

"I had always wanted to coach at Notre Dame," he says. "When I was at St. Gabriel's we wore green shamrocks on our uniforms and the rest of the uniform was purple."

Phelps is now firmly entrenched in the record books at Notre Dame. He became the winningest basketball coach in Fighting Irish history on December 19, 1987, when his Irish team defeated Valparaiso, 88-49.

Yet, Phelp's career at Notre Dame has encompassed far more than simply wins and losses. In fact, no college coach in the nation has more effectively combined on-the-court basketball excellence with in-the-classroom academic success than Phelps has in his 19 years as director of Notre Dame's program.

His on-the-court coaching performance has resulted in a 69%-winning percentage in 20 years of being a head college coach. He has taken 15 teams to the NCAA tournament, a figure surpassed by only four coaches - active head coaches Dean Smith of North Carolina (20) and Lou Carneseca of St. John's (16) plus former greats Adolph Rupp of Kentucky (20), and John Wooden of UCLA (16).

Considered a master of psychology on the bench, Phelps relishes the challenge of preparing his teams for the games against highly-regarded opponents. His Irish have upset the current number-one ranked team or the defending national champion nine times during his tenure in South Bend.

But Phelps' record off the basketball court is even more impressive. In fact, it's perfect. Every player who has competed for four years under Phelps at Notre Dame has received his degree. Few other coaches can match that impeccable 50-for-50 graduation rate.

A master technician of building winning teams, Phelps credits his philosophy of keeping things in perspective, both for himself and his players, as instrumental in his success.

"I hate to say it, but basketball is still a game, he says. "After it's over, it's time to get back to the real world. No matter whether you win or lose, the sun is going to come up the next day."

He continues discussion on his coaching philosophy.

"We're coaches, but we can't lose sight that we're supposed to be helping to educate these young people," Phelps says. "A couple of years ago when we played in New York, we took a tour of Wall Street. When we were in Washington to play Maryland, we toured the White House, we went to the Lincoln Memorial and showed them where Martin Luther King made his great speech and we saw the Vietnam Memorial. About a month later when we played out at Utah, we went to see the movie "Platoon" and we talked about how it all ties in and why that monument in Washington is there."

A tenure as an assistant coach with Phelps has also proven beneficial in moving up to the head coaching ranks. Ten of his former assistants left Notre Dame to guide their own college programs, including Danny Nee of Nebraska and Scott Thompson at Rice University, both of whom have chapters in this book.

Born on July 4, 1941, the Beacon, New York, native competed in football, basketball, baseball and track at Beacon High School. He attended Rider College in Trenton, New Jersey, where he played basketball for four years. As a senior, Phelps helped the Rider squad to an appearance in the 1963 NCIA Tournament in Kansas City.

Following graduation in 1963, Phelps remained as a graduate assistant and helped Rider gain national recognition for its stunning upset of New York University, which ended the Violets' homecourt winning streak that dated back to 1941. He was awarded an honorary doctorate of the arts degree by his alma mater in 1981.

After a brief stint as a junior high school teacher and high school coach at St. Gabriel's in Hazleton, Pennsylvania, (winning the Pennsylvania Class C title), Phelps moved on to the University of Pennsylvania as an assistant to Dick Harter in 1966. During his four years as freshman coach, his squads compiled an overall record of 65-20, including one undefeated 21-0 season.

Phelps left Penn to begin his head coaching career at Fordham in 1970. Taking a team that had finished 10-15 the previous year, Digger molded it into a 26-3 squad that upended the Irish 94-88 in Madison Square Garden and placed third in the NCAA East Regional.

Notre Dame then came calling. Phelps, who in 1966 while at St. Gabriel's had written a letter to Irish football coach Ara Parseghian saying "My big dream is to coach at Notre Dame," got the job he aspired for in 1971 at the age of 29.

A sometimes controversial, often candid and outspoken personality, the 48-year-old Phelps has co-authored two books and dabbled in television by serving as a color analyst on several basketball game broadcasts, including teaming with Keith Jackson to describe men's basketball action for ABC Sports at the 1984 Summer Olympic Games in Los Angeles.

He is a member of the Board of Directors of the National Association of Basketball Coaches and is also a member of the NABC Recruiting Committee. He has worked closely with the Legislative Committee of the NABC in the areas of academic problems and recruiting. An avid stamp collector, he currently serves on the Citizens' Stamp Advisory Committee of the United States Postal Service.

An active volunteer with the Special Olympics program, Phelps and his wife Terry, who received her doctorate degree from Notre Dame and teaches in the School of Law, have three children: Karen, a 1987 Notre Dame graduate married to Chicago Cub pitcher Jamie Moyer; Rick, a junior at the University of Toledo, and Jennifer, a sophomore at Holy Cross Junior College in South Bend.

Taking time out of his busy schedule, Digger welcomed the opportunity to discuss the key elements of building successful teams.

Here are Coach Digger Phelps' thoughts...

...on Motivation

Recruiting players to Notre Dame indicates to most individuals that Fighting Irish players are highly motivated to begin with. Phelps agrees partially with a statement like that, but says it's not all that easy.

"Yes, we get a higher quality person coming to Notre Dame," he says. "Student-athletes at Notre Dame understand that there's something special about the place. But you can't expect any person to stay highly motivated all the time. You must allow for ups and downs in everyone's life."

Digger defines motivation as a combination of factors.

"Organization, job description and game strategy all contribute to motivation," he begins.

"If you are organized in your approach to the game and in conducting the day-to-day business, players appreciate that and tend to stay motivated for a longer period of time.

"By job description I mean roles that players must adjust to and accept if the team is going to be successful.

"Finally, game strategy and successfully implementing game strategy is highly motivating for our players. Notre Dame has a history of playing great games against great opponents. We believe that implementing our game strategy with enthusiasm by the players has been a motivating factor for our success," Digger concludes.

Coach Phelps believes that simple methods are the most effective when motivating people.

"Keeping it simple is the best way to motivate," he points out. "I have three things that are important for a basketball team to be successful. One, you've got to listen. Two, they have to talk to each other, especially on the floor. Three, they've got to concentrate on each situation. If players are able to handle those three things, I believe they are motivated."

In summary, Coach Phelps defines motivation as a combination of organizational skills, defining player roles and implementing game strategy. He believes that the most effective motivation methods are the simple methods, giving players clear understanding of what needs to be done.

* * * * * * * * * *

...on Team Cohesion

Digger sells "the Notre Dame family atmosphere" while recruiting student-athletes to South Bend. He stresses the point that team cohesion is built and maintained through an environment where every person is made to feel like a vital link to the overall success of the program.

"When I arrived at Notre Dame my first year, the first thing Ara (Paraseghian) said to me was, 'If there's anything I can do, let me know'," Phelps says. "I was impressed with that, and I've made it a point of establishing an atmosphere of caring and support for our players ever since."

Digger also believes that giving each player his job description is the best way of building team cohesion.

"Discussing with each player how he can best help the team and himself through his role on the team has been very effective for us," he states.

Coach Phelps utilizes several methods of building team cohesion, most of which are activities involving all team members.

"We have several team and individual meetings where goals are discussed," Phelps says. "We have team meals at home and on the road. On most trips, we try to take the players to some cultural event or location which has some educational value for them.

"We value our player's opinions concerning the recruits we bring in. Even though I make the final decision, we want to know how the players feel about the people we bring in for a visit.

"So involving the players in team decisions has much impact in building team cohesion."

In summary, Coach Phelps believes that team cohesion can be strengthened by establishing a family atmosphere within the program. He says each member of the team must be made to feel like a vital link to the success of the organization.

Effective methods for building team cohesion include team and individual meetings, team meals, social activities that involve all players, and giving players participatory rights in the decision-making process.

* * * * * * * * * *

...on Discipline

Discipline is the trait of the championship team and individual, and Coach Phelps understands the importance of discipline in today's changing world.

"Many athletes today come from one-parent homes or broken marriages, and the drug scene is destroying the promise of a better tomorrow for our young people," Phelps notes. "It's important that our players understand the role of discipline in their lives.

"Notre Dame student-athletes are mainstreamed with the regular student body as soon as they arrive on campus. They live in the dorms with the other students and eat with the other students. They are students who happen to be athletes. It's up to the players to obey the rules of the university in addition to any team rules that are established."

Digger defines team discipline as simply what will be the reaction of others on or off the court.

"We have rules which the team has designated are important to the basketball program and how the program is perceived by the university administration and student body," he states.

Any deviation from those rules involves some form of discipline, Digger says.

"If there is a problem with a player, we will sit down and discuss the situation first," he says. "We attempt to prevent any reoccurrence and we give the athlete their time to explain their side of it. Steps are taken and choices are given to the athlete.

"After taking these steps, we believe it is the responsibility of the athlete to carry through. If the athlete falters again, we then implement some of the options that we discussed with the athlete initially," he concludes.

Coach Phelps admits that discipline problems made public are very disruptive to the team. But he understands that student-athletes at Notre Dame are aware of those kinds of pressures when they decide to attend the school.

"Because you are an athlete at Notre Dame seems to give people the impression that your life is important to them. You may not like that, and it's terribly unfair to the athlete, but it's also a part of the life of a student-athlete on our campus," he says.

In summary, Coach Phelps believes that discipline is extremely important for the long-term success of the program. He thinks that team discipline involves public perception and that rules need to be established and enforced fairly and expeditiously by the head coach. He also believes the student-athlete is responsible for self-discipline at all times.

* * * * * * * * * *

...on Mental Preparation

Coach Phelps takes a different approach when explaining mental preparation for his players. Game preparation is his forte and his love, but preparing his players for life is his top priority.

"I don't let basketball control my life or my players' lives," he begins.

Phelps quickly mentions how he prepares the Irish players mentally for all games during the season.

"First, our scouting report is dissected into fundamental parts: offense, defense, specials and personnel. Some of that report may be the result of videotape; but in most instances, it's not.

"The staff then decides upon a game plan for that opponent and we then assemble the scouting report into a document we can distribute to the players and one that they'll understand."

Digger says effectively utilizing daily practice sessions is the key to all preparation.

"Now, we will set goals for each game, we use relaxation techniques when it's appropriate, and we'll use a little visualization when I think it'll help," he says. "Mostly, we expect the players to concentrate on what we're trying to accomplish while we're on the court."

Digger insists that mental preparation must also be the responsibility of the players.

"We only have so much time to practice on the court," he says. "So the players must take that information with them and think about their roles for that game after practice is over."

Coach Phelps returns to his initial response of getting players ready for their biggest game: life.

"I try to tell kids that when you quit basketball at age 25, you've got 50 years to try to do something," he says. " They're blinded to that and we've created a monster. We spoil them in high school. It's a shame what they're doing to those kids. I try to educate them to the real game and yet still have the big moments you're looking for on the court."

He concludes his thoughts by reiterating his philosophy of taking the players to educational locations when the team is playing on the road.

"This is why when we travel, we look for other things to do in the city. I mentioned we go to Wall Street when we go to New York City. I'll continue to explore those kinds of activities with the players because I think those are the most important parts of preparing them for life after basketball."

In summary, Phelps believes that mental preparation is important and that practice preparation is the best way of mentally preparing for the opponent. He thinks that the coaching staff needs to develop the game plan and that the players need to concentrate on their roles for that game.

But Coach Phelps insists that mental preparation includes getting ready for life after basketball. He does not want basketball to control his life, nor his players' lives. He punctuates those thoughts by explaining how the team visits locations of educational and historic importance when the team travels to different cities.

* * * * * * * * * *

...on Mental Toughness

Digger's motto is "You weren't born to go undefeated. You were born to learn how to survive in everyday life." The mentally tough person, he says, has the ability to get the most out of himself in every situation.

"Mental toughness," he insists, "is nothing but concentration, application and getting the most out of yourself."

Digger believes that the experiences of his youth have sensitized him to the meaning of mental toughness.

"You understand, my father was an undertaker, so I grew up in the business. I grew up dealing with death. I learned something from seeing people come home in a box.

"I worked the door when I was 13, and if there were two funerals going at once, I'd work the other one. I could make all the arrangements, but the embalming I couldn't handle."

Digger concurs with the thoughts of the other coaches in this book who believe that mental toughness can be developed in a person.

"Oh yes, mental toughness can be acquired," he says. "But it takes the right person with the right kind of personality to allow it to develop."

Ultimately, though, mental toughness must come from within the person himself, and not from an overt plan to develop the trait, Digger says.

"If a person applies himself to a task, concentrates on what he's trying to accomplish, and pushes himself to the physical and mental limits, then that person is mentally tough in my book."

In summary, Coach Phelps believes that mental toughness is an important trait in successful persons. He relates that during his youth when he assisted his father at funerals that he was sensitized to dealing with death and dying and that it made him aware of the elements of mental toughness.

Finally, he lists concentration, application and getting the most out of yourself as three mental toughness traits that can be developed by each person.

* * * * * * * * * *

...on Communication

Coach Phelps has never been accused of having only a few words to say. Most of the time he has a lot of words to say: To his staff, his players, the media, and the fans. He loves to talk to people, and effective communication is the lifeline of his successful program at Notre Dame.

"Communication has to be very simple," he insists.

Digger lists his three rules concerning communication.

"Don't assume, followup, and always have a backup," he states.

From a leader's standpoint, he says, you should never assume that your players understand everything they hear from you.

"That can be the biggest mistake you can make," he begins. "You must constantly make sure that what you're communicating to the players is being understood, and you must constantly ask them if they clearly understand what you've said."

That brings us to the idea of following up a major point of discussion with another inquiry.

"As I just said, keep your thoughts simple and direct, but insist upon the players that they explain to you what you just told them. You'd be amazed at how some of your ideas are translated by the players."

The third element of effective communication is to have a backup plan of attack, he says.

"The players must understand that if everything fails, there must be a backup plan to utilize. This is the responsibility of the coaching staff to have these plans ready to implement."

Digger believes that these three elements of communication are vital during halftime adjustments and post-game reviews.

"Those three strategies can be used in any situation, including halftime talks and post-game reviews. It makes the entire communication process much simpler when the players know how you're going to be communicating with them," he concludes.

In summary, Coach Phelps believes that effective communication is the lifeline for all successful organizations. He thinks that the best way of communicating ideas is to keep things very simple and direct in nature.

He insists that his rules of communication have worked very well for him over the years. Those rules include not assuming the players understand everything they hear, following up all important information with inquiries asking the players to repeat what they just heard, and having a backup plan of attack ready for all situations.

* * * * * * * * * *

RON POLK
Mississippi State University

Position
Head Baseball Coach

Career Record
765-329 (19 seasons)

Education
B.S. 1965 Grand Canyon College
M.S. 1966 University of Arizona

Team and Personal Highlights
* Head Coach of USA Team in 1991 Pan American Games.
* Winningest baseball coach in Mississippi State history with 610-265 record.
* Assistant coach of 1988 USA gold medal-winning Olympic baseball team.
* Two-time (1973, 1985) National Coach of the Year Award from American Baseball Coaches Association.
* Recipient of 1988 Lefty Gomez Award, the highest honor presented by the ABCA.
* Five College World Series appearances (1973, 1979, 1981, 1985, and 1990).
* Twelve NCAA Regional Tournament appearances (1973, 1974, 1978, 1979, 1981, 1983, 1984, 1985, 1987, 1988, 1989, and 1990).
* Three Southeastern Conference Championships (1979, 1985, and 1987).
* Twelve All-American and 30 All-Southeastern Conference players at Mississippi State.
* Fifty-four former Bulldog players have signed professional contracts, including Will Clark, Rafael Palmeiro, Bobby Thigpen and Jeff Brantley from the 1985 CWS team.
* Author of *The Baseball Playbook*, the leading textbook for coaches and instructors in baseball coaching classes.
* Past President of the American Baseball Coaches Association (1985-86).
* Seven 30-plus win seasons, seven 40-plus win seasons, and three 50-plus win seasons in 19-year career.

Ron Polk

Introduction...

He smokes his aromatic Hoyo de Monterrey Honduran cigars, reads while he drives on the interstate, wears colorful clothes, fashions a slick-down hairstyle, and writes Christmas cards all year long. Add a workaholic mentality to the list, and you have some general character traits of the most influential and possibly the best baseball coach in Southeastern Conference history.

Ron Polk, the 46-year-old bachelor who leads one of the most successful college baseball programs in the country, shrugs at the mention of his workaholic nature.

"I think that's fine," he says, "I am. But I'm a productive workaholic. Productive workaholics are the reason the world exists as it does today. Show me a non-productive workaholic, and I'll show you a person who is non-productive and doesn't like his job."

Being productive, not wasteful, is one of Polk's unwritten rules of life. His players are highly supportive of that rule, especially on the playing field.

Pete Young, a Bulldog third baseman-relief pitcher who is probably State's next high major league draft choice, likes Polk's demeanor.

"I love playing for him because he's so laid-back," Young says. "We wait for big innings to happen. He doesn't recruit many bunt-and-run type guys. He recruits guys that play for big innings, and our fans love it."

Yes, those Mississippi State fans do love Polk's Diamond Dogs. In 1989, a record 4,294 season tickets were sold. In 1987, an NCAA record 14,378 fans watched a State-LSU doubleheader.

The Southeastern Conference Tournament in Starkville in May 1987 drew a record 43,068 fans and provided the SEC with a $50,000 profit to be divided among the 10 conference schools. An additional $25,000 was split between the tournament participants. Also, State has sent $100,000-plus payouts to the NCAA for the past three NCAA Regionals held in Starkville.

State's success has spawned a 25-station radio network and a 14-station television network that carries Polk's coach's show. Three years ago, State rebuilt Dudy Noble Field at the coast of $3.5 million. Approximately $1 million of the cost came from the sale of chairback seats in the main grandstand, ranging from $250 to $1,000.

Since Polk came to State, every SEC school except one has built a new stadium or made stadium improvements. Beginning with the 1989 season, the SEC has a televised Game of the Week on the SportsChannel cable network.

Said Kentucky coach Keith Madison, a former State graduate assistant, "Ron's done the same thing for baseball that Adolph Rupp did for basketball. People got tired of Rupp beating them. So they built bigger coliseums, hired better coaches and recruited better players."

Polk's formula for recruiting players is simple, he says.

"I like neat-hair all-American types," Polk says. "They must care as much about academics as they do baseball. Make sure the players follow the simple rules - always hustle on the field and act classy on and off the field."

Ron was the second of three boys born to Robert and Ruth Polk. Born in Boston, the family also lived in Buffalo and Phoenix when Ron was growing up. Polk now calls Phoenix his hometown. Since his father played semi-pro baseball, it was unofficially adopted as the family sport.

Polk played second base at Grand Canyon College, an NAIA school of approximately 1,600 students in Phoenix. His former coach, Dave Brazell, remembers Polk as "an excellent fielder with a great arm and an OK hitter."

"He was very intense," Brazell says. "You never caught him sleeping out there. His head was always in the game. And he always wanted to discuss strategy."

Polk's storied 24-year coaching career began in 1966 as a graduate assistant under the legendary Frank Sancet at the University of Arizona. Upon the completion of a six-month tour of active duty with the Marine reserves, he accepted a position as a graduate assistant at the University of New Mexico in 1968.

Polk stayed one year at New Mexico, then began a three-year stint (1969-71) as an assistant coach at Dade-South Community College in Miami, Florida.

In 1971, he received a call from the late J.I. Clements, the athletic director at Georgia Southern. Georgia Southern, once an NAIA baseball power, was to go Division I the next season.

"What they were looking for was a young coach who would take them Division I on an NAIA budget," says Polk.

He took the job, led the team to a 31-19 record his first year at the school, and in 1973, took the team to the College World Series. He was named National Coach of the Year following the 1973 season.

Resigning from Georgia Southern in 1975, Polk served as an assistant to Ron Fraser at Miami for the summer before being hired to replace Jimmy Bragan as head baseball coach at Mississippi State University in November, 1975. And the rest is Bulldog history.

Polk maintains a steady year-round pace as a much sought-after banquet speaker at alumni gatherings, and rates as a favorite on the baseball clinic circuit both throughout the nation and abroad.

The highly personable coach didn't waste a minute in beginning his discussion on the psychology and strategy of successful team building.

Here are Coach Ron Polk's thoughts...

...on Motivation

Coach Polk believes that outside influences have an effect on the motivation of today's athletes, but he also thinks that each person is responsible for self-motivation.

"Motivation to me is the will to do the very best one can do within the restrictions of one's mental and physical capabilities," he says.

"Motivation should also be a self-made trait," he continues. "But at the same time, outside influences like the crowd, aspirations to play pro baseball and peer influence, can play a big part in a young man's motivation to succeed both on and off the athletic field."

Through his coaching experience, Polk has found what works and what doesn't work in the motivation techniques he has observed over the years.

"The least effective techniques are embarrassing a player in front of his peers or in the press or on radio or television, he says. "Another is establishing unrealistic goals by the coach."

Coach Polk lists several techniques that he has found to be highly effective in motivating his student-athletes.

"First, you have to treat each player with love and kindness," he states. "But you must also set rules for discipline.

"You need to provide a positive program for him to develop his skills, and you need to organize his practice plan so that he sees progress within each practice session.

"It's also motivating to surround him with quality people, both in the coaching staff and teammates," he says.

Fan support, bringing in outside speakers, and personal evaluation periods are additional motivational techniques.

"Build a program around fan support, the radio network, and television," he says.

"I also like bringing in former players to speak with him and the team about what athletics has done for them both on and off the athletic field.

"I enjoy visiting with each player two times a year for 45-60 minutes, evaluating his performance both in the classroom and on the baseball field," he says. "We also have his teammates as well as the coaching staff evaluate his performance."

Finally, Coach Polk motivates his players by discussing the player's future in baseball.

"We try to establish the fact that outstanding skill development might lead to a pro baseball future," he states.

In summary, Polk defines motivation as the ability of a person to utilize his mental and physical capabilities to the utmost degree. He also believes that outside influences can have a motivating effect on a person.

Polk lists two methods as being ineffective when motivating athletes. Those methods include public embarrassment of the player in front of his peers or the media, and establishing unrealistic goals for the player.

Effective motivation techniques include treating each player with love and kindness, providing a positive program in which the athlete can develop his skills, and organizing practices so that the player can see consistent improvement.

He lists additional effective motivation techniques, such as bringing in former players to discuss the positive effects of athletics and academics at Mississippi State, utilizing personal evaluation meetings with each player twice a year, providing each athlete with evaluation data from other coaches and teammates, and surrounding each player with quality teammates and coaches.

Finally, Coach Polk believes that building a program through fan support and media coverage can be highly motivating for his players, as can be discussing with each player the possibility of a future professional baseball career.

* * * * * * * * * *

...on Team Cohesion

Team cohesion is a vital ingredient for ultimate team success, but Coach Polk believes that team chemistry is most beneficial when a team is having problems on the field.

"Good cohesion and good chemistry plays a significant role when a team is struggling on the field," he says. "But talent is still the primary ingredient in team success."

Ron defines team cohesion as the ability of each player to accept each team member as an important part of the team.

"I define team cohesion and team chemistry as the degree of acceptance each team member has for the entire team, regardless of personality differences, " he says. "Cohesion and chemistry might also assist a team to reach certain positive goals."

Polk mentions that his techniques for building team cohesion are similar to those he uses to motivate his players.

"I believe that team meetings where positive comments are the rule helps build team chemistry," he says. "I also think that most players living together in a dormitory setting can build team cohesion."

The most important element, however, is the understanding each player has concerning his role on the team.

"Making sure each player understands his role on the baseball team at every opportunity has been very helpful in building team chemistry on our clubs," Polk says.

In summary, Coach Polk defines team cohesion as the degree of acceptance each team member has for the entire team, regardless of personality conflicts. He also believes that team cohesion is most effective when teams are struggling on the field.

Effective methods for building team cohesion include activities in which all players are participants, he says. He lists team meetings, living together in a dormitory, and each player understanding his role on the team as the best methods of building team chemistry in the Bulldog program.

* * * * * * * * * *

...on Discipline

Coach Polk has established himself as a no-nonsense type of person, and his philosophy concerning discipline reflects that attitude.

"Team discipline is very important on any team," he says. "Rules and regulations must not only be talked about, but each player needs to receive a copy of the rules at the first team meeting of the year."

Ron reinforces the discussion of his discipline philosophy with illustrations of some Bulldog baseball rules.

"We follow a strict time schedule for both practices and games," he states. "We have a dress code on the road.

"We believe class attendance reflects individual and team discipline. We also believe that maintaining a clean locker room both at home and on the road reflects team discipline.

"We have a strict curfew on road trips. We think the manner in which the players come on the field at both practices and games is discipline-related.

"Finally, the manner in which the players handle themselves with the press and fans says a lot about self-discipline," he concludes.

Coach Polk believes that effective discipline is a result of team participation in the rules-making process.

"Most effective for us has been discipline that is fair due to the fact that team rules have been set," he says. "We encourage each player to discuss any team rules that might not be in the best interest of the entire team."

Least effective discipline methods would include arbitrary and vindictive kinds of rules enforcement.

"Any discipline that is spotty and only enforced when a team is struggling just won't work," he says.

Showing favoritism in the enforcement of team rules can also cause problems.

"Violation of any team rule will be dealt with immediately and without any concern in regard to the value of the player to team success," Polk says.

In summary, team discipline is very important in Coach Polk's program. He believes that team rules should be set by team members and that each player should receive a written copy of the rules at the first team meeting of the year.

He illustrates his philosophy on team discipline by listing several rules of the Bulldog baseball program.

Finally, he believes that effective discipline methods include fair treatment and immediate enforcement of team rules, while ineffective discipline methods include arbitrary rules enforcement and showing favoritism in the enforcement process.

* * * * * * * * * *

...on Mental Preparation

All successful coaches say that mental preparation is an important element for team and individual success. Coach Polk agrees with that statement, but states that mental preparation holds many definitions.

"Mental preparation means different things to different people," he says. "At Mississippi State, we want each player to be relaxed at all times, but also play aggressively."

Polk believes that practice and repetition assist the athlete in more ways than one.

"Skill development and repetitive training in practices help the player develop a baseball instinct," he states. "The better a player's skill level, the more positive he feels about himself as a player. Good results breed confidence and poor results breed lack of self-esteem and confidence."

Mental preparation also means keeping a balanced mental approach to each game.

"We do not want our players to get too high when things are going good for him or the team," he points out. "We also do not want him too low when things are going bad for him or the team."

Polk claims that mental preparation is an individual responsibility, but that the atmosphere surrounding the Bulldog program makes it easier for the players to prepare.

"Each player must find his own manner to prepare for each game or series," he says. "Here at M.S.U. , we have led the nation in average daily attendance the last couple of years. We do not have a difficult time getting our players to play hard since they have many people rooting for them. This is also the case for non-conference games."

Late-game stratetgy is practiced daily, but it still is important for the players to be relaxed when a crucial situation arises during a game.

"We never build up one game or one series that we must play harder," he states. "Baseball is a sport that one must be relaxed playing. When one presses, the skill level generally drops."

In summary, mental preparation is important for team and individual success. Coach Polk defines mental preparation as being relaxed, but playing aggressively at all times.

He believes that skill development and repetition training in practices assist the player in gaining confidence and self-esteem. This confidence and self-esteem is essential for mental preparation and correct execution, he says.

Finally, Polk wants his players to keep a balanced mental attitude for each game, not getting too high nor too low depending upon the situation. He stresses the importance of playing relaxed aand not pressing when crucial situations arise during games.

* * * * * * * * * *

...on Mental Toughness

Mental toughness is a trait found in the highly-successful athlete. Coach Polk believes that mental toughness is an on-going test for a player.

"Mental toughness to me means that a player must be able to withstand prosperity and despair each time his skill level is tested," he says. "That might be pitch by pitch, game by game, or season by season."

Polk thinks that there are several characteristics of a mentally tough individual.

"Mentally tough players get after it at all times," he states. "They always play with enthusiasm and aggressiveness."

Coach Polk also believes that mentally tough players avoid any kind of slumps.

"They are not generally slump-prone due to the fact that they understand their limitations," he says.

Consistency and being a positive role model are the final two characteristics of mental toughness.

"The mentally tough players are consistent in the way they handle themselves at all times, on and off the field," he says. "They also pick up other members of the team by the way they go about their business on a daily basis."

In summary, Coach Polk believes that mental toughness is the ability of a player to react in a positive way when his skill level is tested. This test can occur pitch by pitch, game by game, or season by season.

Finally, he lists several characteristics of a mentally tough person. Those traits include being enthusiastic and aggressive, not being slump-prone, being a good role model for other teammates, and being consistent in their behavior at all times, on and off the field.

* * * * * * * * * *

...on Communication

Coach Polk will never be accused of a lack of communication. He prides himself in the fact that he keeps the lines of communication open at all times, with his players, with his correspondence, and even with opposing players.

"I have a policy that before I leave each night, every letter is answered and every phone call returned," he says. "If somebody says I didn't return a phone call, then I never got the message."

His open-door policy with players is very important in keeping communication lines open.

"My players know that I hate wasted time during the day," he says. "But they also know they can come in at any time and discuss anything with me. That's important to me and always will be."

He also keeps in touch not only with former players, but some opposing players. He personally types each letter.

"I'll write Dale Murphy, because I've known him for years. And I'll write Roger Clemens, who we played against when he was at Texas. Sure, those guys get thousands of letters, but it's important to let them know that you care how they're doing.

"And I think it's especially important to keep in touch with kids in the minor leagues. It might be one of my former players or a guy who used to play at Alabama. I get *Baseball America* and *The Sporting News*. If I see where a kid went 3-for-4, I'll drop him a note and tell him 'Congratulations. Hang in there.' Why not? It only takes a minute. I know what they're going through."

Polk believes that once a game begins, the motivation of the players must be the primary source of inspiration, and not a speech from the coach.

"Baseball is not a 'locker talk' type of sport," he says. "Football, basketball, wrestling or those sports where one must maintain physical strength and endurance are dealt with by motivation techniques."

Post-game comments are always positive in nature, he asserts, unless the effort level of the players was not very good.

"We always find good things to say about a loss unless one player or others might not have played hard to achieve team success," he states. "We try to give them confidence in themselves and in the team by asking them not to do anything they are not capable of doing. Performance is reflected by practice preparation and instincts."

In summary, communication skills are very important in Coach Polk's program at Mississippi State University. He enjoys communicating with his players, former players, and opposing players.

He strictly adheres to a personal policy of answering every letter and returning every phone call on a daily basis. He personally types each letter that leaves his office.

He believes that motivational speeches are not appropriate or effective once a game has begun. He says it is the responsibility of the players to keep self-motivated during games.

Finally, Coach Polk keeps all post-game comments positive in nature. The exception to that rule would be evidence of a lack of effort on the part of one or more players. His post-game comments are meant to build confidence in the players, and he believes that player performance is reflected by practice preparation and instincts.

* * * * * * * * *

JACK RAMSAY
Former Head Coach
National Basketball Association

Position
Television analyst for Philadelphia 76ers
basketball games

Career Record
1208-906 (38 seasons)

Education
B.S.   1949 St. Joseph's University
M.S.   1952 University of Pennsylvania
Ph.D.   1963 University of Pennsylvania

Team and Personal Highlights

*   Second on the all-time NBA victories list with 864 wins,
    trailing only Red Auerbach's 938 wins.
*   Coach of four NBA teams: Philadelphia 76ers (1968-72),
    Buffalo Braves (1972-76), Portland Trail Blazers
    (1976-86), and Indiana Pacers (1986-88).
*   Won NBA Championship in 1977 with Portland.
*   League record of 1,640 games as an NBA coach.
*   Coach in the NBA All-Star game in 1978.
*   Player-coach in Eastern Basketball League in 1950's.
*   Author of two books: *Pressure Basketball* and *The
    Coaches Art.*
*   Champion triathlete in 60-and-over age bracket.

Jack Ramsay

Introduction...

Jack Ramsay needs a business card the size of a free throw line to adequately cover his many work titles: Television Analyst, Doctor, Author, Triathlete, Teacher, Husband, Father, World Champion, among others.

The svelte 65-year-old Ramsay has established himself as one of the truly great teachers of the game of basketball. In 38 years of coaching, he has amassed over 1200 victories, ranking him as one of the winningest coaches of all time.

John T. "Jack" Ramsay was born February 21, 1925, in Philadelphia. He soon moved to Milford, Connecticut, where he grew up shooting baskets at a goal nailed to the side of a barn.

As a sophomore in high school, Ramsay and his family moved to Upper Darby, a suburb of Philadelphia. An all-around athlete, he earned letters in basketball, baseball, and soccer. He received the school's outstanding athlete award as a senior and was named to the all-county basketball team.

Ramsay earned a starting berth at St. Joseph's College in Philadelphia in 1942, but after his freshman season he entered the Navy. He was commissioned an Ensign in 1944 and served with underwater demolition teams as well as captain of an inter-island cargo vessel in the Pacific prior to his discharge in 1946.

He returned to St. Joseph's to continue his career in basketball as well as baseball. He captained the Hawks' cage team as a senior and made the all-Philadelphia team as a junior and senior.

Ramsay received his Bachelor of Science degree in social science in 1949 and began his teaching and coaching career at St. James High School in Chester, Pennsylvania, that fall. Coaching did not stop him from continuing his education or his playing.

He enrolled at the University of Pennsylvania where he obtained his Master's degree in education in 1952 and ultimately his Ph.D. in education in 1963.

Ramsay continued to play competitively for six years in the Eastern Basketball League for Harrisburg and Sunbury.

After three seasons at St. James, Ramsay moved to Mt. Pleasant High School in Wilmington, Delaware. In three years there, his teams were 40-18 and he was rewarded with the head coaching position at St. Joseph's in 1955.

In his first season, Ramsay led his alma mater to a 23-6 record, the school's first Big Five championship, and a trip to the National Invitation Tournament, the school's first post-season tourney.

He stayed at St. Joseph's for 11 years, compiling a record of 234-72 with 10 post-season tournament appearances. While at St. Joseph's, Ramsay had stints as athletic director and baseball coach, in addition to a full load of classes as a teacher and student.

He moved across town in 1966 and got his first taste of the NBA as general manager of the Philadelphia 76ers. In his first season there, the 76ers won an NBA record 68 games enroute to the world championship.

After one more year in the front office, Ramsay was urged to return to the sideline. The 76ers went 55-27 in 1968-69 and Ramsay had them in the playoffs three out of four years.

He moved to the Buffalo Braves as head coach in 1972 and in four years there took teams into the playoffs three times, winning 158 games in the process.

Ramsay became the head coach of the Portland Trail Blazers in 1976. He inherited a team which not only had never made the playoffs in the franchise's six years of existence, but had never had a winning record, either.

In his first year in Portland, he guided the Trail Blazers to a 49-33 record and the NBA Championship. He followed that with a 58-24 mark in 1977-78, the best record in the league. In 10 seasons at Portland, his teams made the playoffs nine times.

Ramsay was named the Indiana Pacer's head coach on August 8, 1986. He compiled a record of 79-85 over the next two seasons. But after the 1988-89 team started the season with seven consecutive losses, Ramsay resigned. He remained with the club as a consultant for the remainder of the 1988-89 season before assuming his present position as television analyst for Philadelphia 76ers games.

A vocal proponent of physical fitness, Ramsay maintains a vigoroius exercise routine. He has made numerous long-distance bicycle rides and has been competing in triathlons for several years.

Ramsay broke the three-hour barrier in the triathlon, which usually includes a one-mile swim, 25-mile bike ride, and a 6.5 mile run, all done without any rest in between. He has finished as high as 11th in the 60-and-over bracket of the national triathlon championships.

Ramsay's family includes five grown children: Three daughters and two sons. Jack and his wife, Jean, live in New Jersey.

The highly-articulate former coach was most enthusiastic in his response to discussing successful team building.

Here are Jack Ramsay's thoughts...

...on Motivation

Motivation is a prime ingredient for success within all organizations. Coach Ramsay believes that motivation has a direct impact on the productivity level of the athlete.

"Motivation is the psychological impetus that increases the productivity level of the individual in reaching his established objectives," he says.

Having dealt with athletes from all levels of competition during his 38 years of coaching, Ramsay says effective motivation techniques vary with each athlete.

"The most effective motivation techniques are those which reach the individual in ways he relates to directly," he says. "Those techniques can vary, and it's the responsibility of the coach to discern which techniques work best for each player."

Least effective motivation techniques are those which the athlete cannot relate to.

"I've found that the ineffective motivation techniques are those which the recipient doesn't understand or which don't reach him directly," he points out.

In summary, Ramsay believes that motivation is a psychological impetus that drives an individual to a higher productivity level.

He states that it is the responsibility of the head coach to discover the best motivation methods for each player. That is the reason why techniques will vary for each person, he says.

Finally, Ramsay says effective motivation methods are those which reach the individual in ways he relates to directly, while least effective motivation techniques are those which the player cannot relate to or understand.

* * * * * * * * * *

...on Team Cohesion

Team cohesion is a vital ingredient for ultimate team success, and Coach Ramsay believes team chemistry is just a matter of player knowledge and practical usage.

"Team cohesion is closely related to timing and understanding of objectives," he says. "Then after that, it's a matter of practical usage."

Building team cohesion includes three important elements: visual examples, practice and defining roles on the team.

"You need to constantly stress the need for team play to be able to win," Jack states. "Then you need to show the players examples of effective team play."

Those examples can be videotape highlights of the team or occasionally the use of examples of an opposing team.

"We would show the team highlights of past great teams, or highlights of the present team in the area of team play," he says. "We would also utilize a great opponent for examples of team play if we thought it would help get the point across to our players."

Ramsay is a proponent of the adage "practice what you preach."

"You must practice to reach team play level of performance," he says. "It doesn't come naturally."

The third important method of effectively building team cohesion is defining the roles of the players.

"Each player must have a clear definition of his role on the team," he says."Then the player needs to accept that role and execute that role to the best of his ability if the team is going to be successful."

In summary, Coach Ramsay defines team cohesion as a relationship of timing and understanding team objectives, then putting that knowledge into practical usage.

Effective methods of building team chemistry, he says, include the use of videotape highlights to show examples of effective team play, and daily practice to reach team play level of performance.

Finally, in order for the team to be cohesive, the head coach must clearly define the role each person is to play on the team, and the player must accept and execute that role to the best of his ability.

* * * * * * * * * *

...on Discipline

Discipline is a trait of the championship team and individual. Ramsay-coached teams have built the reputation of being highly-disciplined in addition to being highly-successful.

"It was important for our teams to demonstrate a level of self-restraint and discipline on and off the court," he says.

Ramsay mentions that effective team discipline must be handled in only one way.

"You must be firm, fair and universal," Jack says. "It is the only way."

Discipline with professional athletes is different in some areas, but Ramsay says that you handle each situation the same.

"You must handle each discipline case on an individual basis," he says. "Each person has the right to explain his side of the story.

"But once the player's side is explained, the head coach must implement team discipline policy in the same way, whether it involves the team star or the 12th player."

Ramsay says that inconsistent implementation of team rules is the least effective method of discipline.

"Any spasmatic or inconsistent administration of team discipline rules is highly ineffective," he says. "That kind of action can also lead to team dissension."

In summary, Coach Ramsay believes that team discipline is a very important element of team success. He also states that players need to show self-restraint on and off the court.

Finally, he says that effective methods of discipline include being firm, fair and universal with all players when handling discipline matters. Ineffective methods of team discipline involve inconsistent and spasmatic administration of team rules.

* * * * * * * * * *

...on Mental Preparation

Mental preparation for professional athletes differs from high school or collegiate athletes. For the professional athlete, the process is continuous.

"The professional athlete really has no off-season when it comes to mental preparation," Ramsay says.

Mentally preparing for the grind of a professional basketball season begins long before training camps start in the fall.

"The 'grind' is really a short one," Jack says. "There is only one week of training camp and then three weeks of pre-season games. The athlete must begin mentally preparing himself for the season long before he reports to training camp."

Reporting in top physical condition is a priority for the players in the eyes of the coaching staffs. Jack also believes that the physical condition of the player when he reports to training camp says a lot about the player's mental approach to the upcoming season.

"We stressed summer conditioning prior to camp so that the players came to camp in top shape," he says. "We also had voluntary training sessions of four or five days during the summer which the players could attend on their own.

"But I always thought that the players reporting in top shape had a better mental approach to the coming season than the players reporting in less-than-ideal physical condition."

Late-game strategy is an on-going process for professional athletes and coaching staffs.

"We thought that critical situations involving late-game strategy occurred 40-50 times each season," Jack says. "Therefore, we needed to practice those kinds of situations on a daily basis. Much of that strategy was practiced during pre-season games, and we made adjustments as the season progressed."

In summary, Coach Ramsay believes that the top athletes in professional basketball have a continuous and consistent mental training approach. This approach spans the season and, most importantly, the off-season.

Professional athletes on Coach Ramsay's teams were expected to report to training camp in top physical condition. He thought that the individuals reporting in top physical condition were more mentally prepared for the upcoming season than the players reporting in less-than-top physical condition.

Finally, late-game strategy was practiced on a daily basis, with the bulk of that practice taking place during pre-season games. Coach Ramsay then made the necessary adjustments involving late-game strategy as the season progressed.

* * * * * * * * * *

...on Mental Toughness

Mental toughness is a trait found in all highly-skilled athletes. On a professional level, the degree of mental toughness separates the good players from the great players.

"I think that mental toughess means persevering through tough game and psychological situations which require concentration and high-pressure execution," he says.

In addition to concentration and performing successfully in high-pressure situations, Ramsay lists two additional characteristics.

"The mentally tough player makes the big defensive and offensive plays that decide games," he states. "He makes these plays consistently."

In summary, mental toughness is a trait that separates the good players from the great players on the professional level. Coach Ramsay defines mental toughness as the ability to persevere through tough game and psychological situations.

He lists four characteristics of the mentally tough individual. He says the mentally tough person executes successfully in high-pressure game conditions and has the ability to concentrate during critical times of a game.

Finally, he mentions that the mentally tough player makes the big defensive and offensive plays that decide the outcomes of games, and that the mentally tough player makes these big plays consistently during the course of the season.

* * * * * * * * * *

...on Communication

Communication with athletes and staff during times of adversity is extremely important for all organizations. Coach Ramsay believes that poise during the heat of battle is a vital characteristic for the head coach.

"It is vital that the head coach keeps his poise during tight situations and that he direct his team properly," he says. "He must give his team every chance to win because of his direction."

These tight coaching situations can be found during halftime (when adjustments need to be made) or during the closing seconds of a highly-competitive game. In either case, Jack says, the head coach must show leadership in communicating his strategy to the players.

Post-game comments following a tough loss or a poor team performance are handled in a consistent manner.

"Post-game comments must be honest, brief and applicable," he says. "Tough losses must be given an up-beat treatment by the head coach."

A poor team performance will bring a more critical evaluation from Ramsay.

"A poor performance must be evaluated as such and the specifics of such performance must be briefly described," he says. "It cannot be passed off lightly, nor with an attitude that it is acceptable. On the professional level, a poor performance is never acceptable."

In summary, Coach Ramsay believes that communication is very important within all organizations. He also contends that it is the responsibility of the head coach to exhibit poise during all critical game moments.

Post-game comments following a tough loss will be handled in an up-beat manner, he says. Comments must be honest, brief and applicable during this time.

Finally, post-game comments following a poor team or individual performance will be approached in a more critical way, Jack says. The head coach must be specific in his comments to the player(s) and the team must be impressed with the attitude that poor performance is not acceptable. Passing off poor performance lightly will do more harm than taking a more critical evaluative approach, he says.

* * * * * * * * * *

LARRY RIBBLE

Millard South High School
Omaha, Nebraska

Position

Head Boys Basketball Coach
Social Sciences Teacher

Career Record

351-162 (25 seasons)

Education

B.A.   1965 Nebraska Wesleyan University
M. Ed. 1975 University of Nebraska-Lincoln

Team and Personal Highlights

* 1989   Nebraska Coaches Association Basketball Coach of the Year
          Award; *Lincoln Journal and Star* Coach of the Year Award;
          Metropolitan Area Basketball Coaches Association Coach of
          the Year Award.
* 1988   Nebraska Coaches Association Basketball Coach of the Year
          Award; *Omaha World-Herald* Coach of the Year Award.
* 1985   Head Coach of the Nebraska All-Start team that participated in
          the summer Las Vegas national high school basketball tournament.
* 1984   Nebraska Coaches Association Basketball Coach of the Year
          Award.
* 1982   Metropolitan Area Basketball Coaches Association Coach of the
          Year Award.
* 1980   Head Coach of North team in Nebraska Coaches Association
          All-Star game.
*   Eleven teams have qualified for the Nebraska Boys State
          Basketball Tournament.
*   Twenty-nine former players have played college basketball.
*   Pawnee City teams won back-to-back Class C State Championships in
          1970 and 1971.
*   Millard South teams won back-to-back Class A State Championships in
          1983 and 1984, and 1988 and 1989.
*   Elder in Hope Presbyterian Church.
*   Active member in Fellowship of Christian Athletes.

Larry Ribble

Introduction...

Larry Ribble has established himself as one of the most successful coaches in Nebraska prep basketball history. The Nebraska native is highly respected by his peers because he has demonstrated team-building excellence in both small-enrollment and large-enrollment schools.

The 46-year-old Ribble graduated from Nebraska Wesleyan University in Lincoln in 1965 and started his teaching and coaching career at tiny Holmesville High School that fall. After one year at Holmesville, Larry moved to Dorchester High School as head basketball coach.

For three years, Ribble led the Longhorns and then moved to Pawnee City High School in the fall of 1969. His four-year stint at the Class C school included back-to-back State Championships in 1970 and 1971.

Moving up to a larger-class school, Ribble left Pawnee City after the 1973-74 school year to take the reins of the basketball program at Falls City High School in southeastern Nebraska near the Nebraska-Kansas border. After two successful years with the Tiger basketball teams, Larry pursued the opportunity to coach in Class A, Nebraska's largest enrollment schools.

Ribble's move to Class A Hastings allowed him to keep not only the same school nickname, but the same school colors. The orange and black Hastings Tigers reached the state tournament during Ribble's two years at the central Nebraska school.

Following the 1977-78 school year, Ribble applied for and earned one of the elite Class A coaching positions in Nebraska at Millard South High School. The suburban-Omaha school is presently the largest and fastest-growing Class A school district in the state.

With four state championships under his belt at Millard South, Ribble has risen to the top of his profession. His proudest moments have been associated with back-to-back state championships in 1988 and 1989 with son Dale at a starting guard position. Dale is currently playing NCAA Division I basketball at Southwest Missouri State University under Coach Charlie Spoonhour, a former assistant coach at the University of Nebraska.

Larry and his wife, Joy, have three children: Dale; Heather, a junior at Millard South; and five-year-old Amber. An Elder in his Presbyterian Church, Larry volunteers much of his time to community and church functions.

Possessing a sharp wit and colorful sense of humor, Ribble was happy to have the chance to share his ideas on successful team building.

Here are Coach Larry Ribble's thoughts...

...on Motivation

Motivation on the high school level is a very difficult job for any coach. The high school coach does not have the luxury of recruiting the highly-motivated student-athlete. The high school coach must play with the hand he has been dealt. But Coach Ribble believes that the high school coach still has a responsibility concerning the motivation of his/her athletes.

"I believe that motivation is what enables players to be as good as they can possibly be," he says. "Some players are very self-motivated and are usually the best players. Other players need to have their 'hot button' pushed to help them along."

Finding each player's 'hot button' is often a long, concerted process for the head coach. But Ribble contends that each coach must find his player's 'hot button' if the team is going to be successful.

"I think a coach must know what type of motivation to use with each player," he states. "That motivation can be praise, sarcasm or chewing out.

"Some respond to praise, some respond to getting yelled at, and some respond to sarcasm. The coach must know what works with each player."

Ribble says that today's student-athlete responds best with one kind of motivation method.

"In today's society, praise seems to work best," he says.

Coach Ribble lists another method as being successful in motivating today's athlete.

"Most players today are pretty intelligent," he states. "So just sitting down and talking with them on Mondays and Tuesdays is a good practice to follow."

In summary, Ribble defines motivation as a quality that enables players to be the best they can be. He believes that some players are highly self-motivated, while others need some motivational assistance from the coaches.

Coach Ribble says that each coach must discover what motivates each athlete. Some of those motivational methods include praise, sarcasm or chewing out. Even though each athlete is different, Ribble contends that praise is the best motivating technique for all athletes.

Finally, Ribble believes that today's high school student-athlete is intelligent and relates well to a coach-athlete discussion as an effective motivation technique.

* * * * * * * * * *

...on Team Cohesion

Team cohesion is a vital ingredient for ultimate team success. Coach Ribble equates team chemistry with personal sacrifice.

"To me, team cohesion means getting every member of the team to sacrifice for the good of the team," he says.

As many of the coaches in this book have stressed, Ribble also believes that the most effective method for building team cohesion is to make the environment surrounding the program into a "family" atmosphere.

"We really try to stress team play and verbally reward good passing," he states. "We emphasize it and praise it during practice, videotape sessions, to the news media and during games."

Outside social activities play a major role in building team cohesion, Ribble says.

"We try to do some outside things together. We'll go to a college game and have the kids over for a meal. We really try to get them to look out for each other off the court as well."

In summary, Ribble believes that team cohesion means each member of the team is willing to sacrifice personal reward for team success.

He says that the best method of building team cohesion is to take a "family" approach with the players and reward team play with praise during practice, videotape sessions, in the news media and during games.

Finally, combining team social activities with a caring attitude toward each player is an additional effective team building technique, he says. Activities can include attending a college basketball game together or the head coach hosting the players for a meal at his home. He points out that it is important for the players to assist each other off the court as well as on it.

* * * * * * * * * *

...on Discipline

Discipline is a trait of the championship team and individual. Larry states that team discipline must be established on and off the court if the program is to be a total success.

"I believe that team discipline is getting your players to do what they are supposed to do on the court," he says. "Off-the-court team discipline is more difficult to control."

Because of the high public profile of Coach Ribble's teams within the community, he contends that players need to be responsible for their actions and set good examples for others to emulate.

"We emphasize to the players to be good examples and to do nothing that would embarrass our team," he says. "We feel that our basketball players must be model citizens because they are looked up to by all members of the community."

Ribble long ago established his philosophy of effective discipline practices.

"Be firm, but fair!" he states.

Coach Ribble says that making the players a part of the rules-making process is important in developing team discipline policy. But he quickly points out that the head coach must be quick and consistent in administering the rules.

"If rules are established, they must be followed," he says. "Within some 'gray' area parameters, the head coach must make the final determination."

In summary, Ribble believes team discipline extends from on-court behavior to off-the-court behavior. He says it is most difficult for a coach to control the discipline of team members off the court.

Larry emphasizes to his players the importance of being good role models within the community. He also tells the team that they must be constantly aware that they represent the Millard South basketball program and that behavior that embarrasses the player personally is also embarrassing the basketball program.

Ribble's philosophy of "being firm, but fair" has been the most effective method when dealing with team discipline problems, he says.

He thinks that team members should have some input into team rules-making, and that players are more likely to follow team rules if they have a voice in making team discipline policy.

Finally, Ribble contends that within the "gray" areas of team discipline, the head coach must make the final determination concerning team rules and implementation.

* * * * * * * * * *

...on Mental Preparation

All successful coaches say that mental preparation is essential to team and individual success. It is Coach Ribble's belief that mental preparation means having an understanding of one's role and responsibility.

"Mental preparation is being able to understand what you are trying to do and how you are going to do it," he says.

Unlike college teams which have six weeks of pre-season practice time, high schools around the country have three weeks to prepare for the first game. For coaches, that time usually goes by quickly. However, to the players, three weeks can be an eternity. Therefore, it is important that coaches organize pre-season practices to lessen the "grind" effect on the players.

"We try to have some intersquad game scrimmages with officials and videotape," Larry says. "We usually do this on Saturdays during pre-season."

The Nebraska State Activities Association, the ruling body governing high school sports in the state, relies on a "wild card" point system to help determine state tournament-qualifying status for teams which don't win their respective district tournaments in Class A. The philosophy behind the "wild card" points is to reward teams which have successful regular seasons, but slip during state-qualifying district tournaments.

This "wild card" system makes every game important, Ribble says.

"Because of wild card points, each game is important, whether it's a conference or non-conference game," he says.

Ribble agrees with the concept that the success of late-game strategy is a result of successful practice of those situations.

"We spend five minutes every day in late-game and game-ending strategy and situations," he says. "We don't ever try anything in a game that hasn't been at least covered in practice."

In summary, Ribble defines mental preparation as the ability of each player to understand his role and responsibilities during each game.

To lessen the grind of pre-season practices, Larry incorporates intersquad scrimmages on Saturdays into the practice schedule. These scrimmages include the use of referees and are videotaped to enhance the learning process for team members.

Because of Nebraska's "wild card" point system which allows Class A teams to qualify for the state tournament without winning a state-qualifying district tournament, every conference and non-conference game is important to his team, he says.

Finally, late-game strategy is practiced on a daily basis, Ribble says. He will not implement any late-game strategy during games that the team has not practiced during the week prior to the game.

* * * * * * * * * *

...on Mental Toughness

Mental toughness is a trait found in all highly-successful individuals. Coach Ribble believes that players who possess this trait are the ones who inspire their teammates and carry their teams to victory. He says it also helps build self-confidence.

"Mental toughness is that trait that enables a player to not give up when things are tough and not going well," he begins. "It is that little trait that enables teams to win when they probably shouldn't. It is the trait that allows a player confidence to shoot a game-winning shot when he has a 2-for-13 shooting night going."

Larry lists four characteristics of a mentally tough player.

"A mentally tough player is good at 'crunch time,'" he says. "A mentally tough player is highly-conditioned, competitive, and has a lot of drive. A mentally tough player is usually self-motivated."

In summary, Coach Ribble states that players who possess mental toughness have the ability to cope when things are not going their way during games. He also believes that mentally tough teams have the ability to win some games against more-talented opponents.

Ribble also points out that mental toughness can build self-confidence in a player, alowing him to take a game-winning shot even though his shooting percentage has been below average that night.

Finally, Ribble lists four characteristics of a mentally tough player. Those characteristics include being highly-conditioned physically and mentally, having a highly-competitive nature, possessing a high level of drive, and being highly self-motivated.

* * * * * * * * * *

...on Communication

Communication with athletes and staff within any organization is an important psychological factor. During times of adversity during games, effective communication becomes a vital ingredient for success. Coach Ribble understands the power of communicating effectively during these critical times.

"If we're behind at halftime, we try to look at our problems logically," he says. "We will make the needed technical adjustments offensively and defensively, and pretty much leave it at that. There's very little time for any kind of pep talk."

Ribble maintains the philosophy that the head coach must keep comments positive during halftime and at critical times during the game.

"If we are losing, we try to cut the deficit in half by the end of the third quarter. We try to be as positive as possible with the players at all times."

Post-game comments will differ, he says, depending upon whether the team suffered a tough defeat or if a poor performance occurred because of a lack of effort.

"We try to be as positive as possible. If we win, we sometimes get on them pretty good, but never after a tough loss.

"However, if it's been a poor performance because of a lack of effort, we will get on them hard and give them specific examples to prove our points."

In summary, Coach Ribble believes that effective communication with athletes and staff is extremely important during critical times of a game.

Halftime talks center around technical adjustments and a logical approach to cutting the deficit, if one is present. Larry's approach is positive in tone to the players, and not very often does he resort to any kind of pep talk to motivate his players for the second half of the game.

Post-game comments will vary, depending upon the outcome and level of effort the team exhibited during the game. Ribble says that after a tough loss, he is positive in all of his comments. If the team wins, he will incorporate critical comments in his evaluation in addition to positive statements.

Finally, post-game comments following a poor performance from a lack of effort will draw severe criticism. He keeps his critical comments general in nature, and will not single out individual players at this time. However, he makes it a point to discuss lack of effort with individual players during private conversations the day following the game.

* * * * * * * * *

DEBBIE RYAN

University of Virginia

Position

Head Women's Basketball Coach

Career Record

270-119   (13 seasons)

Education

B.S.   1975 Ursinus College
M.S.   1977 University of Virginia

Team and Personal Highlights

* 1989-90   Investors Classic Tournament Championship; Bell Atlantic Holiday Tournament Championship; Atlantic Coast Conference Tournament Championship; NCAA East Regional Championship; Final Four participant.

* 1989   Head coach of U.S.A. Junior World Championships team.

* 1988-89   NCAA Tournament.

* 1988   Head Coach of U.S.A. Junior National Team that won the Junior World Qualifying Tournament.

* 1987-88   Atlantic Coach Conference regular season championship; NCAA Tournament; Top 20 final ranking.

* 1986-87   Atlantic Coast Conference regular season championship; NCAA Mideast Regional semi-finals; Atlantic Coast Conference Coach of the Year Award; Converse District III Coach of the Year Award; Top 20 final ranking.

* 1987   Coach of gold medal-winning West team in U.S. Olympic Festival in Chapel Hill, North Carolina.

* 1985-86   Atlantic Coach Conference regular season championship; ACC Coach of the Year Award; Converse District III Coach of the Year Award; *Shreveport (LA) Journal* National Coach of the Year Award.

* 1984-85   NCAA Tournament.

* 1983-84   NCAA Tournament; ACC Coach of the Year Award.

* 1980-81   Association for Intercollegiate Athletics for Women Tournament; VAIAW Coach of the Year Award.

* 1979-80   National Invitation Tournament.

*   Member of USA BASKETBALL Women's Games Committee for 1989-92 quadrennium.

*   Member of NIKE Advisory Coaches Committee.

Debbie Ryan

Introduction...

When Debbie Ryan succeeded Dan Bonner as Virginia's head women's basketball coach in 1977, aspirations of national rankings, Atlantic Coast Conference championships and NCAA tournaments were far off, shrouded in a fog of uncertainty within the program. But after 13 seasons in Charlottesville, she has turned those lofty goals into reality and established herself as one of the top coaches in the country.

Ryan's 270-119 career record includes 12 straight winning seasons, nine trips to post-season play, national rankings, and ACC regular-season and tournament titles in five of the past six years.

The 1989-90 team climaxed a 29-6 season with an NCAA East Regional Championship and a trip to the Final Four in Knoxville, Tennessee, the first trip to the Final Four in the history of Virginia women's basketball. Ryan's team also won three tournament championships: The ACC Tournament, the Investors Classic, and the Bell Atlantic Holiday.

During the 1988-89 season, the team compiled a 21-10 record and played the 1989 National Champion Lady Volunteers of Tennessee in the NCAA Tournament's "Sweet 16" round.

The 1987-88 Cavaliers played "the toughest schedule in the nation'" as tabbed by the top basketball writers. Virginia grabbed the ACC regular-season title for the third consecutive year and appeared in the ACC Championship game for the second year in a row, only to lose to Maryland in the finals.

In 1986-87, Ryan directed Virginia to a 26-5 record, a second consecutive ACC regular-season title, a first-ever appearance in an ACC championship game, a fourth straight trip to the NCAA Tournament, and a No. 11 ranking in the final Associated Press national poll.

The 1985-86 Cavaliers enjoyed a successful 26-3 season, winning the regular-season title, advancing to the NCAA tournament, and finishing the year ranked sixth by the Associated Press.

For her efforts, Ryan has been honored three times as ACC Coach of the Year, winning the award in 1984, 1986 and 1987. She also won back-to-back Converse District III Coach of the Year awards in 1986 and 1987. She was also named the Virginia Intercollegiate Athletics for Women Coach of the Year after the 1980-81 season.

Coach Ryan has distinguished herself on the national and international coaching scene. She was the head coach of the gold medal-winning West team at the 1987 U.S. Olympic Festival in Chapel Hill, North Carolina.

In May of 1988, Ryan was named head coach of the USA Junior National team. With a task of putting together a competitive team in only 10 days, the Under-19 National team defeated Brazil in an exciting 70-68 victory to win the Junior World Qualifying tournament and earn a berth to the 1989 Junior World Championships. Ryan's 1989 Junior World team finished seventh in the Championships in Balboa, Spain.

Her list of honors does not stop at the coaching position. In April 1989, she was named to USA Basketball (formerly ABAUSA) Women's Games Committee for the 1989-92 quadrennium. The committee is responsible for staff and player selection, as well as for establishing guidelines at competitive events. Members of the committee are appointed by the constituent organization they represent, in this case the NCAA, with USA Basketball determining the number of at-large representatives.

Born in Baltimore on November 4, 1952, Ryan and her family eventually moved to Pennington, New Jersey, where Debbie became a standout student-athlete at Hopewell Valley Central High School. She won three letters each in basketball and field hockey and was named captain of both teams in 1970-71, her senior year.

Named Most Valuable Player in both basketball and field hockey following her senior seasons, she was ultimately honored as the Outstanding Senior Athlete at Hopewell High School in 1971.

Following graduation, Ryan continued her athletic career at Ursinus College in Collegeville, Pennsylvania, playing guard on the basketball team and earning a bachelor's degree in physical education in 1975.

She then moved to Charlottesville, earning a Master's degree in physical education in 1977 and assisting with both the women's basketball and field hockey programs. After Bonner's resignation, Ryan was named head women's basketball coach.

The 37-year-old dynamo is a Nike Advisory Coach and has been a speaker at Nike coaching clinics for nine years. She is the author of three books: *Virginia Defense, Virginia Summer Development Program*, and her most recent *Women's Basketball Drills-Conditioning*, which is one part of a series in conjunction with other coaches. She conducts her own highly successful basketball camp at Virginia each summer and is a regular speaker at camps and clinics nationwide. For relaxation, Ryan enjoys fishing and golfing in the off-season.

The high-energy coach with the non-stop lifestyle was very excited to share her ideas on successful team building.

Here are Coach Debbie Ryan's thoughts...

...on Motivation

Motivation is a prime ingredient for success within all organizations, and Coach Ryan believes that each player must be self-motivated in order to reach her goals.

"Motivation is a desire to do or perform a particular task," she says. "It is a personal thing that lies within each individual."

Least effective motivation techniques include any kind of system that reinforces good performance with some type of reward. Ryan believes that method sends the wrong message.

"Trying to extrinsically motivate your players is not a good motivation method," she states. "Eventually, the player performs only for the reward and nothing else."

The only kind of effective motivation is self-motivation, she asserts.

"Each team member must understand that they are responsible for themselves and their own motivation. I find that if I worry only about getting myself up, others will follow."

Ryan adds that motivational speakers may be effective in teaching self-motivation skills to the players.

"I do believe that a person can be motivated through listening to a speaker who educates the player on how to motivate themselves. Sometimes a speaker can use a key phrase that helps an athlete realize what motivates them. This helps in gaining personal control of this particular aspect."

Ryan believes that her players must motivate themselves on and off the court without her supervision.

"I cannot 'motivate' others to do certain tasks," she says. "Our players work hard at motivating themselves both in school and on the court. We are fortunate to get the student-athlete who excells in both areas."

Ryan likes to utilize motivational slogans and phrases to illustrate key points.

"'Happiness is a decision we make every morning we get up'," she concludes.

In summary, Coach Ryan believes that motivation is a desire to perform a particular task. She adds that motivation is personal for each athlete.

Least effective motivational methods are those in which extrinsic rewards are used to get the players to perform at their best. She thinks that any kind of reward system like this is sending the player the wrong message.

Ryan believes that the only effective method for motivation is self-motivation. She says that each player must be responsible for her own motivation, and that it is not possible for the coach to motivate all players at all times. She adds her thoughts that motivational speakers that teach self-motivation skills can also be helpful. Finally, she states that self-motivation is the key factor in success both on and off the court.

* * * * * * * * * *

...on Team Cohesion

Team chemistry is a vital ingredient for ultimate team success, and Coach Ryan believes that team cohesion is built around the theme of honesty within the program.

"Team cohesion or chemistry is the way that players, coaches and team members interact and relate to one another," she says.

Effective methods for building team cohesion include total honesty with each person and activities that involve all team members.

"We purport being totally open and honest with one another," she says.

"It may hurt at times and we may say things that are not complimentary, but we think that if a problem sits inside the player, it will fester and be expressed as anger inadvertently. So we believe that cohesion and chemistry grow through honestly and openly getting to know one another."

Ryan incoporates the use of activities that promote team cohesion. Those activities will include pre-game meals, team movies, community involvement, and any activity that will bring the team together for a worthwhile purpose.

In summary, Coach Ryan understands the importance of team chemistry and believes that building a program around the idea of total honesty is the most effective way to do it.

She concedes that total honesty includes comments which at times are not very complimentary to the player. But she is a proponent of the theory that lack of total honesty with players can result in stored-up anger that eventually can be very destructive to the player and the team.

Finally, Ryan utilizes activities that build team unity. Those activities include team meals and movies, involvement with community projects, and any other activities that will bring the team together for a worthwhile cause.

* * * * * * * * * *

...on Discipline

Discipline is trait of the championship team and individual, and Coach Ryan believes that team discipline is at the heart of the success of the Virginia women's basketball program.

"I believe a team and players not only need discipline, but want discipline," she says.

From her experiences, Ryan thinks she has a good grip on effective and ineffective discipline methods.

"Least effective methods of discipline incorporate negative, sarcastic or antagonistic behavior," she says. "Using negative comments or physical punishment usually transfers a person's own feeling of guilt and remorse on to the 'punisher'."

Any form of public reprimands is not a very effective discipline method, she states.

"Players want to be disciplined in humane ways. I avoid disciplining players in front of their peers. It is much more effective one-on-one."

Ryan believes that the most effective methods of disciplining players are through honest statements and "team-oriented" punishment.

"I've found that the most effective way of dealing with a discipline matter is using short and honest statements of what the person did wrong," she says.

"Team-oriented" punishment is also very effective.

"I find that using punishment that 'helps the team' is more effective than physical punishment," she states. "For example, helping our manager set up for practice for a specific period of time or performing a task in the office seems to work the best for us.

"It not only helps the player make up for a wrongdoing, but gives her a better understanding of someone else's job and position on the team."

In summary, Coach Ryan thinks that discipline is at the heart of the success of her program over the years. She also believes that players need and want discipline in their lives.

Least effective discipline methods include any form of sarcastic, antagonistic or negative comments from the head coach to the player. She adds that public reprimands of players in front of peers are also ineffective.

Finally, effective discipline methods include private, one-on-one conversations with the player in which an honest assessment of the problem is discussed. Ryan also believes that any form of punishment needs to be "team-oriented." This kind of punishment can include helping the team manager set up for practice for a specific period of time or performing a task in the basketball office. The key, she says, is to make the discipline a learning experience for the player in which she gets a better understanding of the other jobs and responsibilities associated with the team.

* * * * * * * * * *

...on Mental Preparation

Mental preparation is essential to team and individual success, and Coach Ryan spends a lot of time during the season working on this area.

"Mental preparation is having a good understanding of the task at hand and being ready to perform that task on a conscious level," she says.

Organization is one of the key elements when mentally preparing for the upcoming season, she states.

"Our players are informed of what takes place during pre-season, so as to ease anxiety," Coach Ryan says. "They are also given a summer program that eases them into pre-season practice."

Ryan incorporates her experienced players' knowledge when the team prepares for conference and non-conference games.

"We talk a lot about our schedule since it is so competitive each year," she says. "We allow the older, more experienced players to pass on their experiences and thoughts on how to prepare and handle these situations, both at home and away."

Experience, she says, helps when mentally preparing for a specific opponent.

"Experience is the best teacher," Ryan says. "But when you're inexperienced, hearing from someone who has been through the situation before is the next best thing."

She adds that pre-game preparation is also included in these discussions of the opponents.

Late-game strategy is practiced daily throughout the course of the season.

Familiarity breeds successful execution, and Ryan contends that daily practice is the key to her team's past successes during critical game situations.

"We act out late-game strategy consistently throughout the year," she says. "We try to recreate situations and are consistent with the way we deal with each late-game situation. The players are comfortable when they get into these situations because they already know what to do."

In summary, Coach Ryan is a proponent of mental preparation and believes that organization can be very helpful in mentally preparing the team for the upcoming season.

Each player is given a summer development program which has been very beneficial in getting the players both physically and mentally prepared for the grind of a long season.

Ryan utilizes her experienced players to a great extent when she prepares the team for specific opponents. She believes that the information the older players share with the younger players is very helpful in mentally preparing for certain opposing teams.

Finally, late-game strategy is practiced daily throughout the season. Ryan thinks that taking a consistent approach to late-game situations allows the players to gain the needed confidence to successfully execute late-game strategy during critical times in a game. This familiarity with strategy helps each player mentally prepare for the actual execution when it's needed, she concludes.

* * * * * * * * * *

...on Mental Toughness

Coach Ryan believes she has been very fortunate over the years in recruiting student-athletes whom she considers to be mentally tough individuals.

"I guess when a person decides to become a student-athlete at the Univeristy of Virginia, she comes into the program with the pre-conceived thought that she is going to have to work very hard on the court and in the classroom in order to be successful," she asserts.

Ryan has her own definition of mental toughness.

"Mental toughness is not allowing anything to distract you during the performance of your skill," she states. "It's the ability to block out disturbances and perform under adverse conditions, for example, shooting a foul shot away from home with fans screaming and arms waving."

The ability to block out disturbances and perform under adverse conditions are two characteristics of a mentally tough person. Ryan adds consistency and emotional stability to that list of traits.

"I believe that a player needs to be consistent in her effort and have an even-keel type of personality," she says. "The mentally tough person is not susceptible to emotional ups-and-downs."

In summary, Coach Ryan thinks that mental toughness is a trait of all highly-successful individuals. She feels fortunate that many of her Virginia players possessed the characteristic upon their arrival at Charlottesville.

She defines mental toughness as the ability to perform a skill without being distracted, in addition to the ability to perform well under adverse conditions.

Finally, Ryan lists consistent effort and emotional stability as two additional mental toughness traits.

* * * * * * * * * *

...on Communication

Effective communciation with staff and athletes during adverse game conditions is vital if the team is to be successful. Coach Ryan believes that the element of trust must be present among team members and coaches during this time period.

"At halftime and during critical moments in a game, we want to encourage the players and be very relaxed and upbeat with them," she begins. "At that point, they need your support and trust. If we as coaches trust that they will come through and the players read that feeling of trust in you, then in most cases, the players will execute successfully."

Post-game comments are extremely brief following a win or loss because coaches and players are too mentally drained at the end of games.

"I always reserve judgment for the day after," she says. "Players and coaches are both physically and emotionally too 'charged' to be receptive to many comments, win or lose.

"I usually keep my comments short and deal with the rest the following day. Many times you can be misinterpreted if you 'lecture' or make quick judgments immediately following a game."

In summary, Coach Ryan cites effective communication with staff and players as critical during adverse game conditions.

Halftime talks are kept very upbeat and positive with the players. She also says that coaches must convey a feeling of trust that the players will execute successfully when they need to during the game.

Finally, post-game comments are kept very brief. Ryan believes that game evaluation should wait until the following day because players and coaches are too emotionally charged after games and because post-game comments can be misinterpreted by players more easily immediately following a game.

* * * * * * * * * *

RICK SAMUELS

Eastern Illinois University

Position
Head Men's Basketball Coach

Career Record
149-142 (10 seasons)

Education
B.S.   1971 Chadron State College
M.Ed. 1975 Eastern Washington University

Team and Personal Highlights

* 1984-85 Eastern Illinois won 20 games and the Association of Mid-Continent Universities post-season tournament.
* 1981-82 Coach of the Year Award from AMCU; team tied for first place of the league.
* Long time member of the Research Committee of the National Association of Basketball Coaches.
* Three-year starter in basketball and senior co-captain at Chadron State College in Nebraska.
* Received an award senior year from Chadron State Booster Club for "Special Contributions to Athletics."
* Four-year starter in basketball and two-year captain at University High School in Laramie, Wyoming.
* Member of two state championship and one state runner-up teams during four-year high school career.
* Twenty-six of 31 basketball seniors have graduated during Samuel's 10 seasons at Eastern Illinois University.
* Developed NBA draft picks Kevin Duckworth of Portland and Jon Collins of Denver.

Rick Samuels

Introduction...

When Rick Samuels was growing up in Laramie, Wyoming, in the 1950's and early 1960's, about the only thing a boy could do was occupy his time the best way he could. Rick discovered that shooting a basketball was the most fun he could have. Little did he realize that one day he would be leading his own college basketball program.

Under the direction of Samuels, Eastern Illinois University basketball has become a widely respected, quality Division I program in the 1980's. With 139 victories and Association of Mid-Continent Universities coaching honors, the 41-year-old has made the Panther program into a consistent upper-division force within the AMCU.

Not only does Samuels extoll the on-court work ethic of his players, he says he is most proud of the player's results in the classroom. Twenty-six of 31 seniors who have played for Samuels at Eastern Illinois have graduated.

Samuels still carries legendary playing status at University High School in Laramie. He was a four-year starter and was named captain both his junior and senior years. His teams won two state championships and were runner-up one other time during his four years.

Graduating in 1967, he then accepted a scholarship to play basketball at Chadron State College in western Nebraska, a small NAIA school about 200 miles from Laramie.

His four years as a Chadron State Eagle were equally impressive. He was a three-year letterman and co-captain his senior year. The Chadron State Booster Club honored Rick with an award following his senior year for "Special Contributions to Athletics." He earned a Bachelor of Science degree in education in 1971.

Using his basketball status as a springboard, Samuels began his coaching career as head coach at Chadron High School in 1971. He stayed at the school for two years before heading to Eastern Washington University to work on a Masters degree in 1973.

He earned his Masters of Education degree from Eastern Washington in 1975 and promptly was named an assistant coach at the Cheney, Washington, school. After one year, he moved to Ames, Iowa, as an assistant basketball coach at Iowa State University.

From 1976-80, Samuels was a key member of the Cyclone coaching staff. Because of his successes at Iowa State, he was named head coach at Eastern Illinois in May, 1980.

It's difficult not to be a lady's man when Rick arrives home. Usually meeting him are his bevy of beautiful women who are also his biggest supporters: his wife, Jan, and their three daughters, 10-year-old Tiffany, eight-year-old Risa and six-year-old Kassie.

Possessing one of college basketball's "nice-guy" images, the low-key Panther coach was happy to have the opportunity to share his philosophy concerning the elements of successful team building.

Here are Coach Rick Samuels' thoughts...

...on Motivation

Motivation is a prime ingredient for success within all organizations. Coach Samuels believes that motivation must come from within the athlete himself on most occasions, but that an outside force can also be utilized.

"Motivation is an innate or an instilled desire to achieve," he says.

Motivating today's student-athletes is getting more difficult all the time.

"The outside pressures on the players are increasing every year," he says. "Besides the drug and alcohol problems that exist in society, our student-athletes must stay motivated to accomplish their academic goals as well."

Rick lists any form of negative behavior as least effective in motivating student-athletes.

"Fear techniques or any kind of punishment are not very effective when motivating athletes or anyone else for that matter," he says.

Because of his low-key approach to coaching, any form of contrasting behavior on Samuel's part usually results in some kind of motivational response from his players.

"I've found from experience that emotional arousals on my part has been an effective motivational technique," he states. "I don't use them all the time, but when I do, the players usually respond in a positive way."

Another motivational technique that Samuels says he utilizes concerns competitive challenges to the players.

"I call them competitive ploys. I will personally challenge a player or players or the team to outplay the opponents in certain areas of the game. The players have been most responsive to these types of challenges."

In summary, Coach Samuels defines motivation as an innate or an instilled desire to achieve. He thinks that athletes should be self-motivated most of the time, but adds that some motivational assistance from coaches may also help at times.

Finally, Samuels lists negative behavior in the form of fear techniques or punishment as least effective motivational methods. He mentions occasional emotional arousals and player challenges as the most effective methods for motivating his athletes.

* * * * * * * * * *

...on Team Cohesion

Team chemistry is a vital ingredient for ultimate team success, and Coach Samuels believes that team cohesion can make a good team into an even better team.

"If the players are truly interested in team success, then that team will reach its potential in most cases," he says.

Samuels defines team cohesion as a quest for common goals.

"Team chemistry is a unification of goals or directions," he states. "It's a personal caring for your teammates and wanting each teammate to succeed."

Building team cohesion in most cases calls for an attitude adjustment.

"When you recruit student-athletes, you hope that they agree with the concept that 'we' is more important than 'me'," he says. "Therefore, a positive group attitude is instrumental in building effective team cohesion."

He also says group success builds team cohesion.

"If the team has been successful, the players feel better about themselves, too," he says.

Outside group activities are the third method of successfully building team cohesion.

"We do several activities as a group." he begins. "We have team meals home and away. We might go to a movie together. Then there's study hall. We also might visit a hospital as a group or might participate in some other civic activity if time and schedules permit."

In summary, team cohesion is important for the overall success of a program. Coach Samuels believes that team chemistry means that players are unified in their goals and that players have a personal interest in the success of other teammates.

Effective methods of building team cohesion include developing a team attitude toward success, stressing a philosophy of "we" instead of "me."

Finally, Rick incorporates outside group activities to help build cohesion. Some of these activities include team meals for both home and away games, an occasional movie, study hall, or some civic activity which helps bond the team with the community.

* * * * * * * * * *

...on Discipline

Discipline is a trait of the championship team and individual, and Samuels ranks this trait at the top of his success list.

"Discipline is the single most important factor to success," he states.

Discipline embodies several ideas, he points out.

"Discipline is the will to prepare. Discipline is doing what you're expected to do, and discipline is doing something consistently."

Ironically, Samuels finds one-on-one, player-coach conversations the least effective way of dealing with a discipline problem.

"I just don't feel these kinds of discussions are productive," he says. "The results can be even worse if a player misleads the coach, nothing is done, and the other players know that the player got away with something. No one wins in a situation like that."

Effective discipline methods include rewards and encouragement.

"Effective discipline methods put the emphasis on correct techniques and attitudes," he states. "Rewards should be given for excellence in concentration and encouragement should be given for correct behavior."

In summary, Coach Samuels ranks discipline as the most important factor to success. He says that discipline means the will to prepare, the ability to meet expectations, and the ability to act consistently within team rules.

Finally, he believes that talking out a discipline problem with an athlete is the least effective discipline method. The most effective discipline methods include a coaching emphasis on correct methods and attitudes, rewards for concentration, and encouragement for correct behavior.

****

...on Mental Preparation

All successful coaches say that mental preparation is essential to team and individual success. Coach Samuels believes that mentally preparing for a game or season is a matter of focusing in the right direction.

"We focus on three elements in our mental preparation approach," he says. "The first element involves each player focusing on his role on the team. During player conferences early in the year, I sit down with the athlete and discuss what role will benefit the team and the player the most."

Motivation and intensity level are the other two elements that Samuels focuses on for mental preparation.

"We talk a lot about the internal motivation level of each player," he states. "How well a player executes, we think, is correlated to his self-motivation level."

"Finally, mental preparation is effective if the intensity level of the player is high. So our mental preparation approach focuses on those three elements: individual roles, self-motivation and intensity level."

Coach Samuels is quick to point out that mental preparation is an on-going process. His pre-season approach to mentally preparing the team for the grind of the long season has been effective.

"We have rotation days," he says. "We have days of practice away from a high intensity level. We go hard for three or four days, then we adjust practice so that the intensity level isn't as high. The players know the schedule and can adjust mentally."

Panther players are responsible for keeping notebooks during the season. Samuels believes that the notebooks keep each player focused and mentally ready for conference and non-conference games.

"We do have the players keep notebooks," he states. "The information in the books include not only technical information on opponents, but also inspirational thoughts or articles that we think may help the players during the course of the season.

"We also strongly utilize videotape of opponents or of ourselves to mentally prepare for games. And then the 'walk-throughs' before each game of the opponent's offenses and defenses also help us prepare mentally."

Samuels believes that late-game strategy must be practiced on a daily basis.

"We practice late-game situations every day," he says. "We also teach the players to incorporate mental visualization techniques in their pre-game preparation so they can replay the strategy in their minds.

"We also utilize a word stimulus during practice which allows the players to quickly understand what we want executed during a critical point in a late-game situation."

In summary, Coach Samuels is a proponent of mental training for his players. He defines mental preparation as the ability of each player to focus on roles, self-motivation and a high intensity level.

He utilizes rotation days during pre-season to allow players to mentally prepare for high-intensity practices. He rotates high intensity with low intensity practices, which he thinks helps the player through the grind of pre-season.

To mentally prepare for non-conference and conference games, Samuels has each player keep notebooks which contain opponent information in addition to inspirational thoughts or articles for self-motivation purposes. He also utilizes videotape and "walk-throughs" to further assist the players in their mental approach to each game.

Finally, Coach Samuels practices late-game strategy on a daily basis. To augment the players' mental preparation for each game, he teaches visualization techniques to his players and designates "word cues" to be utilized in late-game strategy situations.

* * * * * * * * * *

...on Mental Toughness

Mental toughness is a trait found in all highly-successful individuals. Coach Samuels defines mental toughness as an ability to overcome obstacles.

"Mental toughness is the mental ability to overcome let-downs and moments of defeat," he says. "I think it's also the ability to keep the mind and the will focused on the task through adversity."

Samuels believes that the mentally tough person is endowed with certain characteristics.

"The mentally tough player is resilient," he begins. "He can bounce back from a bad moment instanteously. Nothing affects him for a long period of time.

"The mentally tough person is highly competitive. He hates to lose and will do whatever is necessary to be successful.

"A third trait is intensity. A mentally tough person constantly battles his adversaries. He is relentless in his effort. He overwhelms his opponent with his drive.

"Finally, the mentally tough person is goal-oriented. They are always setting goals for themselves and then resetting goals when they've accomplished the first ones."

In summary, Coach Samuels defines mental toughness as the ability to overcome let-downs and to work through adversity.

Finally, he lists four characteristics of a mentally tough individual. Those traits are resiliency, competitiveness, intensity, and goal-oriented.

* * * * * * * * * *

...on Communication

Communication with staff and players during times of adversity is an important psychological factor within a program. Coach Samuels believes that a positive, consistent approach during these critical times is most helpful.

"During halftime or during timeouts late in a game when the outcome is uncertain, I think it's important to always give encouragement to the players," he says. "We always focus on the positive. But it is also important to be firm and consistent in your comments."

Samuels says that it is the responsibility of the head coach to show the players how they can be successful.

"We really must show the players the keys to success for that situation," Samuels says. "Those key elements are usually technical adjustments: rebounding, getting loose balls on the floor, or taking a charge."

He adds that the players must be reminded of similar circumstances in which the team was successful.

"It's important to illustrate technical adjustments with reminders of past recoveries and successes from similar circumstances," he says.

Post-game comments following tough losses or poor performances are handled in a consistent, low-key approach.

"Following a tough loss, we like to stress the positive aspects of the game," he says. "But we also think it's critical for the players to move on to the next opponent quickly and not dwell on the tough loss."

Comments following a poor team performance takes the same analytical approach.

"If the team has played poorly, we must quickly find out why," he states. "We will usually review our preparation methods, trying to find a flaw there. We also will detail the negatives of the performance with the players. Finally, we stress the need for change, either in attitude adjustments or game-preparation methods."

In summary, Coach Samuels believes that effective communication with staff and players during adverse times is very important to the success of the program.

Halftime talks or comments during late-game timeouts always stress the positive aspects of the situation and encouragement is always given to the players. Samuels thinks it is the responsibility of the head coach to make the key technical adjustments which can lead to victory.

Finally, post-game comments following a tough loss are positive in nature, with a final focus on the need for the team to begin looking at the next opponent. Comments following a poor team performance are firm and analytical. Details of the negative performance are reviewed, and the total preparation plans for that game are scrutinized to locate any flaw. The final comments indicate a need for change, either in player attitude adjustment or game-preparation methods.

* * * * * * * * * *

CURT SHOCKEY

Ralston High School
Ralston, Nebraska

Position
Head Baseball Coach
Social Sciences Teacher

Career Record
362 - 130 (8 seasons, Varsity and Legion)

Education
B.S. 1974 Kansas State University

Team and Personal Highlights

* 1988   American Baseball Coaches Association Midwest Coach of the
         Year Award; finalist for ABCA National Coach of the Year Award;
         Diamond Baseball District Coach of the Year Award; finalist for
         Diamond Baseball National Coach of the Year Award; Nebraska
         Baseball Coaches Association Coach of the Year Award; Nebraska
         State Baseball Champions.
* 1987   Nebraska State Baseball Champions; final national ranking of 30th in
         Collegiate Baseball Magazine; Iowa-Nebraska League Legion
         Champions.
* 1986   Nebraska State Baseball Champions; final national ranking of 27th in
         Collegiate Baseball magazine; Iowa-Nebraska League Legion
         Champions; Coach of the Year Award in Iowa-Nebraska League.
* 1985   Iowa-Nebraska League Legion Champions; national ranking of 23rd
         in *Collegiate Baseball* magazine.
* 1984   Iowa-Nebraska Legue Legion Champions; Coach of the Year Award
         in Iowa-Nebraska League.
* 1983   President of Nebraska Baseball Coaches Association; NBCA Coach
         of the Year Award; Iowa-Nebraska League Legion Champions;
         Coach of the Year Award in Iowa-Nebraska League.
* 1982   Iowa-Nebraska League Legion Champions; Coach of the Year Award
         in Iowa-Nebraska League.
*   Eleven All-state players.
*   Thirty players on college baseball rosters.
*   Published articles in *Inside Coaching*, *Collegiate Baseball* and
         Coaching Digest magazines.

Curt Shockey

Introduction...

Baseball has always been a big part of Curt Shockey's life. He's played it, taught it, watched it. Basically lived it for over 30 years. The dedication to the sport that he so dearly loves has been a driving force behind the phenomenal record of success he has built as baseball coach at Ralson High School in Ralston, Nebraska.

Since being named head coach in 1982, Shockey has established the Ralston Ram program as one of the premier baseball powers in the Midwest. A perennial contender for the state championships during both the Varsity and summer Legion seasons, Shockey has sent 30 former players into the college ranks, many of those going to Division I schools.

The championships and coaching honors began with his first varsity season. The Rams won the first of six consecutive Iowa-Nebraska Legion championships in July, 1982. Shockey was chosen Coach of the Year in the Iowa-Nebraska League that summer, and repeated that honor following the 1983, 1984 and 1986 seasons. From 1982-88, Ralston won over 85% of their regular season games in the Iowa-Nebraska League.

Ralston is one of only two teams to have won three consecutive spring state baseball championship, accomplishing the feat in 1986, 1987, and 1988. Shockey received Coach of the Year honors during that span from the American Baseball Coaches Association, the Nebraska Baseball Coaches Association, and Diamond Baseball. Twice he has been a finalist for National High School Baseball Coach of the Year awards.

The winning and honors have been non-stop: National rankings for the Ram team in 1985, 1986 and 1987, league Division titles, Invitational Tournament championships, District championships, and Area championships. But despite all the notoriety, Shockey remains unimpressed and maintains his philosophy that "you're only as good as your last game."

Born in Freeport, Illinois, on October 1, 1952, Curt played his way to stardom at Freeport High School. A three-year letterman on the baseball team, he was named All-State shortstop following his senior year in 1970.

Accepting a scholorship to play baseball at Kansas State University, Shockey was a standout for the Wildcats as a four-year letterman. Following his graduation in 1974, Curt joined the Wildcat staff as an assistant coach, concentrating on his role as a hitting instructor.

Shockey left Kansas State after one year to take a teaching and coaching position at Ralston High School in 1975. He was an assistant basketball coach in addition to assistant baseball coach for seven years before assuming the head baseball position in 1982.

A Social Science teacher, Shockey has been intrigued with the assassination of President John F. Kennedy since he was a young boy. He not only has an extensive collection of research notes and books on the subject, but teaches a course on the subject as part of his overall teaching assignment. He claims to be a coaching "disciple" of Gary Ward, the highly-successful baseball coach at Oklahoma State University. Ward's comments can be found in a later chapter of this book.

A writer of several technical articles in coaching publications, Curt is also a guest clinician at baseball camps nationwide. He aspires to return to college baseball coaching.

He and his vivacious wife, Shelley, are active members of Beautiful Savior Lutheran Church in Ralston. Curt also volunteers much time to Ralston community projects. They have two sons, nine-year-old Jason and seven-year-old Colin.

Combining a sincere and honest approach to life with a witty sense of humor, Shockey was extremely honored to have the opportunity to share his ideas on successful team building on the high school level.

Here are Coach Curt Shockey's thoughts...

...on Motivation

Motivation is a prime ingredient for success within all organizations, and Coach Shockey believes that today's high school student-athletes need constant reminders along those lines.

"Motivation is getting the players to do what they should already realize they need to do for success," he says.

Effectively motivating student-athletes is a difficult process for the high school coach. From experience, Shockey knows which motivation methods work better than others.

"Two methods are not very effective," he states. "First, yelling at the athlete just doesn't work. It's a totally non-productive method.

"The other least effective method is assumption on the coach's part. Assuming that the athlete is already motivated can backfire on you."

Shockey lists three methods for effectively motivating his athletes: organization, knowledge, and pride.

"I especially appeal to the players' pride," he says. "You need to make the players feel like they are a part of an on-going process of excellence with a past, a present, and a future. In other words, you tell them they are a part of a winning tradition."

Shockey thinks that being well-organized is another effective motivation technique.

"I feel that players are motivated when a coach is organized," he states. "An organized coach sends the message to the players that their time is not going to be wasted, and I think they appreciate that."

Coaching knowledge is the third effective technique for motivating today's student-athletes, he states.

"The players are motivated when a coach is knowledgeable and can explain <u>how</u> and <u>why</u> the team is doing something."

In summary, Coach Shockey defines motivation as getting players to do what they should already realize they need to do for success.

He contends that least effective motivation methods include yelling at the athlete and assuming that the athlete is already motivated.

Finally, Curt believes that appealing to a player's pride, being well-organized within the program, and being knowledgeable in the intricacies of coaching are the most effective motivation methods.

****

...on Team Cohesion

Ralston teams under the direction of Coach Shockey have demonstrated a distinct cohesiveness since his first day as head coach. Shockey believes that team cohesion is a vital ingredient for ultimate team success.

"Team chemistry occurs when each player understands his role and is willing to sacrifice personal glory for the good of the team," he states. "When the team wins, there is plenty of glory to go around."

Shockey stresses the importance of public praise for the "little" things surrounding successful play when he discusses effective methods for building team cohesion.

"I always make sure that the 'little' things get praised in front of everybody," he says. "For example, we praise players when they hit behind a runner or hit a cut-off man to keep the double play in order."

Shockey mentions some additional methods for building team cohesion.

"We have the players over to the house for a meal, or we'll go see a college game together. We've also had our players assist the younger players during our summer baseball camp," he states.

The key to successfully building team cohesion, he reiterates, is that all players are involved.

In summary, Coach Shockey lists team cohesion as an important element for building team success. He defines team cohesion as the ability of a team member to understand his role on the team, and to believe in the concept of "team."

Finally, methods and techniques for effectively building team cohesion include public praise of players who execute sound fundamentals, team meals, attending a college game together, and older players assisting the small youth during summer baseball camp.

****

...on Discipline

Discipline is the trait of the championship team and individual. Coach

Shockey believes that discipline is one of the most important aspects of team building. He also states that the players must understand the definition of term.

"Players need to realize that discipline is <u>not</u> punishment," he says. "It is necessary to show the players that team discipline puts us all on the same page."

Coach Shockey has strong feelings concerning discipline methods which are not effective when dealing with todays student-athletes.

"Disciplining a player in front of his peers or in public in general is a terrible way to handle a situation," he says.

Effective discipline methods combine player participation in the rules-making process with the privacy of a player-coach meeting.

"I've found that involving the players in making team rules has a very positive effect on team discipline," he begins. "Setting down team rules and then following them is most important. Of course, I must be expedient and fair with the players when administering the rules.

"Going behind closed doors to discuss any problem with the individual is highly effective," he says. "The player seems to appreciate the privacy of the matter, also."

In summary, Coach Shockey believes that team discipline is one of the most important elements of successful team building. He states that it is important for the head coach to help each player understand that discipline is not punishment.

Least effective discipline methods involve public reprimands of the players. He says that players react most unfavorably to discipline that occurs in front of their peers.

Finally, the most effective methods of dealing with disciplinary matters involves player participation in making team rules. Shockey contends that when the players help set the rules, they are then more likely to follow them. He also says that it is important for the head coach to act quickly and fairly once team rules have been compromised.

* * * * * * * * * *

...on Mental Preparation

Coach Shockey has been a strong proponent of mental training since he began coaching in 1974. Mental preparation can mean the difference between a victory or defeat as the season progresses. Shockey defines mental preparation as a process that has a beginning and an end.

"I believe that mental preparation is the ability to see yourself being successful," he says. "It's a process in which the body completes what the mind begins."

A high school baseball player in Nebraska begins practice for the spring season in February. There is no discernable break from the spring season to the summer Legion season. In essence, a high school basball player's season in a successful program like Ralston's can extend from February to late August, or a span of seven months. Shockey points out that a correct mental approach is needed to counter any staleness from the grind of both seasons.

"We give the players time off to rest," he begins. "But Nebraska weather in the spring is so unpredictable that it could postpone one game or half the season. So the grind isn't as bad as it sounds."

During a long stretch of season, Shockey stresses to his players that every day offers them an opportunity.

"We must make the players realize that each day of practice is an opportunity to master more of their game," he says.

Non-conference and conference games are prepared for in the same way, Shockey says. He also adds that the approach may seem a little unorthodox to some people.

"We emphasize with the players that you really play against the game and not the opponent," he states. "It doesn't matter who we play. How we execute will dictate the outcome of the game."

Ralston players utilize visualization techniques when preparing for critical game situations. Shockey claims that this element of game preparation is a perfect example of his theory that the body finishes off what the mind begins.

"We try to visualize all situations that could come up in the course of a game, including being behind late in the game," he says. "The idea is to have the feeling that 'we've been here before'."

In summary, Coach Shockey believes in the powers of mental training. He defines mental preparation as the ability to see yourself being successful. He asserts that mental preparation allows the body to complete what the mind begins.

During the course of a long season, Shockey constantly reminds the players that each day of practice is an opportunity for them to improve in every aspect of their game. The successful athletes are the ones who take advantage of those opportunities, he says.

Coach Shockey prepares his Ralston team for non-conference and conference games in the same way. He emphasizes that the players are actually competing against the elements of the game of baseball and not competing against the opponent. In this way, the players can prepare in a consistent manner without experiencing the emotional peaks and valleys associated with individual rivalries.

Finally, Coach Shockey utilizes visualization techniques when preparing the team for all game situations that involve strategy. These situations are practiced on a daily basis. It is Curt's belief that utilizing visualization techniques with physical practice will give the players the confidence in executing correctly when the actual event occurs during a game.

* * * * * * * * * *

...on Mental Toughness

Mental toughness is a characteristic found in all highly-successful players. Coach Shockey believes that mental toughness can be acquired, but that it takes a special individual to actually develop the trait on his own.

"A mentally tough player doesn't become a 'scared rabbit' when the situation gets tight," he says. "A player that is mentally tough believes in himself. He puts in the time and work before the big situation occurs so that he sees the situation as an opportunity to succeed, not as a chance to fail."

In addition to having self-confidence, Shockey lists two additional mental toughness traits.

"A mentally tough person is fearless," he states. "He takes calculated risks and is not afraid to fail.

"The third characteristic is aggressiveness. The mentally tough individual never lets up. He has a strong inner drive to succeed. And most of the time he does."

In summary, Coach Shockey believes that mental toughness is a trait that can be acquired, but that few people actually put in the necessary time or effort to develop the trait.

He defines mental toughness as the ability of a player to effectively handle adverse conditions. He believes that the mentally tough player prepares himself in advance of any critical situation, and views the situation as an opportunity to succeed.

Finally, Shockey mentions a high level of self-confidence, a fearless attitude, and aggressiveness as three characteristics of the mentally tough person.

* * * * * * * * * *

...on Communication

Communication with players and staff during the course of a game is an important psychological element. How the head coach effectively communicates his thoughts and strategy during critical game situations most often has a direct correlation to the actual outcome. Baseball does not allow for halftime talks, so Coach Shockey knows that what little time does exist for communication must be used efficiently.

"During critical times of a game, we remind the players that we have been in this situation before," he says. "Our visualization techniques have helped us prepare for this moment.

"We also tell the players to stay with the fundamentals and not try to do too much. We stress the concept of 'staying within your role'."

Post-game comments following a tough loss or a poor performance follow the same pattern, he says.

"We use the 'sandwich concept'. We start with the positive points of the game, then talk about areas where we didn't execute, and then we finish with a positive statement about working on our problems in the next workout."

After a poor performance, Shockey states that the head coach must be careful how criticism of the team is delivered.

"The coach must remember that you criticize the performance, but never the performer," he concludes.

In summary, communication with staff and players is a critical psychological element during the course of a game. Coach Shockey reminds his players during crucial game situations that they have prepared well for this moment, and to concentrate on the fundamentals and not do things they are not capable of doing. He mentions to each player the importance of "playing their role."

Post-game comments following a tough loss or a poor team performance are handled in identical fashion, he says. Shockey utilizes the "sandwich concept" in talking with his players. The "sandwhich concept" involves beginning a performance evaluation of the team with a positive comment followed by discussion of the problem areas. The final aspect of the "sandwich concept" involves another positive statement.

Finally, Shockey states that it is important following a poor team performance for the coach to be careful in how the team is criticized. He stresses that the coach should criticize the performance and never the performers.

* * * * * * * * * *

STU STARNER
University of Texas - San Antonio

Position
Head Men's Basketball Coach

Career Record
110-95 (7 seasons)

Education
B.S. 1965 University of Minnesota - Morris

Team and Personal Highlights

* 1987 Big Sky Conference championship at Montana State
University; National Invitation Tournament
appearance.

* 1986 Big Sky Conference Coach of the Year Award;
NCAA Tournament appearance.

* Richfield (MN) High School Teams were
Minnesota AA state tournament finalist in 1973
and 1974.

* All-Conference football and basketball player
at Hoffman (MN) High School.

* Three-year letterman in football and basketball at
the University of Minnesota - Morris.

Stu Starner

Introduction...

After seven years as head coach at Montana State University, Stu Starner was named the new head men's basketball coach at the University of Texas - San Antonio in April 1990.

Departing his beloved Northwest and Glacier National Park country, Stu was captivated by the opportunities presented in the Lone Star State. Ponderosa Pines, Western meadowlarks and Bitterroot have been replaced by pecan trees, mockingbirds, and Bluebonnets. The serenity and scenic brilliance surrounding Bozeman has been supplanted by Old World Spanish architecture, the Alamo, and a pulsating Southwestern metropolis bursting with civic pride. The former Bobcat is now a Roadrunner, and he arrived with his running shoes on.

Leaving Montana State as the third all-time winningest coach in the history of Bobcat basketball, Starner's record of success impressed President Samuel A. Kirkpatrick of UT - San Antonio.

"Our men's basketball program is entering a new stage of its youthful development that will be characterized by strong, positive leadership and vision from an accomplished professional, " said Kirkpatrick. "Stu Starner is an excellent coach who is held in high esteem by his associates and peers from across the country, and who sets high standards for student-athletes and his coaching staff."

Starner's exciting brand of basketball helped fill the stands in Bozeman, and athletic administrators hope that trend continues at the Convocation Center in San Antonio.

"We are very pleased to have someone of Stu's ability as our new head coach," said UTSA Athletic Director Bobby Thompson. "He's been successful wherever he has gone as a coach and his many years of coaching experience will certainly give our program the stability it needs to be successful for years to come."

When Starner was named head coach at Montana State, the basketball program had enjoyed only three winning seasons since 1970. The last four years the Fighting Bobcats have gone 71-46 and appeared in one NCAA Tournament, while hosting an NIT game in 1987. Starner was named Big Sky Conference Coach of the Year in 1986.

Starner was born in Hoffman, Minnesota, a small town about 100 miles southeast of Moorhead in the west-central part of the state, on April 8, 1943. He was a multi-sport star at Hoffman High School, earning All-Conference honors his senior year in both football and basketball before graduating in 1961.

He received a scholarship to continue playing at the University of Minnesota-Morris, and was a three-year letterman in both football and basketball. He graduated in 1965 with a bachelor's degree in physical education and social studies.

Starner began his coaching career that fall at Wabasso (MN) High School where his teams compiled a 48-16 mark in three seasons. He then moved to the state's largest high school, Richfield, as an assistant coach for two years before taking over as head coach in 1971. In seven years at Richfield, he compiled an impressive 102-54 record that included Minnesota AA State Tournament runner-up finishes in both 1973 and 1974.

In 1978, Starner decided to make the move to the collegiate ranks and became a part-time assistant at the University of Minnesota where his primary responsibilities were game preparation and recruiting. He spent one season at the Big Ten school before making his first move to Montana State in spring of 1979 as an assistant coach.

Before being named head coach at MSU, Starner returned to the University of Minnesota as a full-time assistant in 1981. As a member of the Golden Gopher's staff, Starner helped the Big Ten team to one conference title and berths in both the NCAA and NIT Tournaments. He then returned to MSU as head coach in 1983.

The outgoing, jovial Starner is a popular motivational speaker at business and educational meetings. He is also active in Special Olympics and service clubs. A veteran of summer basketball camps and clinics, Starner is currently serving as a member of both the Recruiting Committee and Converse Clinic Committee of the National Association of Basketball Coaches.

Stu and his wife Barbara, an accomplished watercolor artist, have three children: daughters Susan and Jane, and son Tom.

The humorous and articulate Roadrunner's coach welcomed the opportunity to share his ideas on the psychology and strategy of successful team building.

Here are Coach Stu Starner's thoughts...

...on Motivation

Motivation is a prime ingredient for success within all organizations, and Coach Starner believes an organized system is most helpful in motivating today's student-athlete.

"When the players see that the program is well-organized and runs smoothly, it gives them a motivational lift," he says.

Starner states that a consistent approach must be taken by the head coach.

"A consistent plan must be utilized so that the student-athletes know the expectations, guidelines and philosophy of the program," he says.

Starner lists four effective methods of motivating the student-athlete.

"I think that goal setting is at the heart of any motivation program," he begins. "Without goals, you really have no focus."

"Complementing a goal setting program is an evaluation system in which the player and coach can chart the progress of the player throughout the season.

"A third effective motivation technique is scheduling individual conferences with players. These conferences are highly effective because you can discuss not only basketball, but academics, career and life in general. And I really enjoy talking with players in a relaxed, private atmosphere.

"The final motivation method I've found to be effective is the use of self-evaluations with the players. It is a tremendous learning experience for the player to honestly assess his progress and come to his own conclusions on how he is going to handle a situation. Self-realization is the best learning tool for all of us."

In summary, Coach Starner believes that organization is the key to motivation. He says that the head coach must have a consistent plan so that student-athletes understand the expectations, guidelines and philosophy of the program.

Finally, he lists four methods of effectively motivating today's student-athletes. These methods include goal setting, a system of evaluating goals, individual player-coach conferences, and player self-assessment procedures.

* * * * * * * * * *

...on Team Cohesion

Team cohesion is a vital ingredient for ultimate team success. Coach Starner believes that team cohesion starts during the recruiting process.

"Team chemistry is really just the ability of all the players to get along and focus on our team goals," he says. "You try to locate those team-oriented players during the recruiting process."

Starner does not foster the belief that successful teams need to be together off the court in order to be successful.

"We don't have camp-outs or team functions," he says. "Sometimes it seems like we're together too much."

Starner asserts that player selection and goals are two important elements in building team cohesion.

"I think player selection has a lot to do with it," he begins. "You've got to have people who have good values and goals. We try to establish who are the leaders of the team. If we can identify two of them, then we try to bring the team together through the leadership of those two players. For some reason, we've been very fortunate in this regard."

In summary, Coach Starner states that team cohesion is an important element for ultimate team success. He defines team chemistry as the ability of the players to get along and focus on team goals instead of individual goals.

Starner says that the recruitment process is the ideal time to begin building team cohesion. He believes that the head coach must recruit players with good values and goals.

Finally, Starner builds team cohesion by identifying the one or two players on the team who are considered leaders among their teammates, and bringing the team together through the dynamics of these individuals.

* * * * * * * * * *

...on Discipline

Discipline is a trait of the championship team and individual. Coach Starner believes that discipline and expectations are closely linked.

"Discipline is a common understanding of expectations," he states.

Least effective discipline methods involve changing the rules for the players, Starner says.

"It's not very effective that when you have players with different personalities, you use different individual approaches to discipline.

"A coach has enough trouble with one set of team rules. You start making up new discipline rules for each player, and you're hurting yourself and the players. Creative discipline is good; multiple disciplinary methods are bad."

Effective disciplinary methods are simple in nature and represent the feelings of the team.

"We have team rules and the players have a part in making those rules," he says. "But the bottom line is that the team is more important than the individual. So when a player's behavior is detrimental to team progress, it's time for a change."

In summary, Coach Starner believes that discipline is a trait of successful individuals. He defines his philosophy on team discipline as a common understanding of team expectations.

He mentions that least effective discipline methods involve using multiple disciplinary approaches to match the personality of each player. Any kind of multiple approach can be most harmful to the team, he says.

Finally, the most effective discipline methods involve team participation in the rules-making process and a consistent administration of team rules by the head coach. He also mentions that the team is more important than the individual. Therefore, when a player's actions are detrimental to team progress, it is time for a change in that player's attitude.

* * * * * * * * * *

...on Mental Preparation

All successful coaches say that mental preparation is essential to team and individual success. Coach Starner believes that mental preparation is again a matter of knowing expectations.

"Mental preparation is a process in which the student-athletes understand what is expected of them and then to prepare for all the variables," he says.

Mentally preparing the team for the grind of a long pre-season and then the non-conference and conference schedule is a difficult task.

"The season is long enough," he states. "Six weeks of practice can be an eternity. And if the team is not playing very well for an extended period of time, the total experience can be disheartening for the players and staff."

Focusing on team and individual goals and telling the players what to expect and prepare for are the most effective mental preparation techniques, Starner says. But he adds another important facet of mental preparation.

"We think it's important to mentally condition the players for travel," he says. "Some players have never been on a plane before, and the time zone changes can affect a person in funny ways. So many times, as we prepare for an opponent, we're also mentally preparing for the flight and conditions associated with the trip."

Starner says that the degree of success of late-game strategy is closely tied to the commitment to practice for critical situations late in a game.

"We practice late-game situations every day," he says. "If we don't, the players will not become confident in what we want to accomplish when that situation arises.

"Some teams feel they don't need to practice late-game strategy because they feel they have the athletes who can execute from a chalkboard play. But at Texas-San Antonio, we're committed to practicing these situations because if we don't, we're not going to be successful when the time comes."

In summary, Coach Starner defines mental preparation as understanding expectations. He says that once expectations are known, then all the variables associated with the expectations can be identified and given adequate preparation time.

Mentally preparing for the grind of pre-season practices and the non-conference and conference schedule is an on-going process, he says. Focusing on team and individual goals is the best mental preparation technique. Starner also adds the importance of mentally conditioning the players for travel as crucial to the overall mental preparation process.

Finally, late-game strategy is practiced daily. Coach Starner believes that daily practice of critical game situations assists the athletes in building confidence in the execution of the strategy when it occurs during a game.

* * * * * * * * * *

...on Mental Toughness

Mental toughness is a trait found in all highly-successful individuals. Coach Starner says that he would like to observe mental toughness traits in all Roadrunner players, but realizes that request is not totally realistic.

"Wouldn't it be great that when you recruit a player, you would know his mental toughness quotient or something to that effect before you sign him?" Starner asks. "But in actuality, you don't know how mentally tough a player is until you've had him in your program for a period of time."

Starner lists three characteristics of a mentally tough person.

"First of all, a mentally tough player is very alert," he begins. "He is very aware and observant of everything that is happening. So alertness is one characteristic.

"A mentally tough player is also a quick thinker. By that I mean a player has the ability to make correct decisions instantly on the court.

"The third characteristic of a mentally tough player in my estimation is consistency of performance. A player who is mentally tough performs at a high level every day during practice and in every game. You can expect him to be good all the time and he doesn't disappoint you.

"So alertness, the ability to make correct decisions, and consistency of performance are my three traits of the mentally tough person."

In summary, Coach Starner believes that mental toughness is a trait found in the highly-successful individual. He says his ultimate goal is to fill his roster with excellent student-athletes who are also very mentally tough.

Finally, he lists three characteristics of the mentally tough player. They include alertness, quick and correct decision-making, and consistent, high-level performance.

* * * * * * * * * *

...on Communication

Communication with staff and players and effectively dealing with adversity are important psychological factors for the success of the program. Coach Starner believes that effective communication within the program and job security are closely linked.

"One aspect of being a head coach on the Division I level is a responsibility to establish a communication system within and without the program," Starner says. "We communicate with the players and staff within the program in specific ways, and we deal with the media and the public in a professional manner. If communication lines break down in either setting, that's when the head coach experiences some problems."

Effectively communicating with the players during halftime or during time-outs late in a closely-contested game can mean the difference between winning and losing.

"The head coach must establish a plan for these situations early in the season," he says. "The players must have an understanding of how the head coach will respond to these situations, and they must have confidence in his approach."

Halftime is a period for technical adjustments, not inspirational messages.

"At halftime, we basically make any adjustments that need to be made offensively, defensively, or personnel-wise," Starner says. "If we need to inspire the players during a game, then we're probably in trouble. If we have to constantly inspire our players during the duration of a season, then we're probably in big trouble."

Coach Starner's post-game comments are extremely brief in nature, with game evaluation taking place later.

"We have a one-minute wrap-up after a game, win or lose," he states. "After careful evaluation of the game film, we make our game comments to the players, usually at practice the next day. It's important to save any critical comments for later so that you have the actual game film to justify your comments."

In summary, Coach Starner has a strong belief in the theory that communication skills are extremely important for a head coach and that any breakdowns in communication within a program can possibly have an effect on job security.

Halftime talks and late-game timeouts deal strictly with technical adjustments. He adds that the head coach and the program are in for rough times if some type of motivational message from the coach is needed during games or throughout the season on a continual basis.

Finally, post-game comments are kept very brief following a victory or defeat. Coach Starner says that it is best for the coaching staff to view game films before evaluating player performance. The day following a game is the most efficient time for the head coach to comment on game performance because he can justify his points of emphasis with actual game film. He adds that waiting the extra day to evaluate performance gives the head coach the necessary time to carefully formulate his thoughts before addressing the team.

* * * * * * * * * *

PAT SUMMITT
University of Tennessee

Position
Head Women's Basketball Coach
Associate Athletics Director

Career Record
475-117 (16 seasons)

Education
B.S. 1974 University of Tennessee-Martin
M.S. 1975 University of Tennessee-Knoxville

Team and Personal Highlights

* 1990 Southeastern Conference regular season championship;
NCAA East Regional Finalist.
* 1989 NCAA National Championship; NCAA Regional
Championship; Southeastern Conference Championship;
Naismith Coach of the Year Award.
* 1988 NCAA Final Four appearance; NCAA Regional
Championship; SEC Championship.
* 1987 NCAA National Championship; NCAA Regional Championship;
Naismith Coach of the Year Award.
* 1986 NCAA Regional Championship; Final Four appearance.
* 1985 SEC Championship; NCAA Regional appearance.
* 1984 NCAA Regional Championship; Final Four finalist; U.S. Women's
Olympic Basketball Coach.
* 1983 NCAA Regional finalist; Coach of U.S. World Championships team.
* 1982 NCAA Regional Championship; Final Four appearance.
* 1981 Association for Intercollegiate Athletics for Women (AIAW) Final
Four finalist.
* 1980 AIAW Final Four finalist; SEC Championship; Assistant Coach of
U.S. Women's Olympic Basketball team.
* 1979 AIAW Final Four appearance; U.S.A.'s Coach in Jones Cup, World
Championships, and Pan American Games.
* 1978 Number One ranking in final AIAW poll.
* 1977 AIAW Final Four appearance; Coach of first U.S. Women's Junior
National team.
*   Co-captain of 1976 Olympic basketball team, and member of 1975
World Championships team, 1975 U.S. National team, 1975 Pan
American Games team and 1973 U.S. World University Games team.

Pat Summitt

Introduction...

The great state of Tennessee can boast about its place in history, its stunning natural beauty, and its famous citizens.

More Civil War battles were fought in Tennessee than in any other state except Virginia. The state has several national military parks including Shiloh, near Savannah, Fort Donelson near Dover and Cumberland Gap near the Virginia-Kentucky border in northwestern Tennessee.

Almost half of the Great Smoky Mountains National Park lies in Tennessee. In all, Tennessee maintains 51 state parks and 13 state forests. Mockingbirds flock the state, irises can be found in abundance, and tulip poplars point majestically to the heavens, enhancing the landscape

Three Presidents of the United States-Andrew Jackson, James K. Polk, and Andrew Johnson-all distinguished themselves in Tennessee. Two great heroes of the Texas Revolution, Davy Crockett and Sam Houston, grew up in Tennessee and served its people.

But when you talk to the folks around Knoxville, they speak proudly of their own native daughter, that active little girl that grew up in Henrietta, about 60 miles northwest of Nashville.

Pat Summitt, the 37-year-old coach of the University of Tennessee women's basketball team, has stayed in her home state to build a hoop dynasty that has become a model of consistency and class among the nation's elite women's athletic programs.

Summitt was an international competitor in women's basketball as a player before she became nationally known as a coach. In 1973, she made her first U.S. national team when she represented the United States at the World University Games in the Soviet Union.

Four games into her senior season in 1974 at the University of Tennessee-Martin, Pat suffered a near career-ending knee injury. One year later, after successful rehabilitation, she earned a playing spot on the U.S. National team that competed in Taiwan and was a member of the 1975 Pan American Games team that won the gold medal. In 1976, she was a co-captain of the silver medal-winning Olympic team.

When Summitt graduated from UT-Martin in 1974, she symbolized the prototype player of the 1980's. She was strong, had great instincts, was awesome on defense, took a charge like it belonged to her, denied the ball all over the court, rebounded with authority, took the ball to the hoop, and then could shoot the lights out over a zone defense.

Her reputation for tenacity and integrity during her undergraduate career impressed the athletic brass at the University of Tennessee-Knoxville. Understanding her desire to earn an Olympic playing berth and confident in her abilities as a coach, the school offered her a graduate teaching assistantship and the reins to the women's intercollegiate basketball team as a 22-year-old.

The position was ideal. It allowed her to pursue her career and stay close to basketball while rehabilitating her knee.

In her first year as a college coach, she led her team to a 16-8 overall record, attended classes as a Master's degree candidate, taught physical education classes, and stayed in playing shape. She also tested the repaired knee thoroughly, earning berths on the World Championships and Pan American Games rosters.

After another summer of international experience abroad, she returned home to coach her Lady Vols to a 16-11 record, a second-place finish in the state tournament and a spot for herself on the 1976 U.S. Olympic team.

No other basketball coach in the country, male or female, has enjoyed the success of Summitt. Her career record of 475-117 includes a 412-113 mark on the college level and 63-4 on the international level. She has won 80 percent of her games in her 16-year career.

A celebrated figure in women's athletics, Summitt is busy off the court as well. She presently holds the following positions: associate athletics director at the University of Tennessee; USA BASKETBALL Council member; Vice President (women) of USA BASKETBALL; member of the Women's Games Committee of USA BASKETBALL; a member of the Board of Trustees and the Executive Board of Directors of the Basketball Hall of Fame; member of the Valvoline Sports Advisory Board; and member of the Target Board of Directors.

Coach Summitt has worn many hats during her career - commencement speaker, color commentator for CBS-TV, clinician, contributor to a film series, and both author and subject of books.

Away from the game, she has been a member of Big Brothers-Big Sisters and was the honorary chair for the Tennessee Easter Seal Society in 1985 and 1987. She is still active as an alumni with the Chi Omega sorority. When she can fit it into her schedule, she enjoys running, water and snow skiing, and racquetball.

The 1970 graduate of Cheatham County High School in Ashland City, Tennessee, is married to R.B. Summitt. They live in Seymour, Tennessee.

The hard-working and highly-personable Lady Volunteer coach was most gracious and accommodating when discussing her ideas on the psychology and strategy of successful team building.

Here are Coach Pat Summitt's thoughts...

...on Motivation

Motivation is a prime ingredient for success within all organizations, and Coach Summitt believes that inner drive and goals play a big part in the self-motivation process.

"Motivation is harnessing an inner drive and pointing it toward the attainment of a specific goal," she says.

Motivating today's student-athletes can be a difficult assignment, but Summitt contends that bringing the right person into the program negates much of that problem.

"We look for quality people to represent Tennessee," she states. "That's staff and players included. When you get good people, you have a strong base to work from."

Summitt says that some motivation techniques are not very effective.

"The least effective techniques are gimmicks or temporary tactics, such as newspaper articles, threats or bribery," Summitt says. "Those kinds of methods just aren't productive."

Effective methods of motivation include all techniques that develop self-motivation.

"The most effective techniques are those which enhance self-motivation," she points out. "The techniques can help develop intensity in the player, they can improve work habits, and they can assist the athlete in maintaining a high level of expectations."

In summary, Coach Summitt defines motivation as harnessing an inner drive and pointing it toward the attainment of specific goals. She adds that self-motivation is enhanced when quality persons are brought into the program, both as players and staff members.

Least effective methods of motivating today's student-athletes include techniques that bring only temporary results, she says. Those tactics include newspaper articles, threats or bribery.

Finally, Summitt states that the most effective methods of motivation enhance player self-motivation. These individualized techniques help the player to develop intensity, improve work habits and maintain a high level of expectation.

* * * * * * * * * *

...on Team Cohesion

Team chemistry is a vital ingredient for ultimate team success. Coach Summitt believes that team cohesion can be developed through leadership and trust.

"I would say that I'm the type of coach that would rely heavily on strong leadership from players," she says. "From our strong base of quality people, we look for strong leaders and I believe that leadership has been extremely valuable to us."

A feeling of trust is also important, she states.

"With players and coaches, I think you have to have trust," she says "You have to trust the players on the floor and you have to trust your assistant coaches."

Summitt characterizes team cohesion as a process involving several elements.

"In order to build team chemistry, you first need to identify individual strengths and weaknesses of the team," she begins. "Players must also recognize and accept their roles on the team. Finally, a plan must be developed for how each individual must respond on and off the court to help the team reach its goals."

Summitt believes that utilizing team leadership and incorporating total player involvement in the rules-making process are the best methods of building team cohesion.

"When you have strong leaders like we do, you learn to delegate responsibilities," she says. "We expect our team leaders and players to identify our team goals and then design a code of conduct to help us achieve these goals. When all players have input in determining team rules, there is a strong commitment to uphold that code."

In summary, Coach Summitt believes that team cohesion can be developed through leadership and trust. She also states that team cohesion includes identifying individual strengths and weaknesses, recognizing individual roles, and committing to a plan for team behavior on and off the court.

Finally, effective methods of building team chemistry involve utilizing player leadership skills and incorporating all team members in making team rules. A code of conduct for the team should then be designed and implemented.

* * * * * * * * * *

...on Discipline

Discipline is a trait of the championship team and individual. Coach Summitt claims that discipline is at the heart of her coaching philosophy.

"Certainly we are a disciplined program," she says. "We are very proud of our discipline. We view it as a positive that we do have discipline. I think the expectation that we have in our student-athletes to accept responsibility for themselves and represent Tennessee is important.

"By establishing discipline, we feel like we're all working toward the same goal, that we have a plan and a guideline for getting there. We're not going to move away from it."

Summitt's approach to discipline has remained the same over the years.

"Be firm, fair and consistent," she states. "Be honest and have open communication at all times."

Inconsistency is the coach's worst nightmare when dealing with team discipline.

"Inconsistent discipline can be detrimental to the team and also ineffective individually," she says.

Effective disciplinary procedures involve peer pressure and consistent application of the rules.

"The most effective discipline happens when the team helps to establish the policies or team rules," Pat states. "Peer pressure can be a very effective form of discipline.

"Each coach must also use their own style or philosophy and remain consistent in disciplinary actions."

In summary, Coach Summitt lists discipline as a top priority within her program. She believes that student-athletes at Tennessee accept the responsibility of representing the university and state in a positive manner.

Summitt's philosophy concerning team discipline has remained steady over the years. She says that the head coach must be firm, fair, consistent and honest during all communication with players.

Ineffective discipline methods are a result of inconsistent administration of the rules by the head coach. She adds that inconsistency can harm the individual as well as the team.

Finally, Summitt states that effective discipline methods include player participation in making team rules, peer pressure, and consistent disciplinary action by the head coach.

* * * * * * * * * *

...on Mental Preparation

All successful coaches say that mental preparation is essential to team and individual success. Coach Summitt believes that mental preparation begins with a basic understanding of team philosophy.

"Mental preparation is a basic understanding and knowledge of our team's system, both offensively and defensively," she says. "Knowledge and repetition are elements of good mental preparation."

Summitt states that goal setting is imperative during pre-season practices.

"The long pre-season practices can wear you down, no doubt about it," she says. "Therefore, we use goal setting to a great extent during this time. The process involves daily goal setting and long-range goal setting."

Mental preparation for non-conference and conference games is similar.

"For both non-conference and conference games, our mental preparation is the same," she begins. "We discuss and review keys for success in each game. It's then up to the individual players as to how they respond to each challenge."

Late-game strategy can lead to victory, and Summitt mentally prepares the team for all possible scenarios.

"We create various late-game situations in practice," she says. "Very rarely do we ever run a play late in a game without first having gone over it in practice."

In summary, Coach Summitt is of the belief that mental preparation is effective when each player has a basic understanding and knowledge of the team's offensive and defensive philosophy.

Mental preparation for the grind of pre-season practice includes daily goal setting sessions in addition to long-range goal setting, she says.

Repetition of key elements for success in each game enhances the mental preparation process for non-conference and conference games, she adds.

Finally, late-game strategy is practiced daily so that the players are confident when the situation occurs during a game.

* * * * * * * * * *

...on Mental Toughness

Many people believe that mental toughness is a trait found in highly-skilled athletes. Coach Summitt begs to differ with that type of thinking.

"I do not totally agree that all highly-skilled athletes are mentally tough," she states. "It's not something you're born with. It's something you have to develop on your own."

She mentions that a mentally tough person reacts favorably to adverse conditions.

"I believe that the mentally tough person has the ability to concentrate and successfully perform in adverse or pressure situations," she concludes.

In summary, Coach Summitt believes that some great athletes are not mentally tough. She asserts that mental toughness is not inherent in players, but must be developed like all other fundamental skills.

Finally, Summitt says that the mentally tough person is able to concentrate and perform well in all pressure situations.

* * * * * * * * * *

...on Communication

Effective communication with staff and players is an important psychological factor for the success of the program. Coach Summitt has always been a strong advocate of open communication with her players and staff.

"As I've mentioned before, open, honest communication is the most important element in building trust within the program," she says. "The head coach must take the leadership role in establishing an open communication policy."

Halftime comments and comments during timeouts late in a game in which the team is losing are positive in nature, she says.

"During these times in a game, we encourage them not to give up and assure them they can still win," Summitt says. "We also give them the needed technical changes in offense or defense that may turn the game around in our favor."

Post-game comments following a tough loss or a poor performance will vary, depending upon the outcome and other factors.

"My post-game response to the players depends on our effort and execution," she says. "I try to evaluate why we lost or performed poorly and respond accordingly."

In summary, Coach Summitt believes that open, honest communication within the program has a positive psychological effect on the players and staff.

Comments at halftime or late during a game in a losing cause will be positive in tone. She says it is important to encourage the players at all times and assure them that they will be successful if they keep working hard. Technical adjustments in offensive and defensive strategy are also made during this time.

Finally, post-game comments following a tough loss or poor team performance will vary, depending upon the outcome of the game and effort and execution
exhibited by the players. She says that it is important to evaluate <u>why</u> the team lost
or performed poorly and respond accordingly.

* * * * * * * * * *

SCOTT THOMPSON

Rice University

Position
Head Men's Basketball Coach

Career Record
29-54 (3 seasons)

Education
B.A. 1976 University of Iowa

Team and Personal Highlights

* 1990   Assistant chairman of the Rules Recommendation Committee of the National Association of Basketball Coaches.
* 1987   Member of USA BASKETBALL Olympic Selection Committee.
* 1986   Assistant Coach of U.S. National Team that participated in World Championships.
* 1976   All-Big Ten selection; Academic All-Big Ten team; NCAA post-graduate scholar; team captain and Most Valuable Player Award at the University of Iowa.
*   Third draft pick of Detroit Pistons following senior season.
*   One-year tour as a player with Athletes in Action.
*   In 12 years of major college coaching, has been associated with nine NCAA championship tournaments, including a Final Four appearance in 1978 while at Notre Dame.
*   Recruited and coached 21 student-athletes that have played in the NBA.

Scott Thompson

Introduction...

Scott Thompson is a prototype of the college basketball coach of the 1990's: hired to build a competitive program; young, confident, polished in public relations and recruiting; committed to graduating his student-athletes; very positive and upbeat in dealing with his players, and schooled in nationally-prominent programs. In essence, a modern-day renaissance man, a man with a mission.

Having been groomed for major college coaching by Digger Phelps at Notre Dame and Lute Olson at Arizona, Rice University's third-year coach has dedicated himself to improving the level of basketball played at the school, as well as creating more popular interest.

In a short period of time, he has exceeded expectations in both areas.

The Owls have succeeded in the initial stages of Thompson's mission after doubling their overall and Southwest Conference win totals in 1988-89 to 12 (12-16) and six (6-10) from 1987-88's six (6-21) and three (3-13).

Team and fan interest have climbed dramatically as well. Rice's Autry Court has been dubbed the "Jungle Gym" by opposing teams and attendance figures have increased over 30 percent since Thompson's arrival at the Houston school.

But Thompson realizes the team's momentum has just begun and that a great deal more force is necessary to achieve the ultimate goal: A rendezvous with the nation's elite collegiate basketball programs.

"We've improved in each of my three seasons here," says Thompson. "But you can't be satisfied with just improving. We want to be successful by not only Southwest Conference standards, but by national standards as well."

At 36 years of age, Thompson is the youngest head coach in the Southwest Conference, but he is no stranger to winning programs. He arrived at Rice in April, 1987, riding a wave of success after helping three of the country's most prestigious and respected basketball programs, Notre Dame, Iowa, and Arizona to Final Four appearances.

"Rice reminds me a lot of the University of Notre Dame in that it's a small private school, and it's a very special school because not everyone can get in," Thompson says. "Rice is very attractive because it offers a fabulous education.

"The program also reminds me of the situation we first encountered at the University of Arizona. The program was struggling, but we recruited good athletes and quality people, established the program, and eventually won the Pac-10 championship."

After serving on Digger Phelps' Notre Dame staff for three years, during which time the Irish earned a Final Four berth in 1978, Thompson joined Lute Olson at his alma mater, the University of Iowa, in 1980. He later went with Olson to rebuild the University of Arizona program. The Wildcats participated in the NCAA tournament during three of Thompson's four years at Arizona, winning their first Pac-10 championship in 1985-86.

Thompson was born on May 27, 1954, in Belleville, Illinois, the oldest of four children of Herb and Ann Thompson. A quietly determined youngster, Scott quickly developed into a top student-athlete under the tutelage of his father.

Herb Thompson was an All-State basketball player at Forest City High School in Forest City, Iowa. He became a basketball standout at the University of Iowa in the early 1950's, being chosen the Hawkeyes' captain and most valuable player his senior season.

After graduation in 1953, Herb Thompson began a highly-successful coaching career in Iowa, first going to Waverly, and then in 1959, to Mason City. In 1964, he moved the family to Moline, Illinois, to take the reins of the basketball program at Moline High School.

Scott became a star athlete at Moline High School, running track and playing basketball for his father. He was named an All-State basketball player in Illinois following both his junior and senior seasons.

After graduating in 1972, he followed in his father's footsteps to the University of Iowa, accepting a scholarship to wear the Black and Gold of the Hawkeyes and becoming one of Iowa's all-time greats.

Like his father, Thompson was the Hawkeyes' team captain and most valuable player his senior season. One of the Big Ten's leading scorers, he earned all-Big Ten honors in 1976. He was an academic all-Big Ten selection and an NCAA post-graduate scholar. He was the third pick of the NBA's Detroit Pistons and spent a year touring with Athletes in Action before embarking on his coaching career.

The ebullient Thompson is a frequent speaker at banquets, civic meetings and alumni gatherings, selling the Owl basketball program to the people of Houston and the state of Texas. He also volunteers much time to charitable organizations and activities. He is assistant chairman of the Rules Recommendation Committee of the National Association of Basketball Coaches.

Thompson and his wife, the former Rebecca Goulder, have a son, Christian Scott, born on August 1, 1989.

A very sincere and open person, Scott was happy to share his ideas on successful team building.

Here are Coach Scott Thompson's thoughts...

...on Motivation

Motivation is a prime ingredient for success within all organizations, and Coach Thompson understands the importance of motivation within a team whose members are primarily very young in age and lack the experience of playing major college athletics.

"Nine of our 12 players this past season were either freshmen or sophomores," he says. "In addition, 90 percent of our scoring came from these same sophomores and freshmen. In our case, the youth of our team contributed in a positive way to our overall level of motivation."

Thompson defines motivation in terms of drive and determination.

"Motivation is the ability to set out and accomplish a particular task with as much drive and determination one can acquire," he states.

Thompson believes that consistent motivation techniques are effective whether the team includes younger players or more mature student-athletes.

"Sometimes it seems younger players are more naturally enthusiastic than the veteran players," he says, "but that's not necessarily always true.

"I think the way to keep players motivated is through a consistent approach and not gimmicks or methods that only give short-term results."

Least effective motivation techniques include excessive negative criticism and public and personal ridicule.

"The least effective motivation methods involve some kind of negative behavior," he says. "Those methods would include excessive negative criticism from the coach or cutting the player down in front of his teammates. Those kinds of techniques can be very destructive with the players, especially the young person just getting a start in major college basketball."

The most effective motivation method is simply keeping a focused, constructive approach with the players at all times.

"Our coaching staff is very young for a major college program," he says. "The best motivation approach we have always taken with the players is the same approach that worked the best when we are playing: consistent constructive reinforcement.

"The coaching staff is young enough that we still relate well to the feelings of the players. As in all teaching environments, we criticize when it is needed. But our criticism is always constructive.

"Plus, you have to be very patient and nurturing with freshmen and sophomores when introducing them to big-time college basketball. It's a slow maturation process. Therefore, constructive reinforcement is the best motivation method, no matter what the age and experience level of the team."

In summary, Coach Thompson believes that motivation is the ability of the player to set goals and accomplish a task utilizing drive and determination in the process. He also states that a consistent approach to motivation has long-term benefits whereas motivational gimmicks only result in short-term effectiveness at best.

Least effective motivation techniques include excessive negative criticism and disparaging remarks to the player in front of teammates.

Finally, Thompson states that the best motivation method is keeping a focused, constructuve approach with the players at all times. He contends that a coaching staff that empathizes with the feelings of the players is instrumental in developing self-motivation traits among the players.

...on Team Cohesion   * * * * * * * * * *

Team cohesion is a vital ingredient for ultimate team success. Coach

Thompson believes that team chemistry is one of the most important elements when building a team with many new faces.

"Some of our guys have now been playing together two or three years," he says. "We've always been a tightly-knit group, and it's even more important to develop team chemistry when the bulk of the team is made up of underclassmen."

Thompson brought a definitive team-building style with him from his former mentors.

"Lute's programs and Digger's programs always stressed a 'family' approach to the team," he points out. "I've tried to incorporate a spirit of 'family' within the Rice program. It seems to be working out well for us."

Thompson defines team cohesion as a blending of player unselfishness with team goals.

"Team cohesion or team chemistry means that each person is working together for a common goal, not trying to outdo themselves or their teammates," he begins. "It's a unification of individuals into machine-like precision."

The most effective methods of building team cohesion involve placing individuals in team roles and allowing the players to participate in some decision making for the team.

"First, you must place the individual players into their appropriate roles," he asserts. "It's very important that each player accept his role.

"Next, use as many 'team' types of situations you can for various things. For example, allow the players to make some decisions, such as which restaurants to eat at on the road. Involve them in these 'team' kind of activities. All of these responsibilities help build team chemistry."

In summary, Coach Thompson is a strong proponent in the belief that team cohesion has a great impact on ultimate team success. He defines team chemistry as a joint effort of all players to put team goals ahead of personal gratification. He also believes that team chemistry can assist the team in reaching a machine-like precision in its execution on the court.

Thompson says that establishing a "family" atmosphere within the program is important in building team cohesion. A "family atmosphere reinforces an attitude of openness and caring among the players, coaches and support personnel.

Finally, the most effective methods of building team cohesion include defining player roles and promoting player participation in various aspects of team decision-making.

* * * * * * * * * *

...on Discipline

Discipline is a trait of the championship team and individual. Coach Thompson believes that discipline begins with the actions of the head coach.

"I think that team discipline must be consistent and appropriate," he states. "The punishment must fit the crime.

"But I strongly believe that the head coach must lead by example in this area. Self-discipline on the head coach's part can be demonstrated to the players through promptness to meetings, never being late, or being hypocritical in word or actions."

Least effective discipline methods are a result of an overabundance of rules.

"A coach that has so many set rules is really setting himself up for a problem," Scott says. "When you have a large number of rules, loopholes can be constantly found."

The most effective discipline methods involve player participation in setting team rules.

"Any time you have rules which are set by the players, you have a better chance of the players policing themselves," he states. "Putting some of the responsibility for discipline upon the shoulders of the players makes it more personal for each player and draws the team together in the process. However, the coaching staff makes the final decisions on all discipline matters."

In summary, Coach Thompson believes that championship teams and individuals are very disciplined in their actions. He also states that it is the responsibility of the head coach to be a role model in this area. He adds that the punishent must fit the crime and that the head coach must be consistent in dealing with team discipline.

The least effective methods of discipline are a result of too many team rules. Thompson says that an overabundance of set rules allows players to constantly find loopholes, which undermines the entire discipline process.

Finally, the most effective method of discipline involves player participation in making team rules. Thompson believes that allowing players to make team rules strengthens the commitment of each player to adhere to the rules they have established. However, the coaching staff makes the final decision regarding all discipline matters.

* * * * * * * * * *

...on Mental Preparation

All successful coaches say that mental preparation is essential to team and individual success. Coach Thompson believes that the degree of commitment to mental preparation is a responsibility of the head coach.

"Mental preparation means taking the necessary time for each player to mentally place themselves in every situation they are about to encounter." he says. "The head coach must dictate the amount of time to be spent on mental preparation during practices."

Thompson designates the 15-minute stretching period before practice as the time for each player to mentally prepare for all aspects of that day's practice session. The technique most often utilized by the players is visualization."

"Fifteen minutes is a reasonable amount of time for the players to have the opportunity to mentally prepare themselves for practice," he states. "It's a quiet time, which makes the atmosphere conducive for visualization and mental preparation."

Mental preparation for non-conference and conference games takes similar paths.

"We go over each scouting report and tell the players what to expect," he points out. "The players understand that all games lead to an NCAA bid. It's important that the players understand they need to play hard, intelligently and together in order for us to be successful."

Late-game strategy is practiced daily for the sole purpose of building self-confidence in the players, Thompson says.

"We practice late-game situations for the positive reinforcement it gives our players during a game," Thompson says. "The players know that we've drilled every situation about to occur in a game daily in practice. That builds confidence, and self-confidence allows the players to correctly execute in a game."

In summary, Coach Thompson believes that mental preparation is essential to team and individual success. He states that the head coach is responsible for allocating the necessary time for each player to mentally prepare himself before practice.

Thompson designates the 15-minute stretching period prior to practice as the time for mental preparation. At this time, players use visualization techniques to ready themselves mentally for all aspects of that practice session.

Mental preparation for non-conference and conference games is similar, he says. Proper explanation of the scouting reports in addition to specific strategy for each opponent assists in each player's mental preparation for a game. The ultimate team goal for each game is to play hard, with intelligence and cohesion, he states.

Finally, late-game strategy is practiced daily. The main reason is to build self-confidence in the players so that when the actual situation occurs during a game, the players will be confident in executing the strategy.

* * * * * * * * * *

...on Mental Toughness

Mental toughness is a trait found in most highly-skilled athletes. Coach Thompson believes that mental toughness is more apparent in some players, but is also a trait that can be learned.

"I think that some young people naturally are more mentally tough than others," he says. "But I do think that a person can develop the trait over a period of time if he works at it."

Thompson defines mental toughness as successfully dealing with adversity and he list two characteristics of a mentally tough person.

"Mental toughness is the ability to succeed throughout all adversity," he states. "First, the mentally tough individual is aggressive. He is very assertive in his actions to get what he wants from life.

"The next trait is confidence. Mentally tough people feel they can accomplish anything they set out to do. They don't flaunt their self-confidence, but they certainly do not back down from any challenge, either."

In summary, Coach Thompson believes that mental toughness is a trait of highly successful individuals. He also contends that mental toughness may be naturally more apparent in some poeple, while others may need to work hard to develop it.

Finally, he lists two characteristics of mental toughness. Those characteristics are an aggressive, assertive nature and a self-confidence that openly accepts all challenges.

* * * * * * * * * *

...on Communication

Communication with athletes and staff and effectively dealing with adversity are important psychological factors for the success of a program. Coach Thompson believes that spontaneity can be very helpful during this time.

"At halftime or during timeouts late in a game that we may be losing, there is no one set strategy that we use to inspire the team," he says. "Different things are used at different times, not one planned strategy. Spontaneity is critical, however."

Halftime or late-game comments usually involve technical adjustments and possibly an exhortation to the players.

"The technical adjustment offensively or defensively is usually a key element of strategy here," he states. "I may also challenge the players to exert more energy, though."

Post-game comments are handled in a consistent fashion, win or lose.

"Consistency is the key to post-game comments," he points out. "We try to be the same after wins and losses."

Thompson also believes it is best to evaluate the game films first before discussing the specific aspects of the game with the players.

"Let things sit for a while," he contends. "Then, after looking at the films, deal with the game and the players in practice the next day. This extra time allows you to take notes and organize your thoughts."

In summary, Coach Thompson believes that effective communication with players and coaches during times of adversity is crucial for the overall success of the program.

During halftime or late-game timeouts during a losing cause, Thompson believes that technical adjustments are a key aspect of the strategy, but also says that spontaneous inspirational comments can be effective at this time.

Finally, post-game comments are kept very brief and the content of each post-game evaluation is consistent in nature, whether the Owls win or lose. Thompson says that game films should be evaluated before player evaluation statements are made. He suggests waiting until the following day at practice to discuss specific aspects of the game with the team.

* * * * * * * * * *

GARY WARD
Oklahoma State University

Position
Head Baseball Coach

Career Record
856-269 (19 seasons)

Education
B.S. 1963 New Mexico State University
M.S. 1968 New Mexico State University

Team and Personal Highlights

*   Second-winningest coach percentage-wise among active
    NCAA college baseball coaches.
*   Midwest Region Coach of the Year Award seven con-
    secutive years (1980-87) from American Baseball Coaches
    Association.
*   Ten Big Eight Conference championships.
*   Seven NCAA Regional Tournament championships.
*   Seven consecutive College World Series appearances from
    1981-87, the only baseball team in NCAA history to
    accomplish this feat.
*   Nine NCAA Regional Tournament appearances.
*   Two national junior college baseball championships at
    Yavapai Junior College (1975 and 1977).
*   Forty-six All-Big Eight players at Oklahoma State.
*   Twelve All-America players, including Robin Ventura,
    the 1988 Golden Spikes Award winner, signifying the top
    amateur baseball player in the nation.
*   Founder and director of Mid-America All-Star School, one
    of the finest baseball schools in the nation for the young
    player.
*   Developer of two instructional baseball videos: "The Hitting Machine"
    and "125 Advanced Techniques and Drills for the Hitting Machine."
*   Teams have average 51 victories per year during the Ward era at
    Oklahoma State University
*   Sixty-seven players drafted into professional baseball.

Gary Ward

Introduction...

The name Gary Ward has now taken on legendary status at Oklahoma State University. Upon recording his 500th win at the Stillwater school in 1987, Ward joined the legendary Oklahoma State basketball coach Henry P. Iba as the only coaches in school history to win more than 500 games in their careers. With 616 career wins at Oklahoma State and 856 wins overall heading into the 1990 season, Coach Ward's team building skills have never been more evident.

Beginning his 13th season, the 49-year-old Cowboy coach continues to produce league championships, NCAA Regional championships, College World Series appearances, academic and athletic All-Big Eight and All-America players, and Major League draftees.

Of the 17 Big Eight baseball titles won by Oklahoma State, 10 of those have been under Ward's direction. Over his previous 12 years at the helm, Ward has had 67 players drafted professionally, which is more than 74 percent of the 90 Oklahoma State players drafted by the major leagues since 1958.

Ward is one of only two college coaches with less than 13 years experience on the major college level to be ranked among the Top 50 Division I baseball coaches in terms of victories. He was at the helm when Oklahoma State recorded its 1,000th school baseball victory with a 1-0 win over Baylor on March 8, 1982 at the Pan American Classic in Edinburgh, Texas.

Ward has sent many proteges to the Major Leagues, including Texas' Pete Incaviglia, Detroit's Mike Henneman, Cleveland's John Farrell, Chicago Cubs' Doug Dascenzo, and Baltimore's Mickey Tettleton, Jim Traber and former Oriole Gordie Dillard. Both Tettleton and Henneman were named to the 1989 American League All-Star team.

He also became the first coach in school history to have one of his players earn amateur baseball's most prestigious honor when Robin Ventura was named the 1988 Golden Spikes Award winner.

Ward was the driving force behind the construction of Oklahoma State's Allie P. Reynolds Stadium, a facility that ranks among the best in the nation. The $2.2 million structure, which opened in the spring of 1982, features seating for 3,000, a $200,00 major-league lighting system and has played host to six NCAA Regional Tournaments. National and regional telecasts have been staged on a regular basis at Reynolds Stadium since Ward arrived on the scene.

Ramona, Oklahoma, a small town about 25 miles north of Tulsa, was where Gary was born on September 9, 1940. He became a multi-sport star at Ramona High School, lettering three years each in basketball, baseball and track. Upon graduation in 1958, Ward accepted a basketball and baseball scholarship to Northeastern Oklahoma A & M junior college in Miami, Oklahoma. After graduating with an associate degee in 1960, Ward accepted a scholarship to continue playing basketball and baseball at New Mexico State University in Las Cruces.

After playing two years of baseball and one year of basketball, Ward's college eligibility ran out in 1962. He stayed at New Mexico State one more year, coaching the freshman basketball team and assisting with the baseball team as a graduate assistant before earning a Bachelor of Science degree in education in May, 1963.

That fall, he returned to Oklahoma to continue his teaching and coaching career at tiny Collinsville High School, a 30-minute drive to the southeast from his hometown of Ramona. He was varsity baseball, varsity basketball, and assistant football coach at Collinsville until 1969.

Yearning to return to college coaching, Ward was named head baseball and assistant basketball coach at Yavapai Junior College in Prescott, Arizona, in June, 1969. During his seven years at Yavapai, Ward's Roughrider teams posted a record of 240-83 and won national junior college championships in 1975 and 1977. Following the 1977 championship, Ward was chosen to lead the Cowboy baseball program at Oklahoma State.

Highly respected among his peers, Coach Ward has developed two instructional baseball videos and is a frequent speaker at coaches clinics nationwide. He is also one of the most popular motivational speakers in Oklahoma, bringing his message of excellence in education and athletics to thousands of students around the state. Ward and his wife Kathy are the parents of three: Sherry, a senior at Stillwater High School, and adult sons Rocky, a former Cowboy player, and Roger.

Characterized as an intense competitor with a professorial approach to the game of baseball, Ward was very articulate in discussing the psychology and strategy of successful team building.

Here are Coach Gary Ward's thoughts...

...on Motivation

Motivation is a prime ingredient for success within all organizations. Oklahoma State baseball players have been highly motivated over the years to accomplish team goals. Coach Ward feels fortunate that the highly-motivated student-athlete has found his way to Stillwater.

"We've had the privilege to have outstanding gentlemen play baseball and get their education at Oklahoma State," he says. "You really can't be successful without having the right people in your program."

Ward believes that each person has a specific reason for doing the things they do.

"Motivation is simply a motive to act or take action," he says. "Each person knows what motivates him best."

Ward says negative coaching behavior or extrinsic rewards are not effective motivation techniques.

"Pain or punishment inflicted by the coach is not an effective motivation method," he states. "Incentive motivation has only short-term effectiveness, also."

He adds that too many coaches take a negative or short-term approach to motivating their athletes.

"Pain, punishment and incentives are overused by most persons in authority," Ward says.

The most effective motivation methods involve educating the student-athlete to ideas and techniques that build motivation.

"The best motivation method is providing a positive education that results in self-motivation of each athlete," he says. "That includes teaching performance enhancement skills to the players and keeping the atmosphere very positive throughout the program."

In summary, Coach Ward defines motivation as an individual's personal motive to act or take action. He believes that negative coaching behavior in the form of pain or punishment is a very ineffective motivation method. He includes the utilization of extrinsic rewards as motivation techniques that result only in short-term effectiveness.

Finally, Ward states that the most effecitive motivation methods are those in which each athlete can continually build his level of self-motivation. Therefore, providing a positive education base for each athlete is best in gaining these results, he says.

* * * * * * * * * *

...on Team Cohesion

Team cohesion is a vital ingredient for ulitmate team success. Coach Ward believes that much of the Cowboy's success over the years can be attributed to team chemistry and he gives the credit to the players.

"Our players have shown a tremendous amount of respect toward each other and the coaching staff," he says. "With those qualities, you can build a highly-cohesive team."

Ward is a strong believer in the theory that team cohesion is built around player acceptance of his role on the team.

"Team cohesion is built and strengthened through the understanding and acceptance of his role as defined by the coach for today and the immediate future," he states.

Ward adds that team chemistry is a result of the sensitivity demonstrated by the players.

"Leadership skills and qualities are developed by a sensitivity to other's needs."

Coach Ward effectively builds team cohesion through the utilization of player seminars, which are conducted in January and February preceding the start of each season. These are no ordinary seminars.

"Since I'm a strong believer in educating the player in all facets of his life, our winter seminars are developed to accomplish a number of things," he begins.

"For approximately 20 hours during January and February, our players are exposed to a performance enhancement program. During this time, we discuss motivation, formulate team goals, develop leadership characteristics, and learn mental training skills.

"It is a very thorough program that our players have enjoyed and utilized not only in their baseball lives, but in their academic and social lives as well."

In summary, Coach Ward believes that team cohesion is a vital ingredient for ultimate team success. He defines team cohesion as the ability of a player to understand and accept his role on the team as outlined by the coach. He also stresses the fact that sensitivity among teammates is needed if team chemistry is to be realized within the context of the baseball program.

Finally, the most effective method of building team cohesion is the development and implementation of a pre-season player seminar in which motivation, team goals, leadership training and mental enhancement skills are discussed and incorporated into each player's program.

* * * * * * * * * *

...on Discipline

Discipline is a trait of the championship team and individual. Coach Ward agrees that team discipline is needed in order to attain the level of excellence the team expects.

"Team rules are substitutes for thought," he states. "Discipline is the result of properly-motivated players who understand their role."

Ward mentions four specific areas in which self-discipline is needed.

"Our players need to be self-disciplined in a social context," he says. "We do not tolerate behavior of our players off the field that will cast a negative impression upon the player and our program.

"The next area that requires self-discipline is that of thinking like an opponent. We want our players to compete aggressively, but fairly and within the rules of the game. If something unfortunate happens to an opponent within the context of the game, for example, not executing a squeeze bunt or not successfully bunting a teammate along, we don't want our players to show delight in the opponent's demise because it can easily happen to them. So our players must show restraint during these incidents.

"A third area in which self-discipline is needed is among peers. We want our players to be well-accepted within the student body. Therefore, it is important that our players are respectful of students, teachers and adminstrators on campus.

"Finally, we want to see evidence of self-discipline among team members. we ask that all players keep a positive approach and tone when addressing each other. This kind of self-restraint also builds team unity."

Coach Ward understands that some discipline methods are more effective than others.

"I believe that the least effective discipline methods involve celebrating with the victory and punishing in defeat," he states.

The opposite approach is the best method of handling team discipline problems.

"The most effective means of team discipline is to reverse the above reaction to success and failure as a coach," he says. "Be somewhat critical when they win and ease off when they lose."

In summary, Coach Ward believes that discipline is a trait of championship teams and individuals. He also states that team rules are substitutes for team thought.

Ward contends that players must demonstrate self-discipline within four specific areas: in a social context, as an opponent, with peers and with fellow team members.

Finally, he states that the least effective method of discipline a coach can utilize is to celebrate with the victory and punish the players in defeat. The most effective method of discipline, he says, is just the opposite: criticize in victory and ease off in defeat.

* * * * * * * * * *

...on Mental Preparation

All successful coaches say that mental preparation is essential to team and individual success. Coach Ward has long been a proponent of combining mental training skills with physical practice.

"Practicing physical skills is essential, but it will not result in top performance on a consistent basis," he says. "Also, practicing only mental training skills without physical practice will not result in a consistent peak effort.

"But combining the two elements gives the players an opportunity to establish a consistent, peak performance every time they step on the field."

Mentally preparing the team for the grind of a long season and for non-conference and conference games is the total responsibility of the head coach.

"When you talk about preparing the players for the grind of the long season and for conference and non-conference games, you're really talking about knowing the psychological make-up of every individual on your team," he concludes.

"As a head coach, you must react to all the variables of competition as they occur, appraise their influence on your players and react accordingly."

Mental preparation for late-game strategy is an on-going process, Ward says.

"We discuss many of these situations during our winter seminars with the players," he says. "Once practice and the season begin, we review these critical game situations during each practice session.

"If the players are familiar with what we want accomplished and have the needed confidence to execute properly, we know we will be successful if and when that situation occurs during an actual game."

In summary, Coach Ward believes that mental preparation is an important ingredient for team and individual success. He says that combining mental training skills (goal setting, relaxation, visualization) with physical practice gives the player the best opportunity to produce a consistent, top performance every time he steps on to the field.

Ward claims that the head coach needs to know and understand the psychological make-up of each of his players in order for mental training to be effective. He says that the head coach must be ready to react to all the variables during a game, appraise their influence on the players, and react with the proper strategy.

Finally, mental preparation for late-game strategy is an on-going process. Ward states that late-game strategy is discussed during his winter seminars with the players and that each situation is practiced daily on the field throughout the season.

* * * * * * * * * *

...on Mental Toughness

Mental toughness is a trait found in all highly-successful individuals. Coach Ward believes that a mentally tough player can carry a team to victory, but that coaches rarely find those kinds of players in large numbers.

"I wish you could recruit only the mentally tough person," he says. "But there's really no way of knowing the mental toughness level of the players until you've had them in the program for a while."

Ward connotes mental toughness with a desire to succeed.

"For a mentally tough player, their 'fear of failure' is not greater than their 'desire to succeed'," he states.

Ward mentions three traits of the mentally tough individual.

"First, a mentally tough player is a self-motivated player with a desire to succeed as his focus," he says.

"Next, the mentally tough player can push back his 'personal discomfort zone' when he is under pressure.

"Finally, the mentally tough player takes personal responsibility for his performance.

"If a person can demonstrate those characteristics, then that's mental toughness!"

In summary, Coach Ward defines mental toughness as the ability of a player to make a "desire to succeed" a bigger priority than a "fear of failure" in his life.

Finally, Ward lists self-motivation, performance under pressure, and personal responsibility as mental toughness traits.

* * * * * * * * * *

...on Communication

Communication with staff and players is an important psychological factor within a program. Effective communication is even more vital during times of adversity during games.

"Late in a game if we are behind, it is my responsibility to communicate my thoughts on what strategy I think will be most beneficial at this time," he states. "Preparation is really just the need to review individual and team goals."

He points out that preparation must take place before the beginning of a game.

"If the players don't understand the goals by game time, then call your local realtor, because it doesn't look too good at that point in time," he says.

Post-game comments following a tough loss or a poor performance are handled in the same delicate manner.

"After losing or playing poorly, each player and coach need to accept personal responsibility for the shortcomings of the performance," he asserts. "This is not a time to rationalize the defeat or poor performance or point the finger at specific individuals."

In summary, Coach Ward believes that effective communication is an important psychological factor within the program. Comments dealing with late-game strategy need to be conveyed in a positive manner by the head coach. He also stresses that all game preparation takes place before the actual contest, and not during it.

Finally, post-game comments following a loss or poor performance are handled forthrightly and in a responsible fashion. Ward says that following a tough loss or a poor team performance, each player and coach must accept personal responsibility for the shortcomings and that rationizing and finger-pointing are not appropriate coaching behaviors at this time.

* * * * * * * * * *

THE FINAL ANALYSIS

The Final Analysis

From the insights gained from each chapter, it is obvious that highly successful coaches use a variety of psychological methods and techniques to achieve their goal of building winning teams. Perhaps not surprisingly, many of the methods are very similiar and differ only to the extent that each coach adds his or her unique touch to the way the technique is employed in his or her sport.

It is the purpose of this final chapter to attempt to collectively gather the ideas and spirit of the coach's comments into a generalized summary for each team building section. Here is the final analysis...

...on Motivation

The coaches defined motivation in a variety of ways, but the central idea was always the same. In general, the coaches defined motivation as a process in which the team or individual strives to accomplish a goal or goals.

The motivation process usually involves the efforts of both the player and the coach. However, many of the coaches stated that the motivation process is, or should be, the sole responsibility of the student-athlete. The successful student-athlete the coaches said, is usually the person who has a strong inner drive for perfection, both in the classroom and on the athletic field.

The methods vary, but the coaches said that the most effective approach when motivating student-athletes is to be positive and upbeat at all times. Research has proven that if a positive approach is taken to any situation, a positive response often results. Every coach reinforced that theory when discussing effective motivation techniques.

In contrast, least effective motivational methods involved negative coaching behavior. Least effective motivational methods included any form of yelling, intimidation, or public reprimand of the players, the coaches said.

To illustrate athlete reaction to negative coaching behaviors, one only has to read the accounts of several Division I basketball programs during the 1989-90 season that experienced player boycotts because of what the athletes claimed were negative, harsh treatments of the players by the coaching staff. Drake University and Arkansas State are two examples. In the Drake case, the head coach was fired and the entire staff dismissed.

The message is getting loud and clear to coaches on all levels: Treat the players with respect and use a positive approach in the motivational process. Or it could cost you your job.

* * * * * * * * * *

...on Team Cohesion

Team cohesion or team chemistry was claimed by the coaches to be one of the most important elements of successful team building. A few of the coaches stated that team cohesion was their top priority in building and maintaining a winning team.

The coaches defined team cohesion or team chemistry as an attitude that the team was more important than the individual. Dale Brown, the head basketball coach at Louisiana State University, sums it up best when he says "the 'we' is more important than the 'me'."

The coaches were in general agreement as to the most effective method of building team cohesion. They said that in order to build and maintain team chemistry, it is important for the head coach to establish a "family" atmosphere throughout the program. This "family" attitude needs to be evident among the coaching staff and all support personnel, they said.

In order to build team chemistry, many coaches expressed the need to establish a personal relationship with each student-athlete. Others stated that open communication lines must be maintained at all times. But the majority agreed that an environment fostering a caring, "I-want-to-help-you-become-a-successful-person" attitude is the most effective method for building team cohesion.

Finally, the coaches listed numerous team building activities. But one common theme threaded its way through the description of the activities: In order to build team cohesion, it is imperative that all team members are involved in team activities. There can be no differentiation between the stars and the starters or the substitutes and second-teamers. Everyone participates; no one is excluded.

* * * * * * * * * *

...on Discipline

The coaches expressed similiar thoughts when discussing discipline within their programs. They considered themselves to be disciplinarians to some extent, and they stated their belief that each player must be self-disciplined in order for the team to experience long-term success.

The coaches mentioned several discipline methods which they stated were ineffective. The methods most frequently mentioned included public embarrassment of the player, physical punishment, and inconsistent enforcement of team rules.

Public embarrassment was defined as a result of a coach harshly criticizing a player in front of his peers or a coach talking negatively about a player with the media.

Physical punishment was defined as extra conditioning, performed either before or after practice or early in the morning.

Finally, inconsistent enforcement of team rules by the head coach causes many problems, the coaches said. Any kind of double standard in which the head coach treated the star player differently from the rest of the team often had a direct negative effect on team cohesion.

Effective team discipline was enhanced when the players participated in the rule-making process. The coaches stated that when the players helped establish team rules and the penalties associated with breaking the rules, they were more likely to follow and enforce the rules they had made. The coaches also added that, in many instances, the players would set stricter rules for the team than the coach would have established. Peer pressure is also one of the best methods of ensuring team discipline, the coaches related.

In essence, giving the players the responsibility of making and enforcing the rules seems to be an effective method of maintaining team discipline. However, the players must realize that the head coach possesses the ultimate authority when making the final decision concerning team discipline policy.

* * * * * * * * * *

...on Mental Preparation

The coaches asserted their belief that mental preparation is very important when preparing for competition. But they had different ways of addressing mental preparation.

Some coaches said that they utilize sport psychology consultants to assist them in mentally preparing their teams, while others said they themselves teach performance enhancement techniques to their players.

Other coaches said that even though they believe in the idea of mental training, they have no formal mental skills training for the players. Finally, some coaches expressed their belief that the athlete is ultimately responsible for his or her own mental preparation.

The coaches stated that there are several methods that can be used to psychologically nurture a team along during the grind of a long season. One method includes innovative practice sessions where drills are rotated and new drills are incorporated so that feeling of staleness is eliminated or lessened.

Another effective method is to establish a practice schedule during the pre-season in which four or five days of hard work is followed by one day free of practice or practice of a less strenuous nature.

The majority of the coaches said that they prepare the same way for conference and non-conference opponents. The basic routine is to view opponent films or decipher scouting reports, establish a game plan, organize practices to work on the game plan, and build the confidence of the players so they feel they will be successful during the game itself.

Finally, the coaches stated that late-game success is a result of hours of practice covering all possible late-game scenarios. The coaches were adamant in their belief that only through practicing late-game strategy can you build the confidence level of the players.

They also said that even though late-game success is often the result of individual player heroics, the team or individual was successful because the players were confident in the strategy they had practiced and performed their roles to perfection.

* * * * * * * * * *

...on Mental Toughness

Since the coaches provided such a tremendous amount of diverse definitions of mental toughness, there can really be no generalized summary of the term. One idea was universally shared, however, and that was the thought that mental toughness is not a trait that each person is born with, but rather is a trait that the student-athlete developes as he or she matures within the athletic experience.

As can be expected, the coaches listed numerous characteristics of a mentally tough person. Without divulging all of them, there were some traits mentioned more often than others. Those traits included enthusiasm, competitiveness, an undying will to win, supreme self-confidence, emotional stability, relentless effort, consistency in performance, and the ability to focus on the positive aspect of a situation.

* * * * * * * * * *

...on Communication

Each coach expressed the belief that communication within the program is both highly desirable and most necessary if long-term success is to be maintained.

Many of the coaches said that they incorporated an "open door" policy concerning communication. This policy was established to reinforce the "family" atmosphere and to subconsciously tell each student-athlete that the coach's door is always open to them to discuss anything that is on the player's mind.

The majority of the coaches stated that they maintained open lines of communication with each player through the use of regularly-scheduled player-coach meetings. These meetings were usually scheduled not only during the season, but during the off-season as well. The coaches who utilized these meetings said that both the player and coach were very satisfied with the results of each meeting.

The meetings, the coaches said, involved goal setting and player evaluation. However, some coaches mentioned that many meetings involved discussions of topics outside the athletic domain. The most important factor surrounding player-coach meetings, the coaches pointed out, was the fact that each player was made to feel that he or she could freely express an opinion without fear of retribution from the coach.

Communication with the athletes during halftime or crucial times late in the game were handled in similar fashion by the coaches. Halftime talks and late-game strategy sessions generally contained technical adjustments followed by a positive, confidence-building statement. Very rarely, the coaches said, did they resort to some kind of emotional appeal to the players to raise their level of performance.

Post-game comments varied, depending upon the outcome of the game or the performance level of the players. Generally speaking, the coaches said that their comments to the team following a tough loss were positive and empathetic in nature. They stated that it was important to keep the comments positive because the players felt badly enough about losing the game. Following a victory, many of the coaches said that they will mix criticism with praise.

Some coaches said that they keep post-game comments to a minimum, regardless of the outcome. A few mentioned that they wanted to see the films of the game before making any kind of evaluative statement to the team.

Finally, the coaches were in strong agreement concerning comments following a game in which player performance was poor because of what the coach perceived as a lack of effort. The comments, generally speaking, were highly critical, and in some instances, caustic and profane.

The coaches admitted that these post-game dialogues are occasionally delivered in a booming voice with some added histrionics. However, they quickly caution the coach to refrain from criticizing individual players during post-game comments.

Critical remarks toward one or more players during post-game remarks can cause irreparable harm, they said. The only time to mention the performance of individual players during post-game comments is after a victory.

About the Author

Steve Brennan, a former teacher-coach on the secondary and collegiate levels, has Masters degrees in Educational Administration and Sport Psychology from the University of Nebraska-Lincoln. In addition to speaking at coaching clinics nationwide, he conducts corporate seminars in motivation, goal setting and stress management. Besides conducting the Mental Edge Clinic, his one day mental training workshop for coaches and student-athletes, Steve has developed a one-day mental training corporate seminar entitled "The Mental Edge Clinic for the Corporate Athlete."

Brennan has been employed by professional basketball scouting services, published numerous articles in professional journals, received teaching and coaching awards, and has spoken at international, national and regional educational and psychological conferences.

Steve is also a listed contributor in *The Basketball Bible*, has research material at the Naismith Basketball Hall of Fame, and is included in the second edition of *The World Sport Psychology Sourcebook* and the *World Sport Psychology Who's Who*.

Brennan's diverse clientele include professional and collegiate athletes and coaches, corporate leaders, professional organizations, and all persons striving for peak performance in their lives. Interests include golf, reading, officiating, and traveling with his wife and children to state parks and recreational areas.

You can contact Steve by writing to Peak Performance Consultants, 14728 Shirley Streets, Omaha, Nebraska, 68144, USA.

More books from Peak Performance Publishing

The Mental Edge: Basketball's Peak Performance Workbook.
A step-by-step manual teaching mental training and preparation. Chapters include goal setting, personal and team mental training, positive self-talk, stress management, and more...
$17.50

Basketball Resource Guide
The most comprehensive resource medium for the sport of basketball. Includes listings for audio-visual tapes, books, magazines, and more... The consummate book for the basketball junkie.
$14.95

Competitive Excellence
A collection of top coaches from across the United States at all levels: professional, college, and high school. Each coach is highlighted in sections on motivation, team cohesion, discipline, mental preparation, mental toughness, and communication.
$19.95

ORDER FORM

	Quantity	Price Ea.	Total
The Mental Edge		$17.50	
Basketball Resource Guide		$14.95	
Competitive Excellence		$19.95	
		Shipping	$3.50
		Total	

Check or Money Orders Only
Foreign Orders Add $5.00